Contents

1 *Not a Word*   5

2 *Almost Two Decades of Spreading Rot*   10

3 *'I Don't Think I Should Know More about This.'*   23

4 *Dr Evil*   49

5 *RIPA*   72

6 *Fishing for Headlines*   107

7 *What £330,000 Will Buy You*   125

8 *'We Don't Need F**king Murdoch.'*   160

9 *Milly Dowler*   182

10 *Arms of the State*   220

11 *Spooks*   264

12 *Postcript*   286

Author's Note   287

Appendix   294

THE
NEWS MACHINE

HACKING

THE UNTOLD STORY

James Hanning

with

GIBSON SQUARE

First published by

Gibson Square

Tel: +44 (0)20 7096 1100

info@gibsonsquare.com
www.gibsonsquare.com

ISBN 978-1908096951
Available as an e-book

Printed and bound by CPI Group (UK) Ltd, Croydon, CR0 4YY

1

Not a Word

For a long time, very little was known for certain about the phone-hacking scandal surrounding News International. It even barely intruded on the nation's radar that some grubby, soulless guy and an accomplice on the News of the World had been sent to prison, for eavesdropping on members of the royal household. Bad business, thought those who did hear about it. But they were punished, so presumably any problem had been nipped in the bud. The problem was that within weeks of the two men's conviction, the person paying their wages, who resigned over the affair, had become one of the future Prime Minister's closest confidants.

To some this was vindication of the move-along-nothing-to-see stance taken by the paper. To others, it smelt, raising ever louder questions of who knew what. The story was to develop into what Labour MP Tom Watson predicted would be Britain's Watergate. He had some understanding of the authority and responsibility that goes with being an editor, it invited suspicion. The insertion of Andy Coulson into the heart of the opposition was smooth enough, but was remarkable for the opportunism shown by those who brought it about. The more that emerged, the more surprising that shame-lessness. The courts have gone some way towards apportioning blame. This book seeks to look at how the *News of the World* got to such a state, and what happened subsequently.

Many have had or will have their say in court. Some have been believed, some not. The one person at the heart of it all, though, has said next to nothing since his arrest on 8 August 2006. When Glenn Mulcaire did apparently say something publicly, his words were drafted by his lawyer. Maybe he had something to say for himself after all?

But, surely, we all know Glenn Mulcaire is the crook whose dirty work caused all the phone-hacking trouble? People may argue about who asked him to do this or that, or what their motivation might have been, but the immutable fact at the bottom of it all was that Mulcaire was an unscrupulous and greedy private investigator who cared nothing for his victims' privacy or feelings? A man who sat in a south London trading estate systematically trawling through the phone, mortgage and medical records of hundreds of people surely wouldn't have the audacity to claim motives other than the lowest, sleaziest and most reprehensible? Yet almost nobody knows what has been going on in Glenn Mulcaire's mind in the years since he was first arrested. It has suited too many people for him not to speak. The phone hacking scandal became both a blame game and a study in deniability. Mulcaire, initially a beneficiary of both, became a victim of both. The more guilty people who said they knew nothing, the more Mulcaire must have been responsible. Because he was unable to speak without risking enormous legal and financial claims against him, all the more filth was piled at his door.

Mulcaire and Clive Goodman both 'took one for the company' in 2007 and pleaded guilty, when more senior people at *News of the World* escaped charges (for the time being, as it turned out). He was dismissed as a lawless rogue, yet his bosses knew his work was responsible for winning awards for his newspaper.

To meet Mulcaire is to be surprised, however, and to know his story is to get a feel for how part of an industry worked. How a public appetite for salacious stories, light and heavy, put so much pressure on those responsible for churning them out that the news machine that they were operating simply went up in smoke. Journalism is full of decent people who start off wanting to make the world a better place but who find themselves steered off course by the demands of the market place. They like the idea of holding the powerful to account and standing up for the downtrodden, but are confronted by a public more interested in Miley Cyrus and Cristiano Ronaldo's latest conquest than poverty and global warming. So an accommodation has to be reached.

Nowhere did this accommodation with the real world go more spectacularly wrong than in the case of Glenn Mulcaire. It may surprise those who read about the 6,000 people claimed to have been victims of Mulcaire's eavesdropping that he too signed up to work for the *News of the World* with good intentions. The streetwise investigator, the man David Blunkett wanted to rot in hell, the dab hand at low-level blagging and company searches, had wanted to use his talents for the general good.

Specifically, from the age of 17, he had wanted to be a private detective and help catch criminals. As he grew into the profession, through bread-and-butter company searches, garnished with some light blagging, he believed the details of his painstaking work could be used in the public's interest. His work was indeed scrutinised by the police, eventually, but not as he had intended. On 7th December 2011 he was arrested for the second time and, again, put on trial, for the unlawful interception of voicemails. By this time, the *News of the World*'s disregard for the law had become directly responsible for the re-writing of the entire rule book of British press regulation. His story, then, is also the story of the modern media.

How did this come about? What sort of man can call himself God-fearing and public-spirited yet behave in a way that leads directly to the disgrace and closure of one of the landmarks of British journalism, putting a bomb underneath not only the media as whole, but the political and police system as well? That is one of the questions this book seeks to answer, calling for the first time on extensive evidence from Mulcaire himself.

It will also look at Mulcaire's involvement in the case of Milly Dowler, the story of the kidnapped and later murdered Surrey schoolgirl that turned the phone hacking saga from a hiccup in media regulation to a national outrage. It will show how Mulcaire 'stood up' one of the biggest scoops of the decade. How he helped ferret out some of the country's most dangerous sex offenders. It will ask David Cameron some hitherto unasked questions about how he could have hired Andy Coulson, editor of the *News of the World* within weeks of the phone hacking scandal first exploding.

Most of this came as a surprise to me. It took me about four years to get to meet Glenn Mulcaire. I had become increasingly interested in the phone hacking scandal and, from my position as comment and then deputy editor of the *Independent on* Sunday had sought to nudge the story on, while of course acknowledging the groundbreaking work of Nick Davies of the *Guardian*. As the story grew from modest beginnings, I found I had got to know some of those involved. If another paper broke a story, I had a rough idea who to call to check its accuracy or otherwise. I tried to sort the wheat from the chaff, and could occasionally break the odd bit of new ground myself, but as time went on and with others having six times as many outlets as a Sunday paper, the returns on my efforts grew more marginal. All the same, increasingly, the person editors wanted to hear about was the elusive figure of Mulcaire. He remained the big catch.

Yet he wouldn't come out to play. I had written to him, as I'm sure hundreds of journalists had done, but it seemed his silence had been bought. The 'out-of-control' investigator who had served 6 months in prison was having his legal fees paid by News International. Lawyers piled up the private claims for breach of privacy against him, hoping to lever him away from his protectors, but News International were paying his legal fees (even if no one, seemingly, told Rupert Murdoch) and he seemed impregnable. Meanwhile, the legal process continued, with lawyers lining up to demand he name his controllers at News International. Its executive Rebekah Brooks told the Old Bailey in March 2014 that her organisation planned to oppose such court orders because they felt Mr Mulcaire was an 'unreliable witness'. 'Financially and reputationally we did not want that to happen... the view was he could say anyone or anything,' she said.

2

Almost Two Decades
of Spreading Rot
The News Story that Grew and Grew

As Glenn Mulcaire remained frustratingly elusive, I often wondered who is this mysterious, purportedly feral figure at the centre of the rot that appears to be spreading from the media to the police and the highest political circles in the country? Those few people who knew him were highly protective. He was said to be a good Catholic family man. 'Glenn's all right,' they would say, as in 'you should know the full story – it's very different from what you'd think.'

It was ever more intriguing, although when I finally got to know him I would occasionally have to correct any sympathy for him. He had, after all, peddled tittle-tattle and sleaze for a very comfortable living, invading the privacy of countless people and helped drag my profession – of which I've always been unfashionably proud – to the bottom rank in public esteem.

As I understood it, he had played a part in eavesdropping on a blamelessly homosexual unmarried MP. In accusing football boss Gordon Taylor of having an affair with the PFA's in-house solicitor, when, his lawyer later pointed out, he was consoling her after the death of her father. And in generally helping build and feed an increasingly ravenous public appetite for inconsequential celebrity nonsense. Who is to say what he might have got up to – with computers, bank accounts and so on – that wasn't in his files?

My frustration mounted as a great many journalists, cynically or innocently, said investigative sleaze wasn't really a story. The sophisticated view – which I struggled to share – was that self-regulation meant a more than respectable amount of self-interest and 'light touch' regulation: if corners have to be cut in order to get to the truth, then let them be cut. No bones were broken, and the greater good had been served.

It's a view I would have happily shared, except this wasn't about noble-cause corruption. If every now and then an investigator had to be used and sailed close to the wind legally in the cause of writing a proper public interest story, fine. But as often as not this was about fishing expeditions – the indiscriminate, lawless trawling of the deep in the hope of picking up a soggy fag end. Being given an inch is one thing. Taking a mile is another.

After Andy Coulson was appointed to work alongside David Cameron in May 2007, the more implausible the official version seemed to me to be becoming and the greater the number of perfectly decent public figures there were prepared to believe it. The only thing that would trump their conviction would be some hard facts from the people who had done it. Yet not only Mulcaire but many in the organisation seemed to have ditched their normally assiduous dedication to disseminating the truth.

He was the story, yet he was unattainable. One figure who was prepared to talk to me – eventually – was a roguish former showbiz reporter called Sean Hoare. He had worked hard and played even harder in the service of the *Sun*'s and the *News of the World*'s features desks. There was very little Sean wouldn't do either for his own gratification or to get a story for his paper. Many were the lost weekends with major-league rock stars, parts of which would then appear subsequently in one of the red tops. The phrase rough diamond doesn't begin to do Sean justice; but in his early 40s his wild man life style was beginning to catch up with him. At one point his doctor gave him 2 days to live and friends were never quite able to gauge just how ill he was.

By mid-2007, Sean was an angry man without a job. He had left the *News of the World*, having fallen out badly with Andy Coulson, with whom he had shared many an adventurous evening in the past. Coulson felt that Sean's excesses were getting the better of him and, to put it as neutrally as possible, he decided to place his professionalism ahead of blind loyalty to Sean, by this time in serious need of treatment for an addiction to alcohol. Sean's resentment was heightened when his friend Clive Goodman ('an absolute gentleman', in Sean's words) was sent to prison and sacked by the *News of the World* for his part in the hacking of the royal phones, the scandal that saw Glenn Mulcaire go to prison. Coulson's behaviour had the effect of isolating Goodman and Mulcaire, portraying them as rogue operators. Sean's sense of decency and justice – more finely honed than he would admit, or than the bosses' caricature of him would suggest – was appalled. He knew better than anyone that redtop journalism was a rough and tumble world, and he had few pious pretensions about it. So when he saw someone he had regarded as one of his kind, a tabloid scuffler, and a treacherous one, alongside the leader of the Opposition, he was affronted. 'What's he doing up there?' he would fume. 'He sent my mate to prison. It's just wrong.'

His marriage was checkered and for all his desire to 'get clean', his friends still needed a lot of convincing that he had beaten his demons. But the Sean I met in 2010 was a pretty convincing one. Before our appointment, he was anxious to satisfy himself that there would be 'no funny business'. He wanted me to promise I would not have hidden cameras or microphones – that our encounter was not just off the record, it was 'not for use'. He had evidently forgotten that most of the broadsheet press can't afford 'funny business'. (Read that as you will, but we did manage to recompense him for his train the fare from Watford.) We met in Kensington, near my office, and had a modest half of something non-alcoholic, I think, but we chatted for ages. This was not a man obviously seething with rage at having been stitched up by his former mate. Nor did he seem to particularly want revenge on behalf of Clive Goodman, although that was a part of it. More, he was rather more coolly aware that an entire industry had taken a wrong turn, and that it needed putting right. Nobody could be in any doubt that he was telling the truth, it seemed to me, and he genially recited tales of monstrous intrusion that now seems to belong to another era.

It wasn't as if Sean had had a Damascene conversion one day, more that as time went on, the party was grinding to a halt. Of course this had much to do with his own health (which led increasingly, tragically, to him being edged towards the party's exit) but also a sense that he owed it to his wife Jo and to the world to get a bit more real. In short, it was time to sober up, but that didn't prevent him enjoying going over old ground. He had tales of how News International executives would hack into the computer system of their rivals to get access to their list of upcoming news stories. This was ultimately the cheat's way of conducting business, the sort of homework-stealing sneakery that earns nothing but contempt in the school yard. Yet in the world of the red top, it was all part of the game. There was no limit on lying and cheating, as long as you got the story.

Sean was a News International man through and through. He lived for the story, but demanded entertainment on the way. So he and his co-conspirators were invariably in the thick of the action if there was a showbiz opening or an after-gig party. He had worked on Bizarre, the training ground for up and coming showbiz journos who wanted to catch the proprietor's eye. Andy Coulson, Rav Singh, Dominic Mohan and Piers Morgan all worked there. It was a testing ground, to test not only a reporter's talent but also their endurance.

Sean knew how to play the system. He was one of many who would tell his boss he needed a certain amount of cash for a story. If the source ends up receiving a rather smaller proportion of that figure, who was to know if the reporter had trousered a commission on the way through? When source protection was vital, it would be counterproductive for the left hand to know too much about what the right hand was doing. But this didn't just work occasionally. It was systematic.

As for the dark arts, Sean was in the thick of it. It was casual, routine. On a quiet day, he would be asked to do a bit of 'finger-fishing' to see what X or Y had been up to. He talked of a 'hack off' between two journalists, to see which one could crack the hardest (most secure) voicemails. Sean, a selfless encourager of young talent, was proud to report that the winner was a protégé of his who went on to occupy a senior position. He used to report, almost absent-mindedly, as if everyone knew, how executives would be forever trying to listen in to one another's voicemails. Partly, he said, they were trying to pinch one another's stories, and partly, if – to put it more decorously than perhaps they would – they were checking on one another's fidelity. Rebekah Brooks (as she then wasn't) and Andy Coulson were to the fore in that category.

But the main purpose of what one journalist tagged a 'handy little trick' was stories. One tale, quite possibly apocryphal, involved somebody having a row in a restaurant with Heather McCartney, later the wife of Beatle Paul, after which the one-legged campaigner left a message on the person's voicemail, the gist of which was 'Don't you ever call me Hoppy again.' The message, wouldn't you know it, was picked up by the red-top papers and shared between them, none wanting to be alone in offending the girl friend of so revered a figure at the height of his happiness with her. It was only after extensive legal threats on a Saturday afternoon that the papers were forced to pull the story.

Another of Sean's tales concerned the breaking of the story about Sven-Goran Eriksson's relationship with Ulrika Jonsson. He and a colleague had hacked the phone of one of them, and had managed to establish they were having an affair. They reported this to the office early one week, where ecstatic *News of the World* editor Andy

Coulson declared the story a certain 'splash' for Sunday, congratulated them on their scoop and told them to take the afternoon off. This they chose to spend celebrating their catch. The problem was, they bumped into a reporter from the *Mirror*, to whom Sean's colleague could not help boasting. The *Mirror* reporter thought the tale too good to wait till Sunday, so reported it to his bosses, satisfied himself of its truth (you may well ask how) and the *Mirror* stole the story, running it in the '3am Girls' column on a Thursday. Andy Coulson's reaction at having such a tale stolen from under his nose does not need to be guessed at.

Sean was torn. He wanted the truth about the extent to which redtop stories were driven by titbits picked up from celebrities' phones to come out, but he was reluctant to go public about what he knew, knowing that he might face a charge himself. The police – who had taken their cue from Prime Minister David Cameron and the Press Complaints Commission – were struggling to believe, let alone prove, the extent of the wrongdoing. The House of Commons Culture, media and sport committee, which included the redoubtable Tom Watson, spent several months looking into the matter, concluding that it was 'inconceivable' that no senior executive knew what had been going on, but admitting it had not been able to lay a glove on Andy Coulson.

This was an affront to anyone who knew the truth, but even the anarchic Sean was disinclined to sacrifice his freedom and his family's peace of mind, recently restored by Sean's apparent return to health, in the cause of press regulation. He fumed quietly to friends, and expressed an earnest hope that the truth would come out. Then, one day in September 2010, he went on Radio 4's PM programme and alleged that phone hacking was 'endemic' at the paper and that the Prime Minister's press spokesman had asked him to hack phones to acquire stories. To most senior staff on the red top papers, it was a childish statement of the bleedin' obvious, but nobody had had the courage to say it publicly.

So now the dam seemed likely to break. Surely others would come forward? News International bosses had been warned that Andy Coulson choosing to take a job in Downing Street would attract yet more fire to David Cameron's decision to appoint him. Surely, now, that judgment would be confirmed?

In the following months, more did emerge. Yet Mulcaire was still the story. Sean's stories were highly entertaining, but he felt he had said his piece. The police did go to see him, but would only interview him under caution that he might himself be subject to arrest. There were to be no deals. Sean was scandalised, but trapped. His wife Jo had only recently reclaimed him from alcohol dependency. The last thing she wanted was him up on a criminal charge.

Yet still Mulcaire wouldn't play ball.

My paper had run the only ever interview with him on 19 July 2009, conducted by Peter Burden, a Shropshire-based journalist who had written a book about *News of the World*'s excesses. Burden had got to know Mulcaire, visit his home in Cheam and gain his trust sufficiently for Mulcaire at least to speak to him. The investigator was coy about his plans, but was clearly in a bad way financially. The treasures that Mulcaire had to offer were not forthcoming. He had lost an enormous amount, but he still had much more to lose. He knew too much about people the police had not even interviewed. Too many people were threatening legal action against him, and he was reliant on News International to help pay his legal bills. Far from receding into the past, the scandal was growing, dogging his escape from it and rehabilitation.

Peter Burden was in pole position with Glenn and occasionally we would speak to exchange gossip. Burden was astonishingly brave, placing on his website flagrant allegations of misconduct by senior people at the *News of the World* which had such a deafening ring of truth that Wapping could only ignore them. Such was the power of the News International lawyers these people generally got away with it – in that the mainstream media failed to air his allegations. Burden had been trying unsuccessfully to persuade Mulcaire to collaborate on a book. Mulcaire had had tentative conversations with a former colleague, who planned to write a racy account of goings-on at the paper, but the deal never got off the ground. Legal concerns trumped any amount of money he might have made from such a venture. Peter Burden also sought to persuade Mulcaire into print, and they reached an agreement, binding for a year, that he would write 'the inside story'. Yet that project also ran into the sand. Burden had other fish to fry and Mulcaire's heart evidently wasn't in it. Plus, publishers were still wary of a book involving a convicted criminal which would doubtless make a number of contentious allegations against some very powerful people.

In late 2012, I was told by Peter Burden that Mulcaire was willing to meet. I wasn't sure what he intended, but to someone with an unhealthy interest in the hacking scandal, any meeting was welcome. We met at Starbucks in Victoria station that autumn. When I arrived at the busy coffee bar, Glenn, gangling, tanned and fashionably dressed, was skittering about nervously. I was to learn that's how he often is, but he was in a high old state. He affected friendliness but kept looking over my shoulder and his. He was convinced we were being watched, at very least, and that I was somehow pulling a fast one. I said something crass about how I had waited a long time to meet him. He mumbled something and asked to see my mobile. He asked me if I would take the battery out. Only that way could he be sure I was not – or somebody else was not – using it as a recorder or transmitter. I know now that he also used an electronic device to check whether I was 'wired', with a recording device.

I would like to say it was not long before he came to trust me. In fact, a year later and about15 meetings on, he was still asking me to remove the battery from my phone. Yet we had progressed. I had a bit more of a grasp of how he was feeling and how misunderstood he felt. I think he gathered that I had no axe to grind, nor any political line to push. I just wanted to get to the bottom of who knew what and how it had all come about.

By this time, Operation Weeting, the police investigation headed by Deputy Assistant Commissioner Sue Akers, was well into its stride. Prosecutions were looming. Would that suit Mulcaire or not, I wondered. Having served time, surely he would not be required to do so again? Maybe he would be required to be a witness, I thought.

In any event, it was not clear where our acquaintance was going. He had failed to overcome the legal and financial obstacles to writing a book, and was in all probability prevented even from giving an interview. Anything of interest would almost certainly risk prejudicing the court cases. I had the impression from a friend that Peter Burden had pretty much given up hope of collaborating with him, and was myself coming to think my interest in Glenn was no more than voyeuristic on my part.

But as we spoke, it became clear how fired up he was, and the more time we spent together, the more I came to feel how real his frustration was. He just seemed to want his story told, clearly and factually, without frills and embellishment. Why, he demanded, had nobody sought his side of the story?

I was hard pressed to explain this. Surely everybody wanted to hear his story, contaminated though he was as a source? He knew the answers as to who had ordered the infringement of the privacy of thousands of people. Wasn't that something my profession wanted to know about? Evidently not, or not on terms that he thought suitable.

It would be a surprise if someone so well versed in the culture of the grubbier end of the newspaper business didn't seek to make as much money as possible from an exclusive. Glenn knew that a lot of people wanted to hear his story, but a lot of powerful, well resourced people didn't. It would take a pretty large cheque to cut that Gordian knot. And he needed such a cheque badly. He had not had proper, sustained work since he was sent to prison.

While one might be sympathetic to someone who knew he had done wrong, had served his time and wanted to turn things around, it was all academic to my mind. My newspaper has never been in the business of paying hefty sums for exclusives, and one or two of its freelance contributors will testify that it feels a bit of a bonus to be paid at all. The idea that our cheque book might be able to fight off the competition to land one of phone hacking's biggest fish was absurd. But we do try to treat stories thoughtfully and credit our readers with an appetite for more than the sex lives of soap stars. And, for any ultra-cynics who might be reading this, at its very lowest, we can't afford private investigators.

And there was another big no-no. Mulcaire was soiled goods. How could he expect to make money from a scandal in which he was a leading participant? Media standards may have declined, and infamy may be the new celebrity, but this would surely be a new low. Besides, a coach and horses had been driven through the press' rules, but one rule at least stood: the media should not enable criminals to profit from their crimes.

Whether Mulcaire was aware of this or not, I do not know. Certainly it had not featured in our conversations about his previous dalliances with those wanting to do a book deal (though they must all have been aware of it). I seemed to be the last person on the dance floor. If anyone was to do a book with him, it was me. (I of course credit myself with a valiant-for-truth persistence in wanting to see the story through – others will put it down to an obsessive and impractical interest in a toxic topic.) So it fell to me to tell Mulcaire that whatever else happened, he would not be allowed to make any money from telling his story. Again, there would be 'no funny business'. If he wanted someone to help present his version of events, I was interested, but, given the low base from which his public credibility was starting, I would need a pretty free hand. He discussed the issue with his wife Alison, and came back to say he understood the situation. (At a later stage, the subject of money was raised again briefly, but again dismissed.)

He wanted the right to be listened to. I said I hoped I could offer that at least, but that he could not expect me to do his PR for him. I would be the reporter of his take on things, but not be an advocate for his position. I told him I would need to be able to ask him any questions I wanted, and he should answer them to the best of his ability and above all truthfully. I said I would be a sympathetic sceptic, and insist on being able to check his version with other sources, to the extent that that was possible. If I ever had any reason to doubt he was telling the truth, the game was off.

We seemed to be getting somewhere. We were both keen the book should not be about Murdoch-bashing, or redtop-bashing. He renounced any thought of making money more easily than I expected. He had come to distrust journalists as a breed, so what he wanted was a fair crack of the whip. He believed that I, in harness with my newspaper, would give him that.

3

'I Don't Think
I Should Know More about This'

News International's first few versions of what happened in the phone hacking affair bore very little resemblance to the subterranean truth. An enormous number of lies were told to sustain the fiction that only two people were in on the law-breaking. It was to take several years before anything approaching the full picture was to appear, and by the time it did, the entire centre of gravity of the privacy versus right-to-know balance had shifted.

That small media story, about a couple of barely known sleuths, was to herald the end of an entire approach to popular journalism. Where popular newspapers had always pushed the boundaries, and however many times they were thrown out of the 'last-chance saloon', they seemed to know that their trade would continue to be self-regulated. So the same mindset lived on, one which essentially saw 'getting the story' as the legitimator of any behaviour. While this wasn't true in all cases, the bigger the story, the greater the latitude afforded the journalist. So among their peers, the journalist who got the big story was rarely criticised, few questions were asked, and the sanctity of source protection meant that plenty else never came to be scrutinised. Editors would be accustomed to saying 'I don't think I should know any more about this', although in the end, in the company of the smallest handful of confidants, they would have to inform themselves sufficiently if, in the worst of cases (a writ), they were required to answer for their actions.

Journalists are by nature inquisitive and acquisitive, and the rise of the cult of celebrity (in part created and fed by the press surely) in a highly competitive market meant more than ever that stories were the only currency that mattered. Greater and greater demands would be placed on journalists and more and more outlandish schemes would be devised to find them. In the old days, Fleet Street's smoke-filled bars used to brim with raucous, irreverent middle aged men in raincoats telling rakish tales of how they cut a corner, slipped a security guard a fiver, impersonated a teacher, guard or relative of 'the victim' in order to get the story and file it for the London edition by deadline time. Of paramount importance would be the getting of the story, but it may not be too romantic to think that a degree of implicit peer pressure was applied by the opinion of fellow journalists. A degree of cunning was always acceptable and if shared among long-time colleagues, admired. But possibly an ethos of what was considered acceptable would play some role. Harold Evans, former editor of the *Sunday Times* and for many an essential guide to journalistic practice and ethics, used to have a rule for journalists considering taking a liberty with the truth or otherwise crossing the boundaries of defensible practice, supposedly with some greater goal in mind. He would tell them to ask themselves if – when they came to write their story – they would be willing to tell the reader what they had done. In other words, would they be confident that the reader would say 'that's Ok – I can quite see why (s)he did that, and it was in the public interest to do so because an important truth has been revealed.' It may just be that anticipated peer disapproval in the bars of EC4 used to play some small part in policing some of Britain's more unruly Grub Street scribes.

But in the age of celebrity and sophisticated eaves-dropping, just having a roguish attitude, a few trusted sources and recycling copy from the news agencies wasn't enough. Boundaries had to be pushed, and technology offered plenty of scope for the imaginative to subvert the rules.

The Leveson inquiry heard the claims of Steven Nott, a sales manager based in South Wales, who in 1999 tried to alert people to the fact that anybody could listen in to somebody else's voicemails as long as they had the PIN number, which was usually on a factory setting and therefore easily known. He contacted the *Daily Mirror*, who told him they were keen on the story, sat on it and in the end never ran it. He then went to the *Sun*, but they didn't bite either. Subsequent events lead him to believe senior executives on the papers knew full well the signif-icance of what he was saying. Either they knew already, or they used it to their advantage. 'It didn't take me long to realise what I had done. I couldn't believe I was so stupid to tell a national newspaper how to get hot news for free just by hacking into someone's phone,' he said. (Nott believes that was how phone-hacking took off, although others have different views.)

Mobile phone scanners, of the sort that had picked up the mobile conversations between Prince Charles and Camilla Parker-Bowles on the one hand, and Princess

Diana and James Gilbey on the other, were extensively used during the analogue age. According to one *News of the World* reporter, they were a vital tool in knowing about the movements of the royals, particularly at weekends: 'The photographers could listen in to the royal protection officers at Highgrove and other country estates because they were the only ones on the airwaves, discussing how to get Diana or whoever out and where they were going. Many staffers and freelancers had them in their kitbags in the 1990s. I remember playing with one in an editor's office.' Seemingly, the royal protection officers had no idea.

In February 1997, the *News of the World* ran a story about Phil Davies, a celebrated rugby player, having an extra-marital affair. Tape recordings of the pair proving the existence of the relationship were 'inadvertently picked up by radio hams', or so the paper said. The reporter in question, Paul McMullan, recalls: 'It was the first time the lawyers told us to be careful with recorded mobile phone stuff.... I spent a whole week disguising the source of the story; we all did for 10 full years before Clive went to jail. Everybody knew this was an executive direction coming from either legal or editorial departments to be careful about writing their story so as as not to reveal their source.' Despite admitting that the news was based on three distinct phone calls, the paper was flagrant in tweaking the law's tail. At the end of the article were the words: 'It is illegal to intercept phone calls intentionally, but not if found at random.' As if all three calls had been picked up by chance.

Journalists have of course always known the value of being able to eavesdrop. But only recently had the technology become so easily available. It enabled journalists not just to discover unsuspected truths in an instant, but also to provide clinching evidence, even if it wasn't adducible in the writing of the story, or admissible in court. Some celebrities were wise to their vulnerability, and took precautions, but many did not. One victim was the former manager of Scotland's national football team, Craig Brown.

As the Euro 2000 tournament in Belgium and the Netherlands drew to a close, the *News of the World* marked the occasion by peering into his personal life. On 2nd July, the paper was able to report that 'former Radio One beauty' Louise Port, 23, was having a secret affair with him, even though 'faithful lover Phyllis Kirk is still waiting at home for him'. It revealed that he had attended two games with her although he hardly ever ventured out of his room in the Holiday Inn on the outskirts of Amsterdam, possibly because he was with Louise. The story continued in customary redtop style, detailing what the couple ordered for room service and tormenting the language with a series of painful football metaphors (he wanted to 'make sure he wasn't caught offside with Louise' by colleagues and had escaped fellow pundits to make 'a few plays of his own and analyse a different set of positions upstairs'). The story spoke gloatingly about how 'Louise thinks she's in love', suggesting this was unwise given Brown's famously roving eye. Helpfully, a 'close friend' of the couple was on hand to talk freely about the minutiae of their relationship.

So how had the paper got the story? He had just passed his 60th birthday, but if senescent inactivity was beckoning, he wasn't rushing to greet it. The previous year the *News of the World* revealed Craig was seeing Ayr church elder Phyllis Kirk and teacher Lynda Slaven at the same time. 'Neither woman was aware he was two-timing them,' the paper clarified. 'Then the bombshell news emerged that the frisky football father figure was seeing a THIRD woman – district nurse Allison Brown.' If ever a man had form and might be good for a headline, it was Brown.

The features desk's Paul McMullan, who was in Amsterdam at the time and was well experienced in the ways of news reporting, was given the job and told, as he had been many times before: 'Make it work'. This is a familiar phrase to many reporters, used to being briefed on a story whose source does not want to be identified and they don't need to know. In this case, says McMullan, it was not source protection that was the issue but the fact that some of the evidence had been uncovered unlawfully. The proof, acquired surreptitiously, was not usable.

McMullan rang the office, saying 'I am never going to be able to prove they are shagging.' 'They said 'we are running this', just write it.' McMullan just needed to get Brown talking and acknowledge the bones of the story to avoid a subsequent libel claim. 'Make it work' meant what it said, and few questions would be asked as long as the reporter produced the goods. The confirmation might not be a straight 'Yes, it's true', but might come in the form of an off the record admission (possibly from 'a friend'), or tell-tale pictures, or an implicit acquiescence. McMullan duly obliged, and the office provided the rest. 'I think the "close friend" quotes were taken from the tapes of mobile phone messages back at the office,' remembers McMullan. Thus the paper had a classic story from next to nothing. It had been based on a hunch, that Craig Brown's libido was undimmed, and was backed up by a spot of 'finger-fishing' and an assured piece of foot-in-the-doormanship by a reporter.

On other occasions, the (usually) women in question were less innocent, and would record their own conversations with their lover, with a view to selling the stories to the papers. In such cases, there may be a degree of premeditation, which on occasion would, in extreme cases, invite speculation as to the women's true motivation.

And the journalists, of course, loved the chase. Journalism may be a vocation for many, and some become addicted to story-getting as if it were a drug. The more prominent the piece, the bigger the high; the greater the approbation of the bosses, the more gratifying the reluctance of congratulations from competitors and the unspoken 'how did (s)he get that?' And while a glow remains for a few days, the hunger to repeat the trick is constant. Success breeds success, but it also breeds desire. The thrill of writing a news story which surprises, subverts, challenges, changes the bigger picture and above all cannot be ignored by colleagues and competitors is immense. What greater vindication could there be for someone who enters the profession (hypo-critically or not) with the words 'the people have a right to know' emblazoned on their minds?

Of course, life couldn't go on without friendly contacts on 'the other side', in parliament, medicine, law or wherever, but journalistic machismo requires that these are regarded as purely means to an end. They are, of necessity, treated with confidentiality. This is of course as it should be, although the protection of a source can be used to hide the fact that, for all the bluster and omniscience, a reporter only has one contact on a given topic, knowledge of whose prejudices might slant a boss against his story.

When onto that 'given' is transposed an unprecedented reader interest in celebrities (and a keenness of those celebrities to exploit this insatiable appetite), a ferocious circulation battle and the availability of hitherto unimagined technology with which to snoop, the pressure on journalists is greater than ever.

Stealing ideas off competitors was the least of it. Paul McMullan recalls how the *News of the World* used to pay someone £500 to acquire the *Sunday Mirror*'s news list every week. 'We knew who had the list and there would be a weekly meeting between the person on the *Sunday Mirror* and our person, and often I would get tasked with writing up whatever story they had. Actually the person in question only received £300 a week. The *News of the World*'s intermediary was creaming off £200 a week, which went into his pocket. When Piers Morgan moved to the *Mirror* he sacked the person who had been passing over the list.'

The *News of the World* always kept abreast of the burgeoning technological possibilities. If another paper was getting the big stories, the bosses wanted to know why. If the dark arts were involved, then Wapping would have to up its game. If it found itself lagging its competitors, soon enough a senior figure from management would crack the whip and push the straggler to the front of the pack. On occasions, staff were hired from other papers for their proficiency in the dark arts, and Sean Hoare cheerfully admitted he was one. News International doesn't do laggards. In its last 10 years it reached new levels of bombast and success. And with the *Times*, the *Sunday Times* and the *Sun* in the same stable, it ensured that the Murdoch world view was well represented on the nation's news stands. It also made Murdoch a figure to be feared, both in journalism and public life.

As mentioned earlier, newspaper journalists are inclined to enjoy the raucousness of office life – the heartless banter, the default cynicism and facetiousness, the finding out of secrets, the labour-saving short cuts and the glib, 'I wasn't born yesterday' knowingness. And under the cover of macho callousness, there is often a camaraderie and a commonly held (but rarely articulated) view that when all is said and done, the job of exposing bad people is a worthwhile one, and most of the people in it do it for decent, or at least defensible, reasons.

But the *News of the World*, the paper that used to claim 'All human life is here', lost sight of much of that. Its ethos was corrupted by unmeetable demands and a culture of bullying. Sean Hoare on the features desk, as we have seen, couldn't take the pressure, although his own temperament made him an unsuitable candidate to try. Matt Driscoll, a football writer on the paper, was eventually awarded £792,736 in compensation for being the victim of 'a consistent pattern of bullying behaviour'.

One reporter recalls the change in the atmosphere at the paper, 'They promoted halfwits and liars. One executive in particular was vile on a daily basis. He loved making you miserable. Plus there were others who didn't have the contacts or the ability. Hacking phones was just a tool to them that made their lives easier. All of them were terrified of Rebekah [Brooks]. They just wanted snippets to tell Rebekah.' And Rebekah would pass them on to Rupert Murdoch, or so journalist Michael Wolff asserts, not that Murdoch, presumably, or Brooks, a jury has found, would have known the source of the gossip.

It became a machine, losing sight of the 'human life' and spitting out those who didn't shape up. The fear of being spat out made more and more journalists do things they 'did not go into journalism' to do. Indeed, the closure of the paper can be traced back from the start of hacking scandal to Clive Goodman – under mounting pressure from his bosses – taking a risk on a story about the royal princes. Newspapers are always high-wire acts to an extent, but with hindsight the degree of pressure that prevailed suggested something was likely to give. One journalist with over 10 years on the paper said its closure as a result of phone hacking was a bit like Al Capone being caught for tax evasion. 'It was routine, and really wasn't that big a deal in the scheme of things – I never imagined something as trivial as that would bring the paper down,' he said.

Hand in hand with the ultra-competitiveness of the red tops was the widespread reliance on private investigators. Their use by journalists had reached a height unimagined by most readers, it is fair to assume, by the late 1990s. It would be extremely unfair to tar all private investigators with the brush of criminality. Many are highly reputable, discreet, professional and honourable, and are to the fore where the regulation of their trade is concerned. Those were generally wary of journalists, who they saw as inclined to print rather more of a story than was discreet, and for a private investigator, discretion was all. 'Most PIs wouldn't work for the media,' one of their number remembers. 'They just wouldn't trust them.'

But others were willing to work with the media, and the work was extensive if not particularly creative. Much of it was routine tracing of individuals or companies, finding of phone numbers and so on, sometimes legally, sometimes not. They had the contacts and knowhow to provide such information, so they would be used, simply, as a labour-saving device by newspapers. The provision of this kind of information was not held in high esteem in the investigators' higher echelons, but it was regarded as invaluable and harmless by the papers. And those who commissioned it tended to do so unchallenged by their bosses, and certainly by their employees. As one for *News of the World* reporter put it: 'No reporter sitting in a car on a story that most of Fleet Street is chasing who gets a call from the desk and is told to go to a certain address is going to say, "Where did you get that address? Are you sure it was legally acquired?"'

In some cases, though, the work was more sophisticated. On occasions the difficult bits of a journalist's trade got farmed out to private investigators, so that the scribes in the office were active only at the beginning of the story (the acquiring of a piece of gossip) and the end, the writing it up. The erection of a buffer between the writer and the fact needing to be discovered or verified suited everyone – the investigator was paid to dig up the nugget without too many questions being asked as to how he had done so, and the journalist got the kudos of his colleagues. One well established former business journalist cheerfully admits to his extensive use of private investigators. 'You would have been mad not to do it,' he said. 'Everyone else was doing it. In a competitive world, not to use PIs was unthinkable. Apart from anything else, it saved so much time.'

The body responsible for overseeing the protection of personal and professional data is the Information Commission. In November 2002 it acquired a warrant to investigate the premises of a private investigator, John Boyall. It became clear that he had been misusing data from the Police National Computer. It was a source of stories for journalists, but one to which they were not supposed to have access. Two inquiries followed as a result of the raid. One, called Operation Motorman, was run by the Information Commissioner, and the other, Operation Glade, conducted by the Metropolitan Police.

The Information Commissioner later described the sort of work that was being performed:

> The 'suppliers' almost invariably work within the private investigation industry: private investigators, tracing agents, and their operatives, often working loosely in chains that may include several interme-diaries between the ultimate customer and the person who actually obtains the information. Suppliers use two main methods to obtain the information they want: through corruption, or more usually by some form of deception, generally known as 'blagging.' Blaggers pretend to be someone they are not in order to wheedle out the

information they are seeking. They are prepared to make several telephone calls to get it. Each call they make takes them a little further towards their goal: obtaining information illegally which they then sell for a specified price. Records seized under search warrants show that many private investigators and tracing agents are making a lucrative business out of this trade.

Having raided the Hampshire home of one investigator, Steve Whittamore, in early 2003, the Commission's 'Operation Motorman' found 305 (mostly newspaper) journalists had asked for over 13,000 pieces of information, over 11,000 of which almost certainly involved breaking the Data Protection Act. The total value to Whittamore was over half a million pounds.

The Whittamore records were broken down into files, known colloquially by their colour. In the 'Blue Book', which detailed Whittamore's dealing with the Murdoch newspapers, were over a thousand instances of his services being used. The files do not in themselves prove unlawful behaviour, and much of the work was clearly lawful. In fact, the figure of a thousand is comparatively small, but it is known the Murdoch papers also used other investigators.

Whittamore was just the point of contact. He had a range of sources in key positions who were able to furnish him with the data his clients needed. He had sources at the Department of Work and Pensions, the Driver and Vehicle Licensing Agency, British Telecom and elsewhere, all anxious to help. As Nick Davies reported in his landmark book *Flat Earth News*, 'These sources, scattered across some of the state's biggest databases, appeared to be peddling their information through at least ten different private investigators, former police officers and petty criminals, who knew each other and worked with each other, swapping contacts and making deals together in their corner of the information black market.'

In early 2005, two investigators, Boyall and Whittamore, pleaded guilty to breaches of the data protection act, while the other two, a Wandsworth-based former police officer and a police press officer, admitted committing misconduct in public office (i.e. procuring confidential police data from the Police National Computer). It is a mark of the scant importance the authorities attached to this topic that the four were given conditional discharges. The press barely covered the story.

Though taken for granted in parts of the media, the extensive use of investigators remained unknown to the public. The findings above, and the rest of the Information Commissioner's report, were not published until some time later.

Publicly, of course, the *News of the World* remained beyond reproach. In March 2003, its former editors Rebekah Brooks and Andy Coulson gave evidence to the House of Commons media select committee. Brooks, seemingly unaware of the law, let slip that: 'We have paid the police for information in the past, and it's been....' Coulson butted in confidently: 'We operate within the code and within the law and, if there is a clear public interest, then the same holds for private investigators, subterfuge, video bags, whatever you want to talk about…' Labour's Chris Bryant pointed out that paying police officers is illegal. Coulson said 'As I said, within the law.' He too seemed either not to know the law or be indifferent to it.

Journalists divide themselves into two essential categories: news people and features people. News people go out, attend press conferences, ask difficult questions to politicians, break bad news to concerned parents, explain motorway pile-ups and generally report hard facts. Features people deal with life's softer, frothier side, expressing opinions, building up conceits, interviewing and often promoting celebrities. They sometimes fancy themselves as being more writerly than their news counterparts, for which they are regarded as belonging in 'the shallow end'. To the more hard-bitten in news, features people are not quite proper journalists, too reliant on help from PR people to get their pages filled, though news people too are hugely reliant on being given press releases and spoon-fed 'the story' by those paid to steer the coverage. Features people, it is said, do not understand that news is something someone doesn't want printed, and that innuendo, opinion and frivolous and ill-sourced gossip are emphatically not news. All newspapers need a bit of both. There's nothing to beat a big news story speedily, comprehensively and digestibly handled, but a stylishly written take on a subject we all thought we knew well, can convey something equally valuable.

Successful newspapers knew not to ignore their readers' interest in who was going out/going on holiday/taking drugs/cavorting on a beach/getting drunk at a premiere with whom. Kelvin Mackenzie, editor of the *Sun* from 1981 to 1994, was a towering figure in popular journalism. He had a knack of touching a public nerve. He was often brutal and raucous, but this was usually mitigated by humour. There are countless stories of 'Kelvin' (as he is known to everyone) going over the top, perhaps the gravest of which was his paper's front page headlined 'The Truth', which reported that many of those who died in the Hillsborough football disaster had been drunk, thieving and urinating on one another, a calumny Liverpool has never forgiven. More entertainingly, he once told the Prime Minister, John Major, who had called meekly to ask how he planned to cover something in the next day's paper, that he was planning to pour 'a large bucket of shit' over him.

He did not worry too much where the story came from or (within reason, and this was before the days of hacking) how it was acquired, as long as it ended up being interesting or funny. The paper he ran was Murdochism at its bawdiest. The proprietor loved it. Whereas many editors in the Murdoch stable felt their boss breathing down their neck, even from the other side of the Atlantic, Mackenzie enjoyed a great deal more latitude. He was free to make mistakes, and though he often did, Murdoch knew Mackenzie needed to be given his head.

The floor of a Kelvin-run office was not a place for sensitive souls. He once shouted across a busy news room to a reporter who he believed was having an affair with one of the secretaries on the *Sun*: 'Oi! I don't want you dipping your pen in the company ink!' He fitted the age of the bully-boy, barrow-boy perfectly, and although not ideally suited to marginally more reflective, liberal times, he exerted a big influence on many careers.

Three talented young journalists in particular learned their trade from the Kelvin textbook. Piers Morgan's first job in journalism was with the *South London News*, but he was recruited by Mackenzie from the *Streatham and Tooting News*, and became editor of the *Sun*'s pop column Bizarre. He had clearly caught Rupert Murdoch's eye and in 1994, at just 29, he was made editor of the *News of the World*.

Andy Coulson started his working life on the *Basildon Echo* and in 1988 moved to the *Sun*, where he worked with Piers Morgan. He fell out with Kelvin Mackenzie, and moved to the *Daily Mail*, but soon came back and took up the editorship of Bizarre in 1994. Rebekah Brooks joined the *News of the World* in 1989 as a secretary, and became a feature writer on the magazine before long.

Kelvin set the standard at that time, and the unconstrained bravado with which he edited became a template. 'They all thought they could emulate Kelvin, but Kelvin was unique,' says one well seasoned News International insider. 'They saw what Kelvin did, and the degree of freedom that Rupert gave him, and they decided they wanted some of it,' says another.

'The people under Kelvin all knew they were being fast-tracked,' says another old hand. 'They knew they'd succeed, and they had seen how Rupert was prepared to indulge the successful. Failure wasn't an option at a company like that. They were big businesses, market leaders, given every chance to succeed. The only question was... they would win, but by how much?'

The trio were often photographed together, and were clearly enjoying themselves. The first to achieve editor status was Piers Morgan, who in 1994 took the chair of the *News of the World* in his late twenties, becoming the youngest national newspaper editor for over 50 years. This was Murdoch publicly announcing that he backed talent, and, as his subsequent career has shown, Morgan is a highly charismatic journalist. His Wikipedia entry reports that he 'quickly gained notoriety for his invasive, thrusting style and lack of concern for celebrities' privacy'. That his judgment can go awry is not in doubt, but he had bucket loads of the Mackenzie chutzpah.

Paul McMullan remembers the Morgan editorship: 'The culture of the *News of the World* was dominated, when I first started, by Piers Morgan…. He was young and in my opinion very talented, but with youth clearly came inexperience and his reckless determination to get a story at all costs is something that set the trend. To be fair, this was the spirit of the day. This was 1994-5. Diana was still alive and it was all good fun. A car chase in St Tropez or through the streets of Paris was something that was done with a smile and a wave. It hadn't yet taken that darker turn.'

In the event Morgan didn't stay long at the *News of the World*. A variety of reasons – to do with those lapses of judgment – have been offered for Morgan leaving the paper, but the truth is not complicated. At the end of 1995, the *Mirror*, always fighting to keep out of the *Sun*'s shadow, came calling. It knew that Morgan, though young and learning his trade as an editor, was likely to be restless. The job that anyone who sought to emulate Kelvin – who, incidentally, was to have his voicemails intercepted later – was editorship of the *Sun*. And Morgan calculated that, while the daily paper was the next logical step in his career, there were a fair few people ahead of him in the queue. He told a colleague at the time: 'It will take me an age before I'd get a chance to edit the *Sun*.'

So Morgan headed across to the *Mirror*, where he was treated like royalty by the management. In the best sceptical tradition, journalists are inclined to express doubt about the success of their peers. For every journalist who applauds Morgan's success at the *Mirror*, there are several who say he 'bought' circulation. One who has watched his career closely says: 'He had 11 months of growth, because so many of the resources of the *People* (the *Mirror*'s stable-mate) had been poured into the *Mirror*, which was doing well as it came up towards being sold. Piers was on the cover of the prospectus. He got what he wanted.'

His reign there was characterised by trouble-making, for better or worse. He had to apologise for a tasteless headline before England's crunch football game against Germany in 1996 ('For you, Fritz, the European Championship is Over!'), and survived allegations of impropriety when he bought £67,000 worth of shares that two of his financial journalists had tipped. He was censured by the Press Complaints Commission, although this did not noticeably dent his self-belief.

As Morgan progressed, so too did his friends Andy and Rebekah. Coulson was on the Bizarre column from 1994 where Sean Hoare was his deputy. The pair enjoyed countless high-octane nights of mischief on the town, and before Sean died he recounted great many of them, some for the sake of entertainment, others because he was aggrieved at the way some colleagues and himself had been treated by the management. It would be otiose to rehearse what would have gone on when two well paid men-about-town got together in the company of highly-paid showbiz personalities, but the pair certainly knew how to work hard and play hard.

While of the three Piers Morgan was the most obviously talented, Rebekah Brooks's ascent was no less inevitable. Five years after turning up at Wapping as a secretary on the magazine (as a 'keen, likeable young girl', recalls a colleague), in 1994 she was made features editor of the *News of the World*. She had become an expert in 'buy-ups', the forking out of money for a particularly sensational story, an arena in which her likeability could be deployed with enormous effect. One of her first successes as features editor was a five-page exclusive interview with footballer Paul Gascoigne, for which she paid between £50,000 and £80,000. It was classic *News of the World* fare, in which Gascoigne admitted 'I've been a violent bastard and a coward and I want the world to know it'. 'Paul is a friend,' explained Brooks at the time. 'He rang me and asked me to see him. Then he poured out his heart.'

One person who worked with Rebekah at that time was Paul McMullan, her deputy, known as Mucky to his colleagues for his willingness to do pretty well anything to get the story. While careful not to make allegations against Brooks, he does point to her inexperience. 'She'd never done an investigation or barely written a news story,' he says. 'She was quite sweet in those days. She knew she was out of her depth and would rely on other people to make her shine. And, funnily enough, it was because she was so hopeless, we wanted to protect her as our boss when we would find out she didn't know what she was doing.'

Brooks's tendency to bring out the protective side in men is a constant in her career. Many speak of someone seemingly anxious for approval, and her apparent vulnerability drove her to work all the harder to impress. A former *News of the World* reporter told *Vanity Fair* magazine: 'She was going at 150 all day…. She was very intense. I thought she was a very insecure woman, actually, desperate for a lot of love and attention…. I was quite friendly with her at some point, as friendly as anyone can get with her, and in her quieter moments she would say, "No one loves me; I'm in a battle here." But even then, she was careful. Even out drinking after work, 'she did not get pissed, ever. She never let her guard down…. She'd get you to do things…. She had this charisma, this magnetic attraction…. She would praise to high heaven, make you feel like you were on top of the world. It was only afterwards that you realized you were manipulated.'

It was not only Paul Gascoigne who was impressed by her. News International executive chairman Les Hinton had also fallen under her spell. As subsequent controversies were to show, the cementing of the pair's relationship was to prove a crucial moment in the company's history. Rupert Murdoch always enjoyed being a hands-on proprietor, but there were limits to what even he could keep his eye on. As one senior figure at the company said: 'The business had got so big and Rupert had to trust someone. The company's first total manager was Les Hinton. Editors always reported to Les. For a prospective editor to succeed, they had to be endorsed by Les. Rupert was very keen to have people validated, and Les liked Rebekah.'

Hinton admired her ability to convert ideas into stories in the paper. She was adept at impressing her bosses, and could show a necessary toughness. In a 1997 memo she wrote to the paper's feature writers: 'The editor and I are very concerned at the standard of the (ideas in the) features list. This morning it was appalling, as it has been for the last few weeks. Some of you are highly experienced and highly paid, however the level of stories and ideas on the schedule would not even make the *Basildon Bugle*, never mind a national newspaper. Some of you are young and have just joined the desk yet I can see no evidence of any effort or enthusiasm which warrents (sic) your posi tion on the biggest selling tabloid.'

The success that Piers Morgan was enjoying at the *Mirror* was worrying the owners of the *Sun*. The *Mirror* was giving youth its chance, and some felt News International should be doing the same. Change was in the air, although *Sun* editor Stuart Higgins was resisting anything too radical. So when the deputy editor's chair became vacant, it was a chance for the management to nudge the tiller in their direction.

Higgins and Hinton were not close and Hinton, Murdoch's right-hand man, wanted changes that Higgins was resisting. At News International, such situations tend not to endure. Before long, the writing was on the wall, and was made all the clearer when in January 1998 Hinton insisted on making Rebekah Brooks Higgins's deputy. Higgins resisted her because he thought she lacked experience and would seek to take the paper away from its natural readership. Brooks wanted, she said later, to make the *Sun* 'less blokey'. In a man's world, which News International's red tops very much were, that would have been an achievement indeed. Les Hinton knew her desire to get rid of 'Page Three', the daily picture of a topless woman, was doomed to failure, and told her if she persisted it would put unnecessary obstacles in her way. She stopped lobbying for it, and it seemed to do the trick.

At Brooks' 30th birthday party in late May 1998, according to media pundit Roy Greenslade, 'Hinton made a speech which all but anointed Brooks as Higgins's successor while Higgins, barely concealing his dislike for Brooks, indicated that he knew he was about to go.' But there was, unusually, disagreement between Hinton and Murdoch as to who should succeed Higgins, Murdoch worrying that Brooks lacked experience. In the end, the job went to David Yelland, deputy editor of the *New York Post* and a former City page editor at the *Sun*.

Yelland set about redesigning the *Sun* in a mildly more cerebral direction. This was a matter of degree, admittedly, but he wanted to reposition the paper and lead it away from the excesses of 1980s bombast, while retaining its sense of humour. Brooks was as disappointed as might be expected of someone who felt she had been promised the job, and did not disguise her disappointment well. She, like Piers Morgan before her, felt the *Sun* was the big prize, and to have a man for whom she had limited respect being given the job ahead of her was hard to take.

But being passed over for the *Sun* was to prove a mere hiccup. In May 2000, Les Hinton got his way. Phil Hall, at the helm of the *News of the World* for five years, was sacked to make way for Brooks. At 32, she had arrived.

One of the least publicly understood aspects of what went wrong at the *News of the World* was the fact that the paper's commanding heights were taken over by a new breed. Phil Hall had had extensive news experience in the 1980s and 1990s at the *People*, as both as an executive and a reporter, so had the wherewithal to be able to judge the truth and weight of a story. Even he, though, was considered by some of the reporters to have initiated a tendency towards a more feature approach of the paper.

The Morgan-Brooks-Coulson trio were certainly more oriented towards features than news. One News International veteran who sneaked a look at Brooks' contacts book was shocked: 'They're *all* PR people!' There were other grumblings, too. One reporter was appalled at Brooks getting the editor's job. 'She was totally out of it and unconnected with the day to day running of her office. She was dismal as an editor, the worst editor I ever had. She shouldn't have been there.'

There are few more damaging phrases, in a trade where professionalism is perhaps surprisingly highly rated, than 'not a proper hack'. Brooks seemed to acknowledge her own lack of news experience by appointing Andy Coulson as her deputy. Coulson, she felt, possessed the harder edge that would complement her strengths in softer, 'human interest' stories – although, in truth, Coulson's main redtop experience was also in features. The pair's sexual relationship, which emerged well over a decade later, had begun by that point, and it seems Brooks had high hopes for it, notwithstanding Coulson's marriage. And professionally she wanted to help him, being conscious that he was not highly rated by the companies' bosses. 'There was a feeling at the time that Andy wasn't editor material,' says one senior figure. 'They just weren't sure about him.' In Brooks' early years in the editor's chair, she was also able to count on the guidance of her mentor Les Hinton, with his lifetime's experience in newspapers behind him.

The senior person in the office full-time with the real news 'edge' was Greg Miskiw. He was old-school *News of the World*, having reputedly said of his work: 'That is what we do – *we* go out and destroy other people's lives'. He was the master of many a vintage sting, often in harness with his friend and fellow Ukrainian émigré Alex Marunchak. But Miskiw was on the cusp of his 50th birthday, an old-school smoker and drinker redolent of the age of naughty vicars, busty blondes, dodgy scout-masters and massage parlours. He was seen as something of a dinosaur amid this keen young features-oriented regime brought up on soap stars and MTV.

Nonetheless, whatever else he was, Miskiw was 'a proper hack'. He believed in robust, the-people-have-a-right-to-know journalism, and had a certainty about what he and the paper had been doing. For all his unforgiving exterior, he was in the main supportive of his staff, nurturing them, bringing them on with the chance of writing up the potentially big stories, having a laugh and not sending them on wild-goose chases (always a plus for weather-beaten reporters). He enjoyed the muscle the *News of the World* could bring to bear to a story – the clout of the paper's credibility, the outnumbering of rivals in reporter strength on a big story, the ability to out-pay. The claim to be 'a proper hack' requires a toughness of mind, and Miskiw had plenty of that, possibly to excess.

'He had very little sympathy for the people we wrote about,' says one of his former reporters. He was a prodigiously hard worker, totally absorbed by his work. He and Murdoch's *News of the World* were a good match.

Christine Hart, a private investigator and journalist who worked with and had a relationship with Miskiw, wrote a novel, *In for the Kill*, which contained a fictionalised account of her links with the paper. She said: 'Executives on the paper didn't really care about the subjects of stories. They used to enjoy the hunt of people they could screw over. They became 'non-people' and the execs used to talk openly about 'the kill'. There seemed to be an indifference. There was something really dark about Greg.'

'Greg and Clive [Goodman, his deputy] just couldn't do the new celebby stuff they wanted,' remembers another staff member. 'To the new regime, they were a couple of old gits, and they were put under enormous pressure as a result. They had not only been passed over for promotion, they hadn't even been considered for the top jobs. It must have been really difficult for them.' That pressure was felt across the office, and passed downwards.

4

Dr Evil
The Family Man

Barrister Robert Jay described phone hacking as Mulcaire's 'sole way of being, his industrial activity… what he lives for, to hack into voicemails'. Clive Goodman said he was 'well known for cracking impossible stories often involving communications'. Journalist Nick Davies called him 'a brilliant blagger'. David Blunkett said he hoped Mulcaire would rot in hell.

Who was this man, who first appeared on the *News of the World*'s full-time payroll soon after Rebekah Brooks's appointment as editor? Mulcaire ascribes to himself the name 'Dr Evil', in ironic reference to how little known and understood he believes himself to be by those who know only what some News International executives have wanted them to know.

He was born in September 1970 into swinging London's most switched-on area of privilege, Chelsea. But his parents were of unpretentious background, and the capital's juxtaposition of extreme wealth and modest means were perhaps at their most pronounced in the streets around Kings Road. The Mulcaires were from the entrenched urban poor of SW10's World's End estate rather than the fashionable bohemian rich of Sloanedom.

Glenn's father was, in the language of the day, a dustman, a rogue of the old school and endowed with caricature Irish attributes, starting with the nickname Paddy (it was really Michael) and extending to a 'top of the mornin' bonhomie and a fondness for socialising. Though brought up in a family of tailors in Thurles, County Tipperary, in Ireland, he was a fount of local SW6 knowledge and someone whose exterior cheery manner would be called upon to help his clients lay his hands on the occasional unconsidered trifle. While convention would not have had him down as an obvious soulmate of Chelsea's better-heeled folk, and those who remember him say he was something of a ducker and diver, he is remembered as obliging and hardworking. He is believed never to have had a day off sick in 40 years, and was once featured on BBC1's Nationwide programme, describing him as 'the fastest dustman in the West'.

He was capable of great feats of entertainment. One party trick was to bounce a golf ball on the head of a golf club for minutes on end, a trick he owes to his heritage among Ireland's hurling champions. Another was seemingly to swallow a lit cigarette and smoke it internally, the smoke blowing out of his ears before he would disgorge it again, still lit. And on an evening out he would still be going strong at 4 a.m., singing his heart out and amusing his friends.

One residence on his beat was no less than Buckingham Palace, which, around the time of Glenn's birth, brought with it concerns about the possible terrorist risk from Irish extremists. Glenn's father's unambiguous Irish accent and loyalty towards the nation of his birth suggested that perhaps he was not someone to be allowed behind the Palace Gates. A number of police checks were felt necessary before he was allowed to be one of the few Irishmen to do the Palace bins.

Another home on his dustcart's route was that of Lady Aitken, mother of Jonathan Aitken, later MP and junior minister in the Thatcher government. Pempe, as she was known, was of the patrician cast of mind that likes to think it treats 'the staff' as equals, or something approaching it. Strong-willed and entertaining, she would invite Paddy Mulcaire for a frequent chinwag and, in the best Ealing Comedy tradition, the pair got along hilariously, neither imaging why their backgrounds should prevent them enjoying the other's company. Paddy recalls the occasions with affection, remembering that his host was not above getting out the whiskey at 9.30 in the morning to fortify his efforts on the cart.

On one occasion he and his colleagues came across a pheasant that one of Chelsea's better-heeled residents had left out. Paddy picked it up and, before loading it into the cart, proceeded to kick the lifeless bird across the street with his colleagues. The house's owner came out and shouted: 'Oi, that's my supper you're playing with!' The bird had been left out to hang, but Paddy had assumed it was surplus to requirements, and there was talk of disciplinary action. The heresy they had committed was forgotten a day or two later when Paddy handed back the pheasant, cleaned up and restored to some sort of presentability. If they had broken a taboo, Paddy was not going to allow the owner to have all the moral high ground. He insisted on reminding the gentleman which of them had actually killed the bird. After he lost his job, he was given a redundancy payoff, but a number of his celebrated clients rallied round to endorse his case, including solo round the world yachtsman Sir Francis Chichester.

But while Paddy Mulcaire was the gregarious public face of the family, at home things were different. He was not demonstrative, and could be distant and uncommunicative. He preferred not to be called 'Dad'. And when, much later in life, Glenn was sent to prison, his father chose not to visit him there.

Paddy could also be violent, towards Glenn, his brother Stephen and Glenn's mother Eileen, an ultra-correct, respectful, dutiful Geordie. Of the two parents, she was the quiet home influence, who insisted her two boys' good behaviour and simple courtesies (as do Glenn's own children nowadays). She had a proud degree of military history in her family, her father having served in the Irish guards and the War Office. She had been a professional ballroom dancer and later a window dresser at Peter Jones. She suffered from a rare bone deficiency in her youth and, during a difficult time in her marriage, had a serious eating disorder. Her weight dropped to five and a half stone and one Christmas day nearly died. On several occasions Glenn had to go and stay with his mother's sister, Rosie Harvey (to whom he remains very close), at her house on nearby Burnaby Street during his mother's bouts of illness.

She was the one who in greatest measure passed on to Glenn a commitment to the Catholic faith. He attended first Servites Primary School on Fulham Road and then St Thomas More, a Catholic secondary school between Sloane Street and Sloane Avenue in Chelsea which traditionally imbued a respect for authority, hierarchy and honesty. He would serve at mass from the age of 11 to

15 at our Lady of Dolours, Fulham Road. On one occasion, at the age of 11, he was selected from his class to recite the whole of Gideon, the Old Testament tale of the Mighty Warrior who was tasked by God to reclaim and free the people of Israel. He was also selected from among his classmates to wave to the Pope John Paul II at Victoria station, when he visited in 1982. His form teacher Mrs Feeney wrote in his school report in March 1983: 'Glenn is a well-mannered, responsible and caring member of my form. Totally reliable, he can carry out tasks honestly and efficiently. He participates fully in the classroom and represents the school at football and swimming. His work is satisfactory but more care is needed with presentation in all subjects. I believe that Glenn could do much better if he organised himself in a self-disciplined way.'

Mulcaire remains close to his mother, but he has no hesitation in saying that the person who most influenced him was his brother Stephen, 10 years his elder. For a start he was a 6 foot 3 inches tall 'gentle giant', who was constantly checking that his sibling was keeping out of trouble. As the youngest printing manager estate agents Hamptons had ever had, teetotal Stephen, a product of the London Oratory, was someone for Glenn to look up to in all senses.

Stephen's own enthusiasms included a devotion to Chelsea Football Club, which in his teens he followed to home and away games. The club was then suffering a drop in its fortunes, but perhaps to compensate, its fans were keen to make their mark off the field. This manifested itself in a continuation of violence at football grounds, not curtailed until the arrival of CCTV cameras and after the Heysel and Hillsborough disasters. Though no boot boy, Stephen was never intimidated by the threat of violence and would insouciantly savour the highly charged games with his friends. Young Glenn found the whole theatre of it an inviting spectator sport, but rarely got the opportunity. 'I used to want to go along just to watch the fights,' he says now, recalling his sense of fear at the thought.

Chelsea games were as testosterone-charged as any. One day, at the age of 8, he sneaked away from home and unknown to his parents managed to get himself into Chelsea's ground for a game against West Ham, whose fans were notoriously violent. A series of fights broke out as the West Ham fans sought to 'take the Shed' (i.e. achieve the impossible by displacing the home fans), with a terrified but still inquisitive young Glenn looking on open-mouthed. As Glenn gawped at the sheer aggression, he found his entire body being lifted vertically. It was Stephen, who had grabbed him by the scruff of the neck and picked him up. 'What the hell are you doing here?' he asked as he was marched the 5 hundred yards to the Mulcaires' home. It was Glenn's guardian angel, who knew the difference between childish mischief and putting oneself in serious danger. Stephen never told their parents what Glenn had been up to, but he knew when to take the side of safety. On two other occasions, Glenn, frustrated by tensions at home, ran away. Stephen, though sympathetic and protective in the face of their angry father, read the riot act to his headstrong sibling, patiently explaining that flight was no answer to anything.

Within a season or so of that West Ham game, Glenn

and Stephen went to a Chelsea match against Spurs, when the away fans looked as if they would overwhelm a hopelessly under-resourced line of police and trample through one of the more genteel parts of Chelsea's ground and hem in the home fans. As angry Spurs fans swarmed towards the flimsiest of temporary barriers, the unflappable Stephen registered the danger, and turned to his young brother in a state of near panic. 'If they come through, you go down there and get onto the pitch. You'll be safe down there,' he said. It was a tender moment between two young men at an age when most young men think first of advertising their masculinity and autonomy. 'How he could be so unselfish at a moment like that?" asks Glenn now.

At home, too, Stephen was Glenn's protector. Paddy was inclined to be aggressive (more than once he threw a Radio Rentals television out of the window, and Glenn recalls his father hitting Stephen with a broom handle). On one occasion Paddy hit Glenn across the back with a bicycle inner tube. Stephen turned on his father and told him with some menace: 'Don't ever do that again.' He didn't.

Paddy, though, was capable of great generosity towards his sons, and brought Glenn an expensive car when he (Paddy) was made redundant. His love was shown in ways that the young Glenn could find embarrassing. When Glenn was playing football, Paddy's enthusiasm would get the better of him and he would swear and shout abuse at the opposition on the touchline, way beyond the accepted just deserts of easily embarrassed adolescents. He was also not above the odd terminological inexactitude in order to get what he wanted. Glenn remembers being ushered onto the team bus of the New York Cosmos football team to shake the hand of two of soccer's greatest ever players, Johann Cruyff and Franz Beckenbauer, a treat most schoolboys would kill for. 'I think my dad told the man on the door I had a terminal illness,' he recalls apologetically. 'That was the sort of thing he did.' Paddy recalls simply: 'It did the trick, though, didn't it?'

On another occasion, Paddy bought a snooker table from Harrods, which he took home to World's End on the No 11 bus. In most people at most times, this would normally be merely eccentric, but Paddy's Tipperary tones at a time of heightened terrorist concern caused some consternation and suspicion.

Looking back, Glenn says he was brought up 80 per cent by his brother Stephen and twenty per cent by his mother. 'My father must be in there somewhere,' he says, 'I suppose my willingness to really graft came from my dad.' In some other respects he was not everybody's idea of an enlightened role model. In hindsight, it seems as if Stephen was something of a family safety valve and an emotional load-bearer.

So what happened on 19th September 1981 was shattering for the Mulcaire family in even more ways than one might have imagined. Stephen travelled up the M5 to watch his beloved Chelsea in a match at Shrewsbury. As he and four friends travelled home on a stormy night in an estate car from the game, their car went into a skid and hit a tree. Stephen, in the middle of three on the back seat, had no seatbelt. Four of the young men were taken to intensive care. Three were to emerge alive, but Stephen, his neck broken, never did. He was 21.

In many respects the family never recovered. Glenn, just 11, was too upset to go to the funeral, although his mother would not have allowed him to witness such grief in any case. Over time Paddy's idiosyncracies became yet more pronounced, and for years Eileen barely went out and suffered a series of major eating disorders. She contemplated suicide, and even thought of taking Glenn with her, as it were, but pulled herself back, remembering some curiously prophetic instructions from Stephen, about Glenn: 'Make sure you look after him.' Glenn says now, simply: 'Stephen would never have forgiven her.' It would be glib to surmise what impact the loss of such a young life would have on a young sibling, but proud tears come readily to Glenn's eyes when he remembers him. 'He was my mentor, my idol. I think about him every day.'

Indeed, it is a loss to which Mulcaire still frequently refers, unprompted. Psychologists are inclined to say that those who lose a parent young in life are often highly motivated achievers, having been taught an early lesson in life's brevity, and Stephen's death may have compounded Glenn's drive and willingness to work hard. Not that he had seemed destined for a drifter's life. His vibrant curiosity would surely have seen to that, but in his teenage years he showed a striking willingness to commit and throw himself into whatever he was doing.

Just as striking, given the infamy he was later to acquire, was his out-of-hours work. In modern parlance, there does appear to have been something of 'an ethic' to Glenn's teenage years, and he spent much of his free time working for the benefit of others. He worked for some time at the Chelsea Boys' Club. A youth-club leader, Teus Young, identified leadership qualities in the young

Mulcaire. He recalls: 'He was excellent at interacting with young people, especially underprivileged kids. Some people just have that quality, and he showed it in organising, planning, helping them to work as a team, in offering one to one support. He was always a strong character, and a fantastic support to me in the boys club. Maybe it comes naturally in some people, but he certainly had it. He commands respect. Leadership came out of him. He was an excellent organiser and planner. I'm not saying he wasn't a cheeky bugger too, with lots of aggression and a strong tackler, but definitely bright.'

He was a better than ordinary footballer, and had trials with several clubs. He was on Chelsea's books at one point, being named Under-16 player of the year and lauded by Chelsea's controversial then chairman Ken Bates, being told he would 'go far'. Two of his contemporaries Jason Cundy and Frank Sinclair, did go far in football, becoming first team regulars for the Premiership team and playing in the same sides as Ruud Gullitt and Gianluca Vialli. Mulcaire showed leadership qualities and conviction as a player, and no little measure of self-confidence. But he fell out over an issue of tactics with a Chelsea coach Gwyn Williams, and was asked to leave, because, Williams believed Mulcaire had an attitude problem. To this day, Mulcaire, though agreeing that he can be stubborn, insists Williams was in the wrong. ('We lost a South East Counties trial game 3-1 because of him. I was proved right. He was playing two players out of position. I was totally vindicated, and the other players all knew it, but Williams hated having to listen to feedback and took against me,' he will explain, at greater length than the casual reader may be anxious to know.) Williams told Mulcaire he would never play for a London team again.

At the age of 17 he won a Community Sports Leaders Award for his work in local boys' clubs. He applied to join the SAS 23rd Territorial Army regiment, but was selected for the 14th Inc Duke of York, passing the entrance tests creditably. But there was a problem. He had been so anxious to sign up that he had lied on his application form, and had been found out when it was compared with his National Insurance documents. He was still only 17, and was rejected as too young, being told 'you are too young to die'. But he had impressed his examiners, who sought to steer him towards an area that best suited his abilities.

He was advised to visit another military person who gave him direction as to how he might cater for his interest in other ways. He prefers not to elaborate on who exactly was advising him. He immersed himself in the world of intelligence gathering, doing a course in forensics, graphology, medicine, first aid and so on. It was at this point he says he learned the argot of 'Humint' (human intelligence, i.e. human sources), 'elint' (electronic intelligence) and 'comms' (communications). He tends to be evasive when the subject comes up nowadays. 'I don't want to sound like Johnny English,' he says, but it was clearly a world that absorbed him.

He spent some time working part-time at Harrods, and is proud to say that he served Walt Disney, selling him a jumper, only realising who it was when he presented his credit card. He is prouder still to recall that the film maker sent a letter, complete with Mickey Mouse logo, thanking the shop for their help and for its obliging service. He also earned money to pay for his courses by working as a youth worker and play leader at Park Walk School on King's Road.

Having acquired some proficiency in research techniques, he was asked to attend a job centre and give a reference number for a job advertising 'investigators needed'. He attended a series of interviews in Hammersmith Chambers and was asked to start work the following Monday.

The company in question was Worldwide Investigations, a large intelligence gathering company, and he describes his work as 'tracing and tracking at corporate and criminal level', plus a bit of credit work and due diligence. His work there also included research for two of their subsidiaries, Unitel and Argen. These companies worked discreetly and never talked about their clients. Mulcaire did a good deal of low-key sleuthing for the two subsidiaries, including equity searches and 'paper trails'.

Argen was an intriguing company. It had been set up in 1968 by a man called John Fairer Smith (born Aug 1939, died 1999), reputedly a former member of MI5 and the South African police who returned to his native UK and set up the investigations company. He was later named in parliament and accused of political and economic espionage, his particular task being to subvert British attempts to undermine the racist regimes of South Africa and Rhodesia. For some time he was the controller of Norman Henry Blackburn, who was sentenced to five years in prison after being caught stealing cabinet papers dealing with Rhodesian sanctions. Argen widened its client base enormously (and its most recent iteration is unrecognisable from its earlier existence), employing many former spies and special forces personnel, specialising initially in protection against the then burgeoning threat of terrorism (in the late 70s he was quoted as saying 99 per cent of his clients were on an IRA hit list, and many others were PLO targets). It opened offices around the world and later became adept at more general business intelligence.

It was a world Mulcaire thrived in. Even after the period of working for pro-apartheid clients, Argen continued to attract some unwelcome publicity. But having several spies on its payroll meant its ethos was highly discreet and intelligence-oriented. And it taught Mulcaire to see the information derived from research as a good in itself. It was not the investigator's job to question the client's motives or lifestyle, although, happily by this time there was probably less reason to do so. A great deal of Argen's work was for the government, and specifically for Serious Fraud Office and MI5. In 1993 Mulcaire also started work for First Legal Financial Services, in Milner Street in Chelsea, and then, in 1995, for LRI Research and Intelligence.

This was to prove a crucial move in his career. The company was run by an investigator called John Boyall. As we have seen, Boyall was later the subject of an Information Commission raid in 2002, which gave rise to the exposure of much of the information-gathering business. In the 1980s, Boyall had run a team of three or four women doing tracing jobs on a small scale. From the basement office in Croydon of Legal Research and Intelligence, he presided over a small team of data-gatherers. To the fore among these was a man called

Andy Gadd. Mulcaire and Gadd did the bulk of the legwork in Boyall's operation, and were used extensively by a variety of newspapers. Their work was largely formulaic, but they were reliable and discreet and gave no cause for discontent among their clients.

During the 1990s, the *News of the World* had also been using the services of Christine Hart. She was also a forceful and resourceful journalist who brought a fresh eye to some of the more mundane work of the private investigator. Personally she found little excitement in the routine unearthing of telephone numbers, company searches, blagging of information from the Police National Computer, and sought to bring a more creative – and possibly more empathetic – eye to the knottier issues that confronted her clients. She did a certain amount of humdrum work for news editor Greg Miskiw (turning around numbers and so on) until, after an office party, she started having an affair with him. The relationship, facilitated by the fact that her flat was a few hundred yards from the *News of the World*'s office in Wapping, was largely based on their work together, and she says in hindsight it was unlikely to endure, not least because of Miskiw's relentless drive, hunger for work and sleeplessness. She also felt that, to a degree at least, she was not getting the credit she deserved inside the paper.

The relationship came to an end, though Miskiw and Hart remained friendly – again, in part, because it suited them to do so for professional reasons. Greg Miskiw, who had an insatiable hunger for new wheezes and methods of uncovering information, found John Boyall, though still in his late 40s but something of a senior figure in the world of private investigation, fascinating.

'John Boyall used to be known as Goldfinger for his high living,' says Hart, who got to know Boyall extremely well. 'Goldfinger was always on the lookout for new devices and ways of putting people under the spotlight. He was a real spy who had worked for [intelligence firm] Hakluyt and the big boys like G3. He had good MI6 contacts.'

Miskiw suggested that he, Boyall and Hart go out for dinner. Miskiw, as ever under pressure from his bosses, seemed preoccupied during the meal, at a swish restaurant near Piccadilly, but was agog at what Boyall had to say. 'Greg used to enjoy the spy business and was impressed by John Boyall's money – property in Aspen and skiing lifestyle paid for by his investigation work,' says Hart. ' Boyall impressed him hugely, and could see there was a vast amount his tradecraft could bring to the *News of the World*. The paper had been using an assortment of investigators, including Jonathan Rees, but it was clear that Boyall had a huge amount to offer. It was agreed that Boyall should sign up with the paper, although it was not going to be cheap.

The relationship worked well, initially at least. Greg Miskiw, Clive Goodman, Neville Thurlbeck and others would all avail themselves of Boyall's expertise, mostly put into practice by Mulcaire or Gadd. Miskiw found himself being increasingly taken with this young man Mulcaire. Although much of the tracing work was low-key and routine, Miskiw was impressed by Mulcaire's ingenuity and obliging nature. Increasingly Miskiw would go direct to Mulcaire and when Miskiw and Boyall fell out in late 2001, Miskiw was reluctant to sever the connection. Then Miskiw had an idea. Why pay Boyall's high rates? Why not hire the man who had learned so much from him for roughly half the price – and put him on an exclusive contract? So that is what he did.

With one exception, Mulcaire had not been unhappy working for Boyall, who had responded positively to his request for his own office at the company's premises in Croydon and provided him with a company Saab. But he had had to stand his ground to win that respect. Boyall's employees were paid by the customary Pay As You Earn arrangement. But one day the boss announced that everyone was to be regarded as freelance and was to make their own tax arrangements. It meant accountants and extra costs for the employees. Mulcaire was not happy, and remembers leading the staff over the road to the pub. After a while, Boyall appeared in the pub and announced that anyone who doesn't come back is sacked. Mulcaire recalls being the only one who stayed in the pub. Peace eventually broke out.

But when the offer came to have 'his own gig' with so celebrated an outfit as the *News of the World*, what could be better? Mulcaire was perfectly aware that as a private investigator he was a long way from being the finished article, but it was a brilliant opportunity. It also meant a more than doubling of his salary and it put him firmly on life's escalator. 'Generally John Boyall always treated me personally pretty well,' recalls Mulcaire, who acknowledges that he was anxious to 'get on' in life. (For some time after Boyall was frozen out of the *News of the World*, he pursued the paper for substantial unpaid bills. However, he was always confident that the matter could be resolved without needless publicity, and in the end, the paper's management gave way and Boyall was paid.)

Mulcaire's move was a big step for a man of barely 30.

Some greybeards felt he had been promoted too fast. After all, he had no training in journalism, and he was unregistered as an investigator. They felt most of his work had been humdrum and routine. 'Miskiw was delighted when he signed Mulcaire,' says Christine Hart. 'He didn't really care about people, although he had a thing about Glenn Mulcaire and what he could do for the paper. But Mulcaire was very green and Miskiw was using him. People in the investigation business regarded Mulcaire as just a tracer, and tracers are supposed to stay in the backroom and not have clients of their own. Miskiw cynically took Mulcaire and told him not to flash his money around, for example, which made Mulcaire think he'd arrived in a world of mystique and mystery, but actually I thought it was just condescending to say that.' Under pressure to save money, Miskiw was doing just that while giving a young man, anxious to impress, his head. For that, Mulcaire owed him a great deal.

Miskiw regarded Mulcaire as rather less of an investigator than Mulcaire did himself. For Miskiw, Mulcaire was a useful in-house blagger, or tracer, of the sort PI firms tend to have on call, who was willing to turn his hand to anything. As Christine Hart, who is sympathetic to what happened to Mulcaire, says of tracers, 'they are usually young people or misfits and they are taught format lies to access different things. As far as Greg was concerned Glenn was a tracer. But Greg rated Glenn because he could do everything, and most 'blaggers' can only do a few blags.'

When he signed up with the *News of the World*, he was ecstatic. He looks back now with an almost painful sense of achievement. 'I was so proud of joining that team. It had done great, really great work in exposing people who needed exposing. It was one of the biggest papers in the world, part of one of the most powerful newspaper groups in the world, and was standing up for and entertaining decent people against corruption.'

Judging solely by the stories in the papers, it is easy to write off Mulcaire as a mere 'chancer' who learned a few tricks and got over-promoted as a result. But his accomplishment at inveigling himself into people's trust made him an ideal candidate to bring in news stories, to help feed a news machine rather than being just any old cog. Certainly he is extremely adept at what might candidly be called dishonesty.

For professional ends, a number of techniques would continually re-present themselves as useful. One was to call an office and get the call rerouted so it looked to the ultimate recipient as if it was internal. Similarly, once that was achieved and the person believed they were talking to a colleague in another department, he would seek to make them believe he was reading the same internal computer file as the person he was talking to. He says Vodafone were the easiest, with BT being a bit harder. 'If they think you're reading it ahead of them, you need no more confirmation than that,' he says. 'Then you say the screen has frozen, and can you check something. If they say 'I'll call you back', you've had it. You need it there and then. It's smash and grab, but you need to be very gentle. You have to execute the plan with confidence, but you'll only get one chance.'

Two stories illustrate his capacity for building trust and then exploiting it. They rest on a metaphor of opening a door, putting a wedge under it and then returning later to gain entry. The first relies on one of the participants being a smoker and requires an ability to react quickly to unforeseen developments, but the gist is clear. Asked by the office to establish if a hospital patient has a particular ailment, Mulcaire would take a 'white coat approach'. 'You have to look as if you belong wherever you go,' he says. 'You never inch into a situation because then you stand out as not belonging.' One trick is to go out of hospital doors outside which people are smoking, muttering 'I'll have a quick one before I go in'. Then, he says, note the name on the badge of one of the doctors, turn and go back in. The next day you check BMA records (then obtainable using a suitable pretext), then ring and check if someone is able to obtain the hospital number that identifies a particular patient (ditto).

'Then, one day when you know that doctor is off, you breeze in with his name badge, taking big files which look like case notes,… wait near reception, making marks on the files… wait till the receptionist goes for a cigarette and follow her out. If she happens to know the person (which he says happens very infrequently), he'd say 'I'm not him, we have the same name, but I'm the new, improved one'. Made contact, cheap joke, and then say 'I must be getting back.'

Then, back in Mulcaire's office, with a CD playing the low chatter of background office noise, he would ring the receptionist.

> M: 'Hi, my name's [false name]. I expect you're frantic.'
> Receptionist: 'Yes but how can I help?'

M pretends to recognise the voice, reminding her that they had met during a cigarette break. He would then reiterate that he didn't want to be a nuisance and needed to be quick.

M: 'My PAS system has frozen and I urgently need some details on a patient…' Mulcaire gives the details, she finds them.

M: 'What medical number comes up?' She gives it.

M: 'And which consultant is dealing with her?… I thought it would be him, let me give him a quick call while you're on.' He pretends to dial. 'Hi, Dr X. You're about to go into theatre? Oh, I'm sorry, but, just quickly, could you wire over some records of one of your patients. Actually it would be easier to get them verbally from the front desk. I'm onto them at the moment.'

Receptionist: 'Yes I heard all that. Ok I'll read what it says.' She reads out details, brief episode details, diagnosis and prognosis.

M: 'Thanks very much.'

Then, to check, he pretends to be the consultant and rings the hospital back, establishing his bona fides by giving the patient's medical number and few details. He says he'll be transferring notes over to them.

M: 'Oh, one other thing, what prescriptions is she on?'

If the answer is consistent with the presumed illness, he has confirmed the story.

Another 'blag' that Mulcaire cites as being fairly 'bog-standard' is the method of getting details of a phone subscriber's 'Friends and Family' list on their phone account. 'Back in 2002 – until journalists started doing it, when they tightened it up – it was comparatively easy. Once you've got the land line, you could get Friends and Family, though not everyone registered them. You'd ring BT posing as the subscriber, and make two calls. The first would ask when the next bill is.

M: 'Do you know how much it is, we're panicking'.

Call centre: 'Oh, it's about £300. Ok, thanks, bye.'

Then you ring later, a second time, again as the subscriber.

M: 'Is it ok to pay by cheque, not direct debit?'

Call centre: 'Yes, that's fine thanks very much…'

M: 'One other thing, can I add another number to my friends and family?'

Call centre: 'Sorry, you're full at the moment.

M: 'Really, oh dear, what have I got at the moment?'

Call centre: 'You've got x, x….'

The key to getting access is gulling the person on the phone into assuming that if you know about the size of the bill, when it's due and so on, you must be who you say you are. It's a technique that no longer works, apparently, as security at phone companies has been considerably improved.

In any event, Mulcaire's mindset – ambitious to provide for his family, morally driven, and socially conservative – made him well-suited to the type of work Miskiw was looking for. To Mulcaire's mind, Miskiw shared his view of what they were trying to do. 'Greg was never that keen on the celebrity nonsense', he remembers. 'Operationally he was always keener on the greater good stuff.' Feeling he had 'arrived' professionally, at the end of 2000 Mulcaire and wife Alison decided to upgrade, moving, with the help of a £1200-a-month mortgage, from their 3-bedroom flat in Battersea to a 4-bedroom semi-detached house in the affluent village of Cheam. Mulcaire had no inclination towards being a journalist, but he had the skills to make a more than decent living as an investigator. He had found his metier.

The fact that someone so accomplished in deceit might have 'a good side' doesn't fit the settled narrative. The intriguing question is, though, where did Mulcaire himself draw the line? Mulcaire remembers that when he worked for John Boyall he was regarded as being always 'one step ahead of the law'. He took it as read that the state does not have a monopoly in defending the public good. It's an assumption that says the forces of light have many faces, including his. (Whether that view can legitimately extend to contravening the state's edicts and breaking the law is another matter.)

Apart from good manners, rectitude is a strong theme in Mulcaire's makeup and the idea of living by a code is important to him. His upbringing had given him a striking trust in those in authority over him, though his mother was inclined to warn him not to allow people to take advantage of him. ('Don't let them use your brain,' she would say.) He has a faith in those in authority exercising a pastoral duty of care. The way he was later abandoned by his former employers would enrage anyone, but having the paternalistic assumptions of the Catholic Church in his blood must have compounded that disappointment.

He makes no claims to sainthood and is reluctant to throw stones at those who breach Catholic morality. But he strongly resists public hypocrisy. However, he also rejects the idea that he was on any kind of moral crusade with his work for *News of the World*. That, he says, would put him into a very different category. Besides, he acknowledges the power of the money he was earning. Any pretence that that didn't have a major role in his thinking would be absurd.

On the specific subject of deceit, his mother brought him up to believe that 'you can have honesty about your dishonesty, but if you're a liar you're a liar'. Thus dishonesty itself was not a wrong if it was used in the cause of good, a notion presumably most spies and even the odd politician and journalist would endorse. Small wonder that Mulcaire's mother was so aggrieved when the judge in 2007 said he was dishonest. The trickery he used in his work, pales, he says, against the deceitfulness of certain journalists. 'The way they would seek to trip each other up and protect their story at all costs – not for source-protection reasons but for petty careerist ones – was a real eye-opener.' 'They would lie and cheat on each other to a degree that astonished me,' he says.

5

RIPA

'When I started, I didn't do much hacking.' The words of Glenn Mulcaire don't fit with the narrative to which his bosses were wedded for a long time. He had been portrayed as the out-of-control rogue who no one knew about, but by the time of the court case, when the facts emerged, things had changed.

There was a substantial refinement of the argument. In early 2014, the judge reported that there were in total 5,600 notes written by Mulcaire. Of these, 2,200 had one name from several *News of the World* executives written on the top left corner. Just 600 were from Rebekah Brooks' time as editor (2000-2003), and of those around 50 were duplicates. A police witness had earlier reported that from that period only 12 contained unquestionable evidence of a phone having been hacked. Among those targeted were TV presenters Amanda Holden and Ulrika Jonsson, singer Charlotte Church and former TV presenter John Leslie, then at the centre of rape claims. Another was TV presenter Natalie Pinkham, who, at the age of 24, was rumoured to be going out with Prince Harry, then just 17.

Mulcaire remembers the Brooks period as one of working on some pretty weighty issues. Intercepting phone messages was the least of what he got up to at the time. Besides, he says, 'I was never actually asked to hack a phone – it wasn't much use, in that terrorists tend not to leave a voicemail message saying "we're putting the bomb at so-and-so."'

Rebekah Brooks had appointed Andy Coulson as her deputy because she felt he was better placed to handle more heavyweight stories. But she also wanted the paper to be more campaigning, a frequent claim of editors around the time of their appointment – but not always one that is delivered. Brooks, though, for all her 'shallow end' background, meant it. After contemplating putting Mazher Mahmood or Paul McMullan in charge, she brought back Greg Miskiw, until recently the news editor, from the US to head an investigations team, which was, perhaps a little grandiosely, to be the equivalent of the *Sunday Times*'s celebrated Insight team. As with Coulson, Brooks felt the seasoned Miskiw's hard edge complemented her own 'Features' outlook. On the surface at least, the pair got on personally better than it suited her later to acknowledge. Occasionally she would turn up for a drink with the reporters in Wapping with him, although privately Miskiw was at a loss to explain how someone with so little news experience could become an editor. Though they were cut from very different cloth, her deployment of him to this specialist role made a certain amount of sense. The same can be said of Miskiw's hiring of Glenn Mulcaire, who he had persuaded to leave John Boyall at LRI Research and who he signed up on an exclusive contract.

Some felt Mulcaire was a boy being asked to do a man's work and seemed to be the main beneficiary of the paper's wish to cut costs. He was considerably cheaper than working through Boyall, though he lacked Boyall's experience and urbanity. Boyall, though, was more than displeased when he learned that a man he had trained up had left him to work for the *News of the World*. One associate of Boyall remembers: 'Boyall then told me he was his office boy who he had trained up in bog standard tracing. He was livid they had plucked out his boy and cut him out of the equation to get the stuff he had trained him to do on the cheap. Boyall was going to take him down.'

But Miskiw was delighted with his hire. He would coo happily about how adept Mulcaire was at triangulating and pinging, the technique of identifying somebody's whereabouts through their mobile phone. And soon a big project presented itself for Mulcaire to get his teeth into. What gave Brooks's first two months in the editor's chair huge impetus and focus was the disappearance of 8-year-old Sarah Payne, on the evening of 1 July 2000 near the home of her paternal grandparents in West Sussex. A nationwide search began, and 16 days later her body was found in a field near Pulborough, about 15 miles away. It emerged later that her murderer was Roy Whiting, who had been convicted in 1995 of abduction and sexual assault and released having served only three-fifths of his 4-year sentence, despite a psychiatrist's fears that he would offend again. Whiting had been interviewed by the police the day after Sarah Payne had disappeared, but he was not charged until some weeks later.

It was a monstrous case, the sort of incontestable affront to decency that newspapers love to reflect and amplify for their readers. The fact that a sex offender known to the police could move into an area and commit so foul a crime would give rise to both righteous anger and media exploitation.

Rebekah Brooks wanted to do more than echo her readers' horror. She wanted to take a stand and get the law changed, to enable parents to know if a paedophile was living in their neighbourhood. Deputy features editor Paul McMullan had recently been sent to Worthing to write a feature about the Scout movement and the precautions it had had to take to ensure that no unsuitable adults came into contact with children. To that end, the movement compiled a list, mainly from newspaper cuttings, of known sex offenders. In a display of ingenuity (often referred to euphemistically as 'journalistic enterprise') typical of both McMullan and his paper, not only did he dutifully take notes but he helped himself to the entire list. 'It was unique, no one else had it,' says McMullan. 'It's the sort of blag we should have been proud of.'

The list was passed on, via Greg Miskiw, to Glenn Mulcaire, and over successive Sundays in July, the paper published pictures of 49 individuals who had committed sex offences, proclaiming that 'Everyone in Britain has a child sex offender living within one mile of their home'. The campaign gave vent to a lynch mob mentality, but concentrated the national debate on the wisdom or otherwise of existing policies. It also boosted sales by 95,000. The overall effect was hard to calculate, but in one case a paediatrician had to flee her house, having been mistakenly identified as a paedophile. ('Not one of mine,' insists Mulcaire, who used to get his information via probation services, benefit agencies and National Insurance numbers. 'We used to look only at the individual, not any labels anyone attached to them')

To the original list were soon added more names (Mulcaire believes there were over 500). He doesn't know where they came from, other than that Greg Miskiw provided them, but they gave rise to extensive coverage in the paper. Someone who knew Brooks well at that time says Brooks self-identified very strongly with abducted children, 'although she got a bit scared of the things she stirred up', he said, struck by Brooks' gift for striking on campaigns that were both admirable and commercially rewarding. 'It was a cynical campaign to start with, but she then got properly friendly with Sarah Payne and saw it as her job to speak up for these people.' In the end, even Sarah Payne's mother (Sara) became a little uncomfortable with the effect the campaign was having.

Certainly, and unsurprisingly, Rebekah Brooks, according to friends, had several wobbles as the heat of the campaign rose. Greg Miskiw, as befits an old-school news hound, was positively brutal in his professionalism. A reporter called him at the weekend to say that her husband had been named as a paedophile in the paper and that he had driven off, saying he was so humiliated he was going to kill himself. The reporter was in tears at the thought, and asked Miskiw's advice. Miskiw, with the certainty of 'a proper hack', was the embodiment of pressure under fire. 'They never actually do it,' he said. 'He won't though, will he?' He didn't.

It is a period Mulcaire looks back on with particular pride. 'I loved what I did there, all the Sarah's law stuff. It was really worthwhile. Rebekah didn't want Greg there, he wasn't her sort of person at all, I gathered, in being too old school for her, but together we did some great stuff.' He was not asking himself questions about the rights and wrongs, and most of his work didn't seem to require that. To his mind, making life hard for paedophiles and keeping the police up to the mark was unassailably the right thing to do. There was always a greater good to protect, and if breaking the law was the only way to locate and catch a child abuser, then it was worth doing.

Beyond work, things were going well, too. The family was growing, and his football was thriving. Although the management of his beloved Wimbledon FC had decided to move the club to Milton Keynes, he and many fans decided to stay put, forming AFC Wimbledon, which started its life in Premier Division of the Combined Counties League. On 17 July 2002 he scored the new club's first ever league goal at Hayes Lane against Bromley, a spectacular volley still available on YouTube. The glory was to be short-lived as he retired due to injury soon afterwards, but that goal lives vividly in the memory.

At work he was helping to break some big stories, so had good reason to feel in demand. He was on good money, although a former colleague says that on a paper used to throwing its money around on 'celebrity buy-ups' and the like, he sold himself short: 'Glenn was very naïve. He had no idea what a story was worth, or how valuable it was to the paper. He provided them with stuff worth a huge amount more than £100,000 a year.'

While listening in to live phone conversations (by means of a scanner, for example) was unambiguously illegal, the advantage of phone hacking, until 2000 at least, was that it was not explicitly illegal, or so many were inclined to believe. But that year the government brought in the Regulation of Investigatory Power Act (RIPA), which said that interception of communications was only lawful if used in the interests of national security or to prevent or detect serious crime. Effectively only branches of the state were in a position to make such a claim, and controversially there was no provision for a 'public interest defence' for journalists seeking to expose wrongdoing. But the change in the law went broadly unnoticed by journalists. Most had little need to pay any attention, some didn't know of the change, and others knew but simply ignored it. Which category Andy Coulson fell into when he told a House of Commons Select committee in 2009 that his paper 'did not use subterfuge of any kind unless there was a clear public interest in doing so,' is an open question.

Mulcaire's assumptions about his 'dual track' approach – sniffing around celebrities but mitigating it by doing serious investigations – was working to his satisfaction in his early years on the paper. At that time, he says it didn't occur to him that what he was doing was unlawful in any event (which some would say speaks volumes for his inexperience at that time).

If it was a matter of finding those who had abducted Milly Dowler or Sarah Payne or Holly Wells and Jessica Chapman, it wasn't an issue. He had operated in a world where some private investigators regarded regulation as optional and where what could be done discreetly tended to stay below the radar, legal or otherwise, so it was not hugely salient. But now, in any event, working at Rupert Murdoch's huge global company News Corporation, he took it for granted that lawyers were on top of everything that went on. Why else, he says, would he have kept such extensive notes? They are now cited as evidence of industrial levels of criminality, but initially they were an aide-memoire for his researches, a way of keeping track of his taskings. Would anyone keep thousands of sheets of paper lying around in his office if he realised they were one-way tickets to jail?

A cynic would say it was a measure of the paper's arrogance that it also afflicted Mulcaire, leading to his getting sloppy. More wizened souls in the world of private investigation would say that real PIs don't keep records. They could be incriminating. Or at least, they don't keep the sort Mulcaire kept. But he says he placed his trust in his employers, and whenever he asked, he was told: 'It's Ok, it's in the public interest' or 'it's a privacy issue, not a legal one'.

One of the most devastating weapons in Rebekah Brooks' armoury was her capacity to get on with the people who mattered. There are countless examples of her 'victims', level-headed men and women who have been targeted and left helpless by one of her charm assaults. It is one of the reasons she rose so fast, and PMs Tony Blair and David Cameron fell hook, line and sinker.

Brooks had a capacity for doing what was wanted and making the recipient an offer they couldn't refuse, not in a Mafioso sense, but simply in a way that had the effect of bestowing an obligation of guilt and gratitude. And of course she was able to deploy this gift for ingratiation in a way that furthered her own, and her company's, journalistic ends. An outstanding case of this came in late 2002 when a strike of Britain's fire service was threatened.

The 'New Labour' government, having by the

admission of some of its senior figures spent its first term in office consolidating rather than reforming, was anxious to push through a programme of public-service reforms. Tony Blair was later to remark that he 'still bears the scars' of his attempts to realise these reforms, and he met with a good deal of resistance from people who felt it was no job of a Labour government to make life more challenging for millions of union members.

Yet any thought of reform in one area, the fire services, was challenged by the fact that many of its employees felt seriously under-rewarded. Ministers attempted to tie in earnings (and the offer of an independent pay review) with the modernising of practices, but the Fire Brigade dug its heels in and was demanding a 40 per cent pay rise, which would have taken the basic pay to £30,000 a year. It was a moment of some militancy, with Bob Crow, general secretary of the Rail, Maritime and Transport Union, pitching in fraternally. He expressed concern that 'inferior appliances and poorly trained operatives will be used in place of the usual highly trained fire-fighters and that this could put the safety of my members and the travelling public at risk,' he said. The threat of a national fire-fighters' strike, the first for 25 years, was a very real one. 'We seriously rocked the government,' recalls one member. 'They had been very arrogant about how they were going to brush us aside, but we offered them much more resistance than they expected. They were really shaken.'

The FBU was led by Andy Gilchrist, an old-style, rabble-rousing union boss. He was a charismatic match for Deputy Prime minister John Prescott, who was old enough to feel scarred by what union militancy could do to a Labour government's capacity to govern. He offered a rise of 11 per cent over two years, but demanded that the union enter into negotiation, which Gilchrist rejected. His members were balloted in October and the first strike took place in early November, with more threatened. The TUC and other unions were supportive. In response, the government deployed the army to help minimise the damage.

Gilchrist recalls his public prominence rising that autumn. He remembers a degree of personal animosity towards him that September, but it was not until the strike started that he felt he was coming under particular scrutiny. He had been used to journalists waiting outside his house in order to have a word with him, and then leaving. Now he was finding people hanging around, apparently not needing to speak to him at all, merely to keep an eye on him. 'I was being followed, that was a given,' he recalls. One day he decided he had had enough of a young man who simply wouldn't leave, so he reported him to the police, who took him to Walton police station. He believes the man, who admitted waiting around outside Gilchrist's house, was working for South East News agency.

Some days later, Duncan Milligan, the FBU's chief handler of the media, got a call from a friendly journalist, warning him that the *News of the World* was pursuing a story about Gilchrist's personal life. We now know that Glenn Mulcaire had been given his details, and the investigator had been put on his case on 4th December. It seemed Wapping was taking no chances, in that both papers seemed to have the union leader on their radar. Gilchrist was later to say that the *Sun* had 'always known where I was going to be', which he 'could never understand'. The phone number of his wife and two colleagues were also found in Mulcaire's files.

'I think they wanted to hear him say "I'll be along later and I'll bring the coke and the hookers," says a colleague, 'but of course that wasn't going to happen.' But there was something in Gilchrist's past. Four years earlier, married with two children, he had begun an affair with Tracey Holland, a rep for the FBU in Wrexham, while at a conference in Mid Wales. The affair seems to have been pursued when work commitments enabled it to, but fizzled out after 12 months. It was in itself unremarkable and, having ended several years earlier, did not seem to reach the usual exacting, marmalade-dropping standards of the *News of the World*.

Just as Mulcaire was deployed, three weeks before Christmas, it began to look as if the threatened strike was off. And at about the same time, the story seemed to go away. One Saturday passed, during which Gilchrist expected to be told the story would run the following day, but the call never came.

On 13th January 2003, Rebekah Brooks moved from the *News of the World* into the editor's chair at the *Sun*. Rupert Murdoch announced that David Yelland had had 'five fabulously successful years' as the *Sun*'s editor, which wasn't quite how his bilious critics saw it. Murdoch said Brooks had 'proven her talent as a great campaigning editor' and he was 'confident she will triumph at the *Sun*'.

Six days later, with the threat of a strike now reignited, a reporter pushed an envelope through Gilchrist's front door. It contained a mocked-up front page reporting in excited detail the fireman's affair. But the paper in question was not the *News of the World* but the *Sun*.

The reader was spared few details of the affair, the reporting of which was a textbook of salacious prurience. With the help of a £25,000 cheque, accepted after much persuasion, Tracey Holland had poured out the details to the paper. She had been taken to a hotel by the paper while the story developed, where she supplied it with the details. Not only did the '31-year-old brunette fall for his charms', but the pair had enjoyed a 'torrid affair' and 'marathon sex sessions', Gilchrist having 'got his fireman's pole out six times a night'. More than that, Gilchrist was dubbed a 'cheat and a liar' by Tracey, who seemingly hadn't known that he was married with children. And, presumably to the delight of his political opponents, Tracey even ventured a view on his suitability to lead the union into another day's strike, happily due to take place the day after the exposé appeared. 'How can the thousands of men and women have any trust in him after this?' she asked. 'Personally, I am against the strike. A 40 per cent rise is an insult to ordinary people.'

Only now, at his moment of greatest influence, was Gilchrist's love life considered of public interest. The story could not have been better timed to maximise its political impact. 'There is no doubt in my mind it was political,' says Duncan Milligan. 'The attacks on Andy fitted absolutely the political profile of the *Sun*. The *News of the World* had barely covered the fireman's strike and it wasn't of that much interest, but getting Andy like that in the *Sun* suited the government perfectly. I have no evidence for this, but I would not have been astounded if someone in government had said to the Murdoch papers that January: "If you have any dirt on

Gilchrist, please throw it now.'"

How much Mulcaire had to do with the eventual story is not clear, but it is an episode that reflects something of Brooks' determination. The tale appeared to follow her. It also reflects an unresolved watershed issue: how much is a public figure's domestic life 'fair game' for lawful scrutiny?

Another high-profile victim of the *News of the World* was Home Secretary David Blunkett, whose private life came to eclipse his role as a minister and he was forced to resign. Blunkett had been made Home Secretary after the election of 2001, having performed creditably as Education and employment secretary in the first Blair administration.

Blunkett's personal life came to the attention of the *News of the World* at around the time the paper was exposing the antics of Boris Johnson, then editor of the *Spectator*. Johnson, married with children, had had an affair with Petronella Wyatt, also a journalist, and their on-off relationship had kept *News of the World* readers on tenterhooks for months. That, too, had been nailed down by Mulcaire. 'It was a "passively probing"' exercise. I was watching Boris for months, as instructed. I remember the breakthrough, which was a really intimate message that he left.' The affair reflected Johnson in a poor light, and when he denied to his party leader's emissary that it had even taken place, he had to resign as front bench arts spokesman.

One of Johnson's colleagues on the magazine was an American, Kimberley Fortier, its publisher, who had married the publisher of *Vogue*, Stephen Quinn, in 2001. Fortier was as famously vivacious as Johnson was ambitious, and her open and engaged manner attracted the attention of a number of middle-aged men. Blunkett, it seems, was among those mightily smitten, and the pair began their affair two months after Blunkett was made Home Secretary, in 2001. His marriage had ended in the late 1980s, and he was spoken of as a possible future leader of the party, should Gordon Brown's rivalry with Tony Blair end his chances. This sense that he was man in the know made him all the more attractive to journalists anxious to stay on the inside track.

Rebekah Brooks was one of those who sustained a professional friendship with Blunkett, although those who worked with him recall his keenness for the boundaries to remain clear. Given what was to transpire, and the fact that one of her newspapers was to hasten the end of his spell as Home Secretary, this is worthy of some attention. Someone who knows them both well says they had more than admiration for Tony Blair in common. 'Rebekah and he were robust in their view of life. They were both a bit outsider-y…. She played down her middle class roots under Labour and played them up under the Tories. She was non-university educated and would often crash through the constitutional barriers, which could cause problems. She was self-made to a degree and shared the same sense of humour as Blunkett. They are both alpha characters.'

Blunkett wanted the *News of the World* on his side, not least because he was regarded as being on the right of his party and needed as many allies as he could find. Gratifyingly for him, most of Blunkett's policies did win the support of Brooks' readers. One insider said people would support them 'if they were explained properly, which we hoped they would be and generally were, but there was also a tension, a degree of implied threat, that things might sour if we didn't do as she wanted.' Blunkett did indeed resist what Brooks wanted on Sarah's Law, a source of pride which those who expect politicians to have minds of their own might find surprising.

When Brooks moved to the *Sun* in January 2003, if anything, they had even more contact than before. Blunkett attended the *Sun*'s annual police bravery awards, and the pair would meet for other dinners. But civil servants who worked with him tell how punctilious Blunkett was about observing constitutional proprieties, and how anxious he was to prevent his private life impinging on his public duties. It is a mark of the emotional tangle into which he fell that those proprieties came to be forgotten, causing him to resign from cabinet twice.

It was reported in court that just 13 people knew about Blunkett's relationship with Fortier. One was Kath Raymond, who was in a relationship with Les Hinton, executive chairman of News International, although there is no reason to think she had been indiscreet. Quite when, or how, Brooks got to know about the targetting of Blunkett's private life is unclear, although she insists she knew nothing until a few days before her part-time lover Andy Coulson, then at the helm of the *News of the World*, published the story. In late July, Blunkett had attended Ross Kemp's birthday party with Brooks. It was a period of some distress for the minister as Fortier was seeking to break off their relationship.

Glenn Mulcaire had had Blunkett under scrutiny since January 2004, and started off by listening in to Fortier's voicemails. 'Greg [Miskiw] and Neville [Thurlbeck] were super confident there was something there,' remembers Mulcaire. 'It was a particularly sensitive case. One false move and the whole thing could have fallen down. We had to be ready for them, in case we were rumbled, so we had a "spoof" plan in place, whereby if we were caught we would be able to give the impression of having been involved but then gone away and given up, while actually maintaining them under surveillance. Spoofing is a very important part of an investigator's tradecraft, to allow the target to drop their guard and get them to go back to behaving normally.'

Mulcaire doesn't know where the original tip about Blunkett's affair with Fortier came from. Some believe that because Boris Johnson was under scrutiny, and he was known to be prone to straying, a belief grew that maybe he was having an affair with Fortier. (There has never been any evidence for this.) Some close to the former Home Secretary believe the Blunkett connection was a bonus that fell into the *News of the World*'s lap when they were looking for Johnson's lovers.

Mulcaire doubts this very much. He says he was tasked specifically to look at Johnson. If anyone was to infer some connection other than the Blunkett-Fortier one, that would be for a journalist to do, rather than him.

He also says that there would have been a free-for-all among journalists in the office hacking Johnson's phone. 'Once I had given them the PIN number, they would all have been having a go. It would have gone on 24/7 for as long as they could, until something changed, like the target changing their PIN or whatever, in which case they would come back to me and ask for a reset to be done.'

Thus it is indeed conceivable that the tip came from hacking, but not on Mulcaire's part, he insists. Another theory exists that Blunkett had fallen out with senior figures in the defence establishment, but that too is doubted by people close to him.

The details of the affair (and Fortier's decision to end it) are painful to behold, and the brutality of the intrusiveness that revealed it uncomfortable. To help ensure the story didn't leak out, *News of the World* reporters spoke of it in code, referring to the couple as Noddy and Big Ears. The second week of August was to be a fateful one. It seems that that was the week the *News of the World* decided to dash for the line, having worked for eight months on the story. The court was told of a note sent by Mulcaire, saying 'need to triangulate calls, build up a call profile make sure it stands up on its own'. On the same day, the court was told, phone billing records showed contact between Andy Coulson, the editor at the time, and *News of the World* reporter Neville Thurlbeck and then with Rebekah Brooks, by then editor of the *Sun*.

The following day, according to one press report at least, Blunkett contacted Fortier to tell her that the *News of the World* knew about the affair. It is tempting to think Rebekah Brooks had alerted him, but she told the court she knew nothing for several more days. She may have wanted to warn her friend of a coming storm. On the other hand, had she done so it might have jeopardised the writing of her lover Andy Coulson's story. (It was claimed in court that at that period in the relationship the pair were close). How she would have felt about that can only be guessed at. Certainly the matter caused some upset between Blunkett and Fortier, who each blamed the other for the relationship becoming public knowledge.

On Friday 13th, Andy Coulson went to Sheffield to confront Blunkett. On the same day, Coulson spoke to Brooks on the phone for 81 seconds, something the editor of a Sunday paper would normally be unlikely to do to a daily counterpart. Coulson told the Home Secretary 'People know about this affair. I'm not saying it is an open secret, but people are aware of it.' He said he was 'extremely confident of the information' but did not admit that it was partly based on voicemail messages left by him on Fortier's phone. Blunkett tried to insist on not confirming or denying the story, saying he had always drawn a line between the public and the private. Coulson told Blunkett that if he doesn't run the story, someone else will. 'You are Home Secretary and I don't think you can use your right to privacy to bat back an accusation that you have had an affair with a married woman'. But he said he was prepared to publish the story, omitting the woman's name, an extraordinary concession in normal circumstances, and doubly so given that her identity was not in doubt. Nonetheless Coulson wanted confirmation. 'You're asking me to say "Yes, I'm having a relationship with a married woman."' Again Blunkett refused to discuss his private life, but did admit: 'I am very happy to confirm that Kimberly is a close friend of mine (and that) we have seen a lot of each other over the past three years....' Normally that would not have been sufficient, but given the recorded proof, Coulson felt he had enough.

There was nowhere for Blunkett to go. The story was heading for the front pages. Blunkett's special adviser Huw Evans told the Old Bailey that he spoke to Andy

Coulson shortly before the exposé appeared, asking him what evidence he had to justify the story. 'I remember his reply and the tone of his voice, which was flat and unequivocal. He was absolutely certain that the story was accurate and he was going to run it. I remember at the time remaining puzzled as to why he would be so certain.' There was no discussion about not using Fortier's name, which under normal circumstances a paper would.

Rebekah Brooks told the court: 'I think Andy told me that he had the Blunkett story late on Saturday', she said. 'He must have told me he wasn't naming her, or when he told me he might not have said he knew the name.' She said she couldn't remember how the *Sun* got the name, later saying it had become evident from reading old gossip columns, such as Ephraim Hardcastle in the *Daily Mail*.

At the end of the week, he flew to Italy, dining with the 'extremely understanding and helpful' Tony and Cherie Blair, staying with the Strozzi family (whose ancestors had kick-started Machiavelli's career), near San Gimignano. The *News of the World* duly published its article on Sunday August 15 2004. On the same day there were 12 'contact events' between Coulson and Brooks. She also spoke to Huw Evans, David Blunkett's special adviser. Brooks was very matter of fact, saying the story was too big not to run. As to the lover's name, she claimed in court 'I just remember having to get it out of Huw Evans', later amending her position, telling the court she had said: '"We are going to name Kimberly tomorrow" and he didn't say "Kimberly who?"' Nobody in Blunkett's office was surprised she had the name.

Fortier was named in the *Sun* on Monday 16th,

although the paper cited little evidence for the story and had no evident confirmation of it, on or off the record, from Blunkett or his office. The following day, it also emerged that she was pregnant (by an unspecified father, later shown not to be Blunkett), something that also features in Mulcaire's recordings.

Brooks was torn between her professional friendship with Blunkett and her professional obligation to her newspaper group. As the *News of the World*'s managing editor Stuart Kuttner was to say later, using a phrase journalists everywhere will recognise as the acknowledging of a paper's not-to-be-crossed party line: 'I think we rather liked David Blunkett.' Brooks sought to sugar the pill by decreeing this was not a resigning matter, and by reflecting that the relationship was a true love affair, rather than a grubby fling. She felt bad enough to ask Blunkett's special adviser Huw Evans how he was taking things, reassuring him about the sympathetic editorial (written by Kuttner) the paper would be running and otherwise seeking to mitigate what had happened to him. It is surely not unfair to place in the same 'this-is-business-not-personal' category the (estimated) £100,000-a-year column he began writing for the *Sun* soon afterwards and the secret award of approaching £400,000 in compensation for having his phone messages hacked, in May 2011.

That was a long way from being the end of Blunkett's brush with the media. In late November 2004 it was reported that Blunkett was the father of Fortier's 2-yr-old son William, and the following month an official report confirmed that the child's nanny had received quicker treatment than would have been expected had the father not been the Home Secretary. Blunkett resigned as a result. After the 2005 election he returned to office as Secretary of State for Work and Pensions, and began a friendship with Sally Anderson, an estate agent who later passed on details of that association to a newspaper.

That friendship also aroused the interest of the *News of the World*. Glenn Mulcaire was deployed, and he recorded messages of Blunkett attacking the 'hyenas' of the press. On another message, he said: 'They're real bastards. They're doing it for money and they're doing it for themselves. It's a sick world.' And in another: 'Someone very, very close has done a really phenomenal piece of work on destroying both our lives at this moment in time and it's vile. 'Whoever it is I hope they rot in hell.' It was said that Mulcaire would be awarded a huge bonus if he could produce evidence that Blunkett was having a relationship with her. The investigator was overheard on one tape uttering the words, 'Just say 'I love you' and it's 25 grand.' Mulcaire's memory is that he was indeed offered an incentive. 'I wouldn't have randomly picked that figure… that was the figure they mentioned to me as what they'd give me if they stood it up. They used to promise all sorts of bonuses, to keep your mind on the job, but actually I don't remember ever receiving any.'

In November 2005, Blunkett resigned from government for the second time, over a conflict between his political and private interests. Like the Gilchrisst story, the Blunkett case might have been designed as a test case for journalism students seeking to compare the competing weight of privacy versus the public right to know. The personal life of a divorced man might be thought his own affair, except that his two ministerial resignations show how much his judgment had been affected by those 'private' matters. But was the intercepting of his voicemails excusable in the public interest? Could it ever be, maybe if he was suspected of doing something criminal or dangerous?

'I don't wince at what I did at all,' says Mulcaire, who is fervent in asserting that he was the agent to the newspaper's principal. 'They know there is something in the bag… it is my job to be professional and do the investigation… it's not my job to decide what is a story… otherwise I'd be a journalist, and I wasn't paid to write stories…. There has to be a chain of command… it's the journalist's call as to whether it's a story, and the *News of the World*'s call as to whether it was legal. They had the biggest legal team. That was an assumption I made – it was part of my own governance…. I was proud to be part of a company that did the right things. I was proud to work for that paper, and I was proud to be the only investigator on the paper ever to have been put on contract. I felt protected by the legal department, one of the biggest anywhere. I was part of the Murdoch elite, which felt great… the *News of the World* had a huge circulation and was doing great work… I loved what I was doing.'

One of the claims against Mulcaire, made by the BBC on 25 June immediately after the 2014 trial but echoing something that had emerged at the Leveson enquiry, is that he was responsible for breaching the government's witness protection programme. The very idea suggests a dastardly degree of indifference to the safety of someone who the police felt it necessary to protect. And the raid on Mulcaire's property provided the police with evidence that he had intruded into the privacy of one of the 'Bulger killers'.

The murder of two year old James Bulger in Bootle in 1993 was one of the most shocking cases in recent criminal history. While out shopping in the New Strand shopping centre in Bootle, young James had wandered off. He was abducted, tortured and murdered by two ten-year-old boys, Jon Venables and Robert Thompson. His body was found on a railway line four miles away.

The case attracted enormous publicity. Everybody is familiar with how young boys can behave mischievously, but this cruelty and indifference to suffering provoked countless articles about the nature of evil and what gave rise to it. The judge said the boys were capable of 'unparalleled evil and barbarity'. The pair became the youngest convicted murderers in modern English history. They were sentenced to custody until they reached adulthood, initially until the age of 18.

A series of political judgments raised then lowered their tariff. The Lord Chief Justice Lord Woolf declared, on the basis of expert reports, that 'these young men are genuinely extremely remorseful about the crime which they committed and the effect which it must have had on James's family.' The pair appeared to pose little risk to the public. 'They have worked hard in pursuing their education and, given their circumstances, have considerable achievements to their credit. All those who have reported on them regard the risk of their re-offending as being low.'

In January 2001, another judge declared they were to be given false identities and enabled, as far as anyone can in such a situation, to start again. The judge said the manager of the secure unit where one boy had been living had received hate mail which threatened: 'To the vermin who killed Jamie Bulger, we don't forget, we will get the job done.' Denise Fergus, Jamie Bulger's mother, was quoted as saying that 'mothers like me will be after their blood', and his father, Ralph Bulger, as saying: 'I will do all I can to try my best to hunt them down.' The pair were released in June 2001, and were required to maintain contact with their appointed social workers, but they were to attempt to reintegrate themselves into normal society. The judge had the *News of the World*'s 'name and shame' campaigns on paedophiles explicitly in the judge's mind when she issued strict instruction that the press were not to find and expose the young men.

It was another classic touchstone issue. Those who believed that attempted rehabilitation was the only possible option ('it's a test of our humanity') against those who were sceptical than any such thing could work, or deserved to work. The police, after all, were a bunch of bunglers, or so it was claimed, so, without robust scrutiny, how could we be sure the public was safe? While outing the pair would be clearly in breach of the law, the redtop papers saw it as their duty to nibble away at the edges. The menacing words 'we know where you live' did not need to be spelled out.

That month the *News of the World* reported on how the mother of one of them and her daughter visited an off-licence 'near the new home' to prepare for his homecoming. 'They looked like an ordinary mum and daughter, dressed in denim skirts.'

The *Independent* reported the *News of the World*'s story

like this: 'A tiny detail, of course, and of no help to a vigilante by itself; but combined with other similarly tiny details, combined with the previous week's issue and combined with Sunday's scandalously provocative headline 'Dead Man Walking' over a story about Venables, it is hardly encouraging restraint. Stuart Kuttner, managing editor of the *News of the World* was interviewed on the Today programme last Saturday in the absence of the seemingly pathologically shy Rebekah Brooks. He justified the *News of the World* telling its readers in which region the two teenagers would be living on the grounds that 'It is of enormous public interest because the taxpayers are funding their future lives. The information that was given was too blurred for anyone to home in on them.'

The *News of the World* promised: 'Whether they are at college, with girlfriends, perhaps working with unwitting colleagues, we shall do all in our power to watch over them.' [This], of course, can only mean 'publish information about' so we can expect months if not years of headlines on 'the woman in love with a killer' 'the teacher whose prize student is a monster' and so on. Each one will put another piece in the vigilante's jigsaw.

There continued to be reasons to think the boys had gone off the rails. The idea that their rehabilitation might be unsuccessful, that the clever-clogs 'experts' had been wrong, fed the pair's awful fascination all the more. 'There was an issue of public safety, and to see whether their own welfare was being given a higher priority than that of the wider public's,' is how Mulcaire remembers it. Liberal sensitivities were all very well, but for a robust free press, leaving 'the experts' to do their work was not enough. Could the politicians, notorious for trying to please their own supporters, really be trusted to hold the boffins to account? Child killers were in a category of their own and any threat to the public needed to be flagged up. The fact that it sold newspapers was given.

In this, the most delicate of stories, Mulcaire admits he played a central role in finding one of the boys. He was accused of breaking the law by subverting Mappa, the government programme which arranges for a person to be given a new identity.

In fact, he completely denies this, and puts it all down to the skills of his trade. 'There was no breach,' he says. 'Whatever your politics, this was a case where we had to be incredibly careful,' he remembers. 'But there was no breach of Mappa [Multi Agency Public Protection Agency], and I don't remember any interception of phone messages in that case.' His memory of the issue is hazy, perhaps unsurprisingly, and he has no access to his papers on the subject, but he has no doubt there was a legitimate public interest in keeping the pair under scrutiny. 'There was a heightened concern around this individual.'

In November 2004, the *News of the World* reported that Bulger's mother Denise Fergus had come face to face Robert Thompson, by then 21, a couple of months earlier, and been 'paralysed with fear'. She said: 'I recognised his podgy face and evil eyes in an instant. I wanted the right to know what he looks like. To know where he is. I wanted to rush up to him and scream, "Why did you kill my child?" Yet I was turned to stone paralysed with hatred.'

It is easy for liberal prejudice to disapprove and to

condescend to the anger of a vengeful mother. Yet 'sophisticated' opinion can claim no vindication (and nor can any other). It was to emerge that one of the boys, Jon Venables, had had an unsuitable relationship during his teen years which seemingly had not been known about by those responsible for him. Later he had to return to prison. He had a considerable appetite for child pornography, and in the early 2000s was having a relationship with a woman who had a five-year-old child. Did the woman in question know about his past? Or his unhealthy tastes? Here, the *News of the World* would say, was the justification for its work. Without such scrutiny, those who think they know best probably don't, the argument goes.

Similar considerations came up when it became known that highly respected author Gitta Sereny was writing a book about Mary Bell, who, as a child, had strangled two smaller children (aged four and three) in 1968. She had been released in 1980, and was the subject of a similar injunction. By collaborating with the book, and being paid for it, she opened herself to the charge of invading her own privacy, and of inviting others to do so.

Mulcaire says, 'As far as I remember the [*News of the World*] investigations unit put a lot of cold cases on the grid. I think we had had a tip that the daughter didn't know the mother's history [before her birth]. The girl was approaching the age of 18 and was pregnant and needed to be told. We identified where she was, where she was working. There was a lot of passive probing to make sure we had the right person, and we eventually reached stage 3 – 'eyes on' – whereby we did discreet surveillance. These people live to have control, but in this case, when they are being watched, they have no control.'

Mulcaire recalls sitting down with Bell herself, and eating fish and chips with her. He is reluctant to elaborate as to what exactly was said, but he is adamant that he performed a public service when he confronted her. 'I put fear of God into her. The blood fell from her face when I spoke to her. She didn't answer, she was in total shock. She was terrified of being exposed, but I explained, if we were going to expose you we wouldn't be talking to you... Greg [Miskiw] knew all about it. Nobody knew where she was, but I found her. Greg let me do it... with a reporter crashing it, it often goes very wrong.'

Because Mulcaire has no access to the relevant files, he cannot be certain of the timing. But it may be that the decision by Dame Elizabeth Butler-Sloss in 2003, to award Mary Bell and her daughter a high court injunction guaranteeing lifelong anonymity, was in part the result of Mulcaire's approach. Certainly, the judge said press intrusion would amount to 'further psychological abuse'.

Again, for Mulcaire, there was no question they were doing good work in the public interest. 'I know we talked about it a lot. 'Should we do this, should we do that? Greg was very much into doing the right thing. Actually I don't know if a story ever came out of it. From my own point of view, the fact that we were marking someone's card was good enough for me.' Asked if it was up to the press to decide in a sensitive case like this, Mulcaire is adamant. 'Oh come on. Look at Baby P... Would you trust the social services? And if it's bad now, what would it have been like then?'

Both cases were absolutely on the *News of the World*'s

home, taboo-busting patch. What is striking is that it is clear in Mulcaire's notes, and was therefore available to the police, that he had the phone numbers of police officers who worked on the witness protection scheme. Further, Mulcaire says he was questioned by the police on the matter, of a sort which the authorities usually take extremely seriously, following his arrest in both 2006 and 2011, yet the matter did not lead to a charge.

In May 2004, the *Mirror* ran a series of pictures of British soldiers of the Queens Lancashire Regiment apparently torturing an Iraqi detainee. One image showed a soldier seemingly urinating on a hooded prisoner, while in another he was being hit with a rifle. The pictures came amid stories of allegations that British troops had been abusing prisoners, so as a story their time had come. The pictures were described by one military pundit as 'a recruiting poster for al-Qaida'. Morgan, whose brother was serving in Basra at the time, had had the pictures in his office safe for some days, musing on their authenticity, before deciding he would go for broke and print them on 1st May.

But the pictures were not entirely convincing, and a lot of people believed them to be fakes. The problem was proving it. Mulcaire was tasked by Greg Miskiw, news executive at the *News of the World,* to get to the bottom of the story. Somehow Miskiw had acquired the names of the soldiers in question. He handed them over, and asked Mulcaire to do the rest. By reference to the soldiers' mobile phones, he was able to confirm that the purported torturers had been in the UK at the time the pictures were taken. In other words, they couldn't have been in Iraq, and the pictures were fakes. If ever there was a case of trying too hard, this was it. *Mirror* editor Piers Morgan was required to fall on his sword, though he maintained that even if the story his paper had run was not true, there was a more general truth behind it, in that, he insisted, British troops were indeed abusing prisoners.

Mulcaire believes he was the first person to establish the pictures were phony, although the *News of the World* records do not support this idea. It is possible, he says, that the proof he provided was used either in another paper in the Murdoch group, or conceivably used to help the Ministry of Defence nail the perpetrators. 'If you'd lost a daughter or a son, you'd want to know who had done that,' says Mulcaire. 'There's no doubt it was my information in my mind and Greg's that it was my information that proved they were fakes. We proved it by triangulation and pinging, but I don't know what use my work was put to. Greg always used to cite it as being responsible for Morgan losing his job.'

Perhaps the biggest headline story of Glenn Mulcaire's career was the tale of David Beckham, national heartthrob, golden boy and family man, and his relationship with a 'stunning brunette', Rebecca Loos, in Madrid. Beckham's wife Victoria was at home in London while David was with his adoring public, playing football for the world's richest football club Real Madrid. The story fell into the category of genuinely big story, exposing the clean-cut, loyal, image of Beckham, which brought him around £10m a year in sponsorship deals, as a sham.

Loos, decidedly middle class and sophisticated by the standards of redtop football exposés, was employed as a nanny-cum-fixer for the Beckhams. She and Beckham were naturally spending a lot of time together, and the first hints that she and Beckham were enjoying one another's company a little too much came in September 2003, when, as the *News of the World* put it, 'the lonely England captain was enjoying female company and the bright lights of Madrid while wife Victoria was 800 miles away in London'. The pair were captured on grainy footage, laughing and drinking together. The bare-shouldered girl 'was being really flirtatious', according to one of the paper's ever-reliable 'onlookers'. Sometimes newspapers persuade one of those in an affair to lure their partner to go to a certain location in order to be photographed by a newspaper. But these pictures do not suggest that. There was no sign that Loos knew the photographers were there, nor that she planned to sell her story.

The Sunday before, the paper had put a story on its front page announcing 'Posh & Becks in marriage crisis', which centred on Victoria's concern about her career and her desire stay in London, having originally said she would move with him and the children to Madrid. Given what is now known, it is fair to assume that Beckham had been under some pretty close scrutiny up till that point, but his personal security was fairly resilient and there had seemed little of note to report in any case. Loos was not identified in the story about the flirtatious drink, but she would not be nameless for long.

The fact that a much admired footballer like Beckham was alone in a hot and glamorous city and had been spotted in the company of an attractive single woman was more than enough to arouse the *News of the World*'s interest. The story went a bit quiet as Glenn Mulcaire set about his work. Six months later, Beckham's world exploded. The *News of the World*, with the boldness and conviction which were its hallmarks, announced its prey. 'Beckham's secret affair' shrieked the headline. 'Lonely star beds aide caught in THAT club pic. Wild romps and txt sex behind Posh's back. The story you thought you would never read.' Chief reporter Neville Thurlbeck, whose by-line appeared on the piece, detailed encounters between the pair stretching back to December. The detail of the relationship, which clinched the prize of scoop of the year at the press awards for that year, was unarguable.

The news story had so far developed along familiar lines. The paper has always been a beneficiary of 'ring-ins', members of the public calling to say that something has happened and it may be that this one began like that. News executives got on the case. The information was given to Mulcaire, who set about it with his customary alacrity. Once the story had been verified (most of the hard data being provided by Mulcaire, but with a lot of consultation at head office), Rebecca Loos got wind of the paper's interest. She decided that if the story was to come out, she might as well make the most of it, and Max Clifford, broker of kiss and tell stories par excellence, later convicted of a string of indecent sexual assaults. 'The deal was done after the *News of the World* were onto Rebecca,' remembers someone who was close to events. 'They had been harassing her. Her father called Max Clifford asking if he could help. It was done very quickly, about two weeks before the story appeared. She hadn't set out to have an affair or sell her story.' But the paper was not going to throw away a tale as big as this.

The 'standing up' of the story had been hugely protracted. In any such tale, the word of the person having the affair is not enough. A celebrity can simply lie and deny a true story, and the newspaper has to produce irrefutable evidence. This was Mulcaire's job. Details of texts sent between the pair appeared in the paper. Surely that said enough? No. It might be claimed that somebody else had sent the texts, maybe as a joke. Why would a happily married celebrity do such a thing?

Mulcaire had to prove that Beckham had been in possession of his phone, and alone, when the texts were sent. Beckham's entourage were of course aware that their boss was a figure of huge interest for the popular press, and had sought to take commensurate precautions. Paul McMullan has been reported as saying of Mulcaire: 'He was hacking masses of phones. We reckoned David Beckham had 13 different SIM cards, and Glenn could hack every one of them.' 'Proving that that number and that phone was in someone's pocket at a given time is enormously difficult,' says Mulcaire. 'We needed to prove it finally, and we knew Beckham had lots of numbers, and two phones close to one another tell their own story.'

To Mulcaire, this was an enormous challenge. 'It was a puzzle not a mystery,' as he often says. Each time Beckham switched his SIM card, Mulcaire was able to follow him, a source of some professional pride to him. Through pinging and call analysis, he was able to identify Beckham's movements. The footballer's space for wriggle room was shrinking, but despite the mountain of evidence, the need to be totally certain of the facts made some people at Wapping uncomfortable. If you take on a nationally adored icon, you need your ducks in line. Was

Mulcaire, seen by some as young and keen but inexperienced, up to it? Emphatically so, said news executive Greg Miskiw, who, Mulcaire recalls, said he would resign if Mulcaire's view was wrong.

It was decided they should go for it, notwithstanding the risk of a complete public denial from the other side. A lot of reputations were on the line. It was no time for faint hearts. As with the Blunkett story, they were confident the story was true, and that they had sufficient evidence to prove it. The problem was whether the use of that evidence would be proof of having broken the law. It was a judgment call for an editor: a footballer's desire to keep his friendship secret versus an editor's need to keep his methods secret.

It is one of the great ironies of the episode is that although Glenn Mulcaire was largely responsible for confirming the story, he believes the Beckhams could have fought harder to oppose the paper. 'If I'd been the Beckhams, I would have called the paper's bluff. I would have denied it outright and demanded to see all the evidence. The paper would have had to show the proof. It is true that Neville [Thurlbeck] was babysitting Rebecca, and that she was by that stage signed up and giving evidence to support the story, but that wouldn't necessarily have been enough to swing it. Her word wouldn't have been enough. They conceded too soon. In my view the key that clinched it was the pinging and the call analysis.'

There was indeed a denial of sorts from the Beckham camp. The player himself was quoted as saying: 'During the past few months I have become accustomed to reading more and more ludicrous stories about my private life. What appeared this morning is just one further example.' As the *Daily Mail* pointed out at the time, 'It was noticeable, however, that he failed categorically to deny any kind of sexual relationship with his former assistant.'

Gerard Tyrrell, Beckham's lawyer, had been tipped off by a source in the world of investigation as to how the paper had satisfied itself of the truth of the story, as well as the investigator they were using, Glenn Mulcaire, and had been among those advising Beckham to keep changing his SIM cards. There followed a major legal wrangle. One source close to the story believes that the *News of the World* came to an arrangement with the Beckhams, which effectively drew a line under the issue. Some years ago the author of this book asked the legal department of the *News of the World* what had happened to the Beckhams' writ. He was told the matter had been resolved. The paper was not notably critical of the player subsequently.

Many suspected that Australian model Elle Macpherson also reached an accommodation with the paper after she was named as one of the original victims of phone hacking in the 2006 trial. She and a number of her associates were known to have been targeted, and in the approximately 30 mentions of Macpherson in the paper in the following years, about half were neutral and half were laudatory, a remarkable strike rate. Any such arrangement was denied, and no independent evidence has been found at Wapping to endorse such a claim.

6

Fishing for Headlines

By 2004 Mulcaire had established his position as a key provider to *News of the World* of electronic data and stander-up of stories from a legal point of view. He says now with great pride that he only deals in facts, and he was building a capacity for picking the wheat from the chaff. Having gained a regular berth and the confidence of some, at least, of his employers, he was feeling reasonably established. Though the *News of the World* 'Special Investigations' department had by now been disbanded, he was able to tell himself that all the celebrity stuff was just a means to an end. In other words, he remained convinced that in the end his skills were being put to a worthwhile cause. It was a delusion, he now recognises, not least caused by his head being turned by the status implied by being on a contract worth well over £100,000 a year.

But at the paper, things were changing. His chief protector, Greg Miskiw, left the London office of the paper to work for it in Manchester. Miskiw had always guarded his asset jealously. 'We always knew Greg had someone who could get stuff, but we were never allowed access to him,' remembers one reporter. The problem was that a lot of people thought they knew as much about the dark arts as Mulcaire, and many were hacking phones for themselves. Why did they need Mulcaire? Without Miskiw, Mulcaire needed someone to explain and defend him in the office, and there were plenty who felt his presence was unnecessary and expensive. Researchers and technology were being sacrificed to help pay for Mulcaire's salary, or so it was claimed.

The arrival of new staff compounded the pressure generally. The new recruits cranked up the pressure on the subordinates all the further. It is the job of news editors to challenge the natural human laziness which can afflict newspapers, to demand more, to make reporters ask the unaskable questions, to push the boundaries, to demand longer and longer hours. Sometimes the news rolls in like the tide. It just happens. At other times, as Fleet Street facetiousness has it, you have to 'make it up'. Only very rarely is this literally true, of course (whatever some might believe), but the demands of filling pages can be relentless.

Some news editors can keep the pressure up yet retain the trust and respect of their reporters, sometimes helped along with the occasional drink, friendly lunch or 'jolly'. Others soon win a reputation for hard-heartedness and cold-bloodedness. Neither counts for much as long as the bosses higher up the chain feel the stories are coming in. *News of the World* royal reporter Clive Goodman told the Old Bailey later that the atmosphere while Andy Coulson was editor was 'competitive, fast and quite bullying and menacing – there was an extreme drive for results… if a reporter did not deliver he would be hauled over the coals'. Goodman said this atmosphere came from the top of the paper, 'from Andy', although in court later Coulson denied being a bully.

Vanessa Altin, a former reporter on the paper, told Lord Leveson: 'I was proud that the paper would pursue stories of national interest without fear or favour and we remained the number one selling English speaking newspaper in the world for many years. I worked there happily until 2004 when I returned from maternity leave to discover a new regime had taken over. The newsdesk …. [was] obsessed with sensational celebrity gossip. I was often asked to insert sensational words and sentences which I knew to be inaccurate or blatantly false. They even demanded I fabricate direct quotes and put them in my copy. My refusal led to several years of intense bullying and unreasonable demands in an attempt on their part to force me to quit.

At the same time they started to employ more inexperienced graduate trainees who would do as they were told without question – leaving me in an unpopular minority. I went into the London office and raised my concerns directly with Andy Coulson – who dismissed them out of hand and said he had complete confidence in the newsdesk.'

That newsdesk was not warmly regarded by many of the reporters. Certainly Glenn Mulcaire was wary of it. The reputation for toughness came in part from a desire to stop the skimming, the widespread abuse of the readily available cash, from which reporters were inclined to trouser a commission. But the demands were constant. Previously, the likelihood was that Mulcaire would be called upon to execute specific, surgical tasks. But as time went on, the jobs became more numerous and the net was cast ever wider.

For better or worse, Mulcaire now saw himself as an

investigator. On good days, this would involve a search to right a wrong – the finding of a kidnapped child, the tracking down of a terrorist, the confronting of a drug dealer. And on others he was a hired hand, an instrument of his bosses' whims, being their eyes and ears rather than establishing facts. In these instances, he would feel no obligation to approve or disapprove of his task and merely churn out the product. This, after all, is the requirement placed on countless employees in most walks of life, he points out.

The category of 'fishing expeditions' grew enormously. These were the indiscriminate trawling of the private lives of (mostly) celebrities, in the hope of catching them doing something worth intruding into. Some time in 1994 (from his memory) Mulcaire met two news executives.. Mulcaire went along for what he took to be a run-of-the-mill session, imagining there would be amicable discussion of a new contract, but he came away worried.

The bosses did not give the impression of wanting to make friends. It may be that they were keener on both Andy Gadd, who signed up with the paper in late 2004 (and with whom Mulcaire had worked in the 1990s under John Boyall) and Jonathan Rees, recently released from prison following his conviction for planting cocaine on an innocent woman, who were also by now doing work for the paper. Anyway, they said they wanted to continue the process that had gone before, with an increased emphasis on celebrities.

Hacking by reporters in the office was seen as a cheap and effective way of getting stoires, but, as someone who worked with Greg Miskiw specialising in in-depth investigations, Mulcaire was decidedly seen as less good value for money. Although he could turn material around quickly, his preference was for longer-term, bigger subjects, which inevitably meant they were more expensive. The use of private investigators was regarded by some reporters as, simply, cheating, and the fact that they cost the company a lot of money – not normally the number one concern of some expenses-happy newshounds – just added to the resentment against the PIs.

Looking back, that restaurant meeting was something of a watershed, a taster of what was to come. 'Nothing serious like the public interest was discussed,' recalls Mulcaire. 'I just didn't like them. They seemed like plastic people to me.' Mulcaire cannot recall exactly when, but says either at that meeting or on the phone later, he was told 'If you don't want to do it, we'll get one of the thousands in who will.' It was a pretty bald assertion that if he thought things had changed, he had seen nothing yet. 'I was caught in no man's land. Either they would make me overwork and make me crack or they would max out on everything they could get. I was boxed in.'

It was a key period in the life and death of the *News of the World*. The Murdoch-owned papers had always had a sense of their own place and importance in the national arena. Some would say they behaved as if they owned the place. Certainly there was an assuredness about what they could do, who they could get access to and so on. If there was mischief to be made, they would push the boundaries, but in a way leavened by humour or populist brilliance. Now the goals were being redefined to keep the machine fed. Asked about it some years later, a very senior *Sun* reporter, hugely respected by his peers – and no stranger to the occasional need to cut corners in the interests of getting a story – turned his palms upwards and raised them as if in a 'stand up' gesture and said 'They just lifted it up and up and up'.

A reporter from the paper recalled the changed climate in the office, which ran counter to the old newsdesk machismo. 'Coulson was inexperienced and had to rely on PI's to stand stories up, which was really expensive and shouldn't have been necessary,' he said. 'The old school way of doing stuff was to sit outside in a van, watching people, sometimes for days, even if it does mean having to poo in a plastic bag.' Another describes how in the past there had been a discreet way of using blaggers and private investigators: 'There wasn't much we couldn't get, in terms of phone numbers, addresses, records and so on. It was Ok when it was done judiciously, but then the halfwits turned up and they went and put it all in the paper.' Another says: 'They didn't have contacts or ability. Doing the phones was a tool which made their lives easier. And they used to say things like 'Wouldn't it be good if Kylie was having an affair with so-and-so', and then they'd try to make it come true.' Yet another reporter mentioned: 'There was no care involved. It was all onwards and upwards, don't look back, smash and grab stuff. There was no feeling that you should bother about looking after contacts. They just wanted results.'

After four comparatively productive and worthwhile years, Mulcaire felt himself to be deluged with requests on stories big and small. In looking back, he refers to this period as 'the spike', spraying the room with imaginary machine gun fire. 'It was relentless,' he remembers. This increase in volume may have been down simply to the newsdesk's insatiable drive, but Mulcaire sensed that he was being tested. Could he deliver on so many requests? Would he crack under the pressure? Although generally 'user-friendly' and obliging, Mulcaire would on occasions ask about the purpose of certain taskings.

The mounting pressure took its toll on Mulcaire. He was working enormously long hours, drinking to excess, suffering from anxiety disorder and panic attacks, and was prescribed with beta blockers and Prozac. Some executives would refer to him as 'Mr Grumpy', because of the occasional question why such-and-such a job needed doing. On other occasions he would be asked to do a job that somebody else had failed to perform, thus rendering it more difficult. 'That used to really aggravate me. Why hadn't they asked me in the first place? I also used to complain about my contract, and whether it would be renewed. Plus, it was the volume of stuff they were asking me to do. I used to work long days, often 15 hours, from Tuesdays to Fridays, and then be off with the kids at the weekend, and free on Monday. But gradually – and quite apologetically, actually – they wanted me to do stuff on Mondays, so they'd be ready for Tuesday morning conference. And then they started wanting me doing stuff on Saturdays as well, when I used to do training with AFC Wimbledon's Junior Dons and reserve team.' Mr Justice Saunders later referred to an email Mulcaire sent, asking his bosses to lighten the load.

But whereas in his early days of working for the paper he would show an interest in the stories that were being worked on, latterly, under the weight of tasks given him by the ever-more demanding news desk, he became more and more of a production line. 'I was getting asked to do something on average about every ten minutes. The phone barely stopped ringing,' he remembers. Mostly the sort of things he was asked to do related to stories of little interest to him personally, usually the private lives of soap stars or other celebrities. One lawyer familiar with Mulcaire's activities said in 2013 as the trials approached: 'I didn't think I'd ever say this, but I now feel a bit sorry for Glenn Mulcaire. From what I understand, he started out doing the sort of work that traditionally public-spirited newspapers do, and under the weight of what he was asked to do he became completely institutionalised and stopped asking questions.'

In the course of preparing this book, Mulcaire on several occasions discussed how it could be that so many shockingly intrusive cases could have come to pass. How could anyone defend invading the privacy of, for example, the mother of a 22-year-old girl who has been stabbed by a jealous boyfriend just hours before? How unfeeling does a journalist have to be to excuse that in the name of the trade? It is a question to which Mulcaire has become inured, possibly through a sense of self-protection. He was accused of deleting the voicemails of Milly Dowler, a claim which left him tearful, sleepless and frustrated at his inability to answer the claims. If his role in that case is clearer now than it was, what about those other cases for which News International has had to pay out substantial damages. How does he explain those?

The conviction with which he confronts the questions might surprise his accusers. When asked about specific cases involving breaches of the privacy of blameless people he doesn't recall, he cites a ready answer. 'If something bad happened, it would have been for one of three reasons,' he says now. 'Either I was given an untrue pretext, in that I was told to go after someone and lied to as to why.' He then named various commissioning people on the paper's news desk. 'Generally, if it was something bad, Greg Miskiw would say nothing rather than lie. He tended to be straighter than the others,' he said. 'Or sometimes they would simply pile the work on me, and slip in something they thought otherwise I wouldn't want to do. Often there would be a VoC (victim of crime) in there. It's called packaging, when you get a pile of work and you just have to plough through it because it has to be done. They don't say what it's about, you just get the number, or whatever it is.' In other words, he argues, his work had become just a 'commodity'. The fact that it might be providing access to someone's intimate, painful secret was overshadowed by the need to keep the beast fed. The job in question would often be 'reversing' a number, that is, finding a name and address from a mobile phone number, or acquiring the PIN number that accompanied a mobile number.

The third category of story on which Mulcaire would sometimes be working unaware would be a 'Special Projects' story. The facts of such a story would be made known only to those who needed to know, such was the requirement of complete discretion. Mulcaire's ability to keep a secret was not, it seems, ever in doubt, but occasionally voices in the office would require a secret to be kept as tight as possible. It was sometimes claimed in the office that for all the secret squirrel work, Mulcaire wasn't that good at his job, and that, as an example, he would not be able to hack the phones of Rebekah Brooks and Andy Coulson, then editors of the *Sun* and the *News of the World*, and of Rav Singh, editor of Bizarre. All three were considered prone to the attentions of story-hungry rivals and had taken special precautions to ensure their phones were interception-proof.

Perhaps to goad Mulcaire, a news executive mentioned these precautions to him in a phone conversation. Whatever the intention, it had the effect of spurring Mulcaire to prove he could get access to their voicemails. 'Within four minutes I had done it,' he remembers with satisfaction. He also recalls providing himself with something of an insurance policy by confirming in an email to the office that he had in effect been commissioned to hack his editors' phones. The email, saying something like 'as requested, here is Andy's PIN number', elicited a prompt and panicky call back from the office, chastising him for making explicit this lawlessness in writing. The email in question has never surfaced. Mulcaire doesn't remember how many times he listened to the voicemails of his editor and deputy editor. He says it is possible, as has been claimed, that it was quite a lot, but he doubts it. 'If that is the case, I will gladly admit it, but as far as I remember, there was no call to do it more than once. I was only working under instruction.' Sean Hoare said there were frequent attempts (by senior executives) to hack one another's phones.

Mulcaire is less certain as to whether the reason he was given was the real reason for his being asked to get into the voicemail box of his and the *Sun*'s editor. 'I always suspected they wanted to know what was going on between them,' says Mulcaire. 'We know they were having an affair, although I admit I didn't know that at the time. It may be that they just wanted to know the gossip, or it may be that they wanted to be in on what stories they were working on, in order to be better prepared professionally.'

It may be difficult to believe that Mulcaire was unaware of the upset he was causing in the carrying out of his duties for the paper. How could he not know? Did he not read the paper?

Well, no, actually, he says, frequently he didn't. Even if 'all human life is here', in the *News of the World*, he had little interest in it, or in the telling of stories. His curiosity was that of a technician, focussed on how best to acquire information, on the establishing of fact. What journalists chose to do with it, how they presented it, was of not the faintest concern. This may be a surprise, but whereas he had begun his spell with the paper doing what he regarded as serious, worthwhile and remunerative digging, by the middle of the decade much of it was just a job. A job he was well paid for and, with a wife and five children, a large mortgage and an ultra-demanding boss, he could not easily walk away from.

That period, at its worst in 2005 and 2006, was, for Mulcaire, the grimmest of his career. Greg Miskiw, the closest thing he had to a protector in Wapping, had gone, although they were still in touch and doing bits of work together. Mulcaire felt trapped.

In hindsight he wishes he had made more effort to cultivate possible employers on other papers. Clive Goodman arranged for him to meet Charlie Rae, a veteran on the *Sun*, then under Rebekah Brooks's editorship, but nothing came of the proposed meeting. His workload piled up as he sought to keep his bosses happy. He was uncomfortable with his brief, but having signed up to it, he felt he had little option. And it wasn't just a matter of 'stay or go'. The costs of jumping ship were incalculable, he believes. 'If I'd not done what I was asked,' he says, 'I would have been blacklisted and unemployable. I would have become a bad name in the trade, so I was perfectly placed to be betrayed. It was damned if you do, damned if you don't. How do you explain to the kids that we can't go on living in this house any more? I couldn't have done that. The carrot got shorter and the stick got longer, and I should have cultivated other outlets.'

Anyone appalled by the extent of lawlessness commissioned and carried out by those working for the *News of the World* may see more mitigation than justification here. Mulcaire, however, knows he broke the law, acknowledges it and doesn't seek to defend it. He pleaded guilty after all to all charges, except one (which was dropped). He does, though, speak with the self-acknowledged frustration of someone who was part of a criminal enterprise for which, for over 7 years, only he and Clive Goodman paid a price. He affects little bitterness at that fact alone, and became indifferent as to whether others came to suffer the same fate. What does rile him is how the whole story has been hung on him and prevented him getting back to a normal life. The refusal of his former bosses to come clean has hampered his prospects of finding respectable employment. Having pleaded guilty and served his sentence, he hoped to return to what he does best – investigative work. Yet the slow dawning on the public consciousness of the fact that phone hacking was not so much the work of a rogue investigator but a veritable flourishing industry has held up that rehabilitation, he feels.

He admits, too, to frustration that he has had to (or felt he had to) keep his counsel for so long. Partly this was down to the confidentiality agreement he had signed, and partly to the many ongoing civil cases being brought against News International (and often against him personally). But, notwithstanding what his lawyers have told him about incriminating himself, his silence may not have been a legal necessity. Looking back, his evidence could have been of great use to the House of Commons Committee for Culture Media and Sport, during their investigations into phone hacking. The same goes for the IPCC's investigation into the Dowler affair, and the Leveson inquiry, but it didn't happen.

After Miskiw left, Mulcaire's place at the paper was under constant threat, and there was regular talk of his contract being terminated. But Mulcaire's record, for one reason or another, made him effectively unsackable, or so it seems. At one point, when it looked as if chief reporter Neville Thurlbeck was seemingly endorsing a plan to get rid of Mulcaire, Mulcaire's sense of natural justice was offended. Mulcaire recalls arranging to meet Thurlbeck to discuss the situation. 'I asked my friend Steve Mills [a football contact] to come along to a pub on Fleet Street and stay out of sight but simply to listen to the conversation,' Mulcaire recalls. 'I told Thurlbeck that was fine – if he really wanted me pushed out, Ok, but he should know that I planned to make public the fact that the Beckham story, for which he won the 2005 British Press

Awards prize for Scoop of the Year, was stood up by me…. After that I think it was pretty much agreed I was unsackable.'

A former *News of the World* stalwart says: 'Mulcaire was too good at his job. He just brought in too much good stuff.' But in his chat with Thurlbeck Mulcaire had touched on another reason why he had become unsackable. 'They couldn't get rid of Mulcaire because he had done the Beckham story,' says a *News of the World* source. 'It has never been confirmed that they did his phone. If he had left the company and let it be known how they stood up the Beckham story, Beckham could have sued Murdoch['s empire] for millions.'

At the 2005 Press Awards in March, which looked back on the previous year in journalism, The *News of the World* won both National Newspaper of the Year award for the second consecutive year and the Scoop of the Year award, for the story of Beckham's Secret Affair. One of Andy Coulson's assets as a manager was a willingness to put professionalism ahead of personal popularity, a huge plus in an industry where affability goes a long way. He always wanted more, so there was to be no complacency as a result of the awards. The usual pressure applied to senior executives and reporters was to be ratcheted up ever further. The following month, Coulson sent a memo to his senior staff, proposing some minor changes to the working week. More importantly, they were being put on notice:

> 2005 has been a great year for *News of the World* awards… and an average one for *News of the World* stories. The truth is we have not fulfilled our brief

this year. Few very good stories, plenty of good stories and far, far too many stories that fall into the 'fine' category.... I've no doubt you are all as aware and concerned about this as I am and I'm not for a moment doubting your efforts. But we need a hit. Badly.

No limits on this in terms of cash or other resources. We should all be coming into the office on Tuesday with two or three potential splash ideas –preferably with a couple of calls already made....

We had an unprecedented year of success in 2004 and your brilliant work has been rightly recognised and celebrated.

On the upside last year we broke Beckham in April, Sven in July and Blunkett in August. Time we got started this year I think...

The pattern in the news machine was for pressure to be passed downwards. Someone who worked on features recalls how the *News of the World* features department was 'put under horrible pressure' by Andy Coulson and his executives, who 'would come and just scream at us – they always wanted more. It had been a fun and exciting place to work but that changed entirely.' The introduction of Dan Evans was a direct response to that pressure, the employee believes. 'We knew they were hacking phones on news, and features had to get into that. Dan Evans's news list used to be unbelievable, he had some amazing stories on it, and compared to that we were failures. We couldn't compete. So they hired this guy who we knew had been doing that dark arts stuff at. There was no secret about it. We talked about it in the pub.'

One of Glenn Mulcaire's targets during this period was troubled Atomic Kitten singer Kerry Katona, whose personal life could fill the *News of the World* for a year. Mulcaire had been in and out of her phones since she split from Westlife singer Brian McFadden in September 2004. This brought the paper up against Max Clifford, who was representing her. In June 2005, he and editor Andy Coulson fell out badly over the paper's handling of Katona. They felt she was too rich a source of stories to ignore, and in December 2005 ran a story headed 'Kerry in New Coke Shocker'. When asked later why he had run the story, Coulson replied crisply: 'Because it was true.'

In redtop land, the Clifford-Coulson split was a big event. Clifford was the king of buy-ups, the man to whom those mistreated by celebrities would go in search of financial consolation. He, indeed, had brokered the deal with Rebecca Loos that exposed David Beckham's infidelity, and the judges who gave the story the Scoop of the Year award were torn as to whether 'a Clifford buy-up' was a fitting winner of such a prize. (In the end, they gave it the award largely because of the level of detail it contained, most of it supplied by Mulcaire.)

Whatever the immediate cause of the argument, the effect was that Clifford's close relationship with News International had been damaged. He decided to withdraw co-operation with its papers. A major source of stories had dried up.

As we will see, Clive Goodman came under mounting pressure during this period, but this was part of a continuing cranking up of demands. At around the same time, Coulson's falling out with reporter Sean Hoare, his erstwhile drinking buddy, became complete, and Hoare left the paper. Hoare had his own demons, and complained that the paper had not shown the duty of care he was owed. His behaviour had certainly become unprofessional, but he maintained in part that the pressure had driven him to it. He said later: 'There is so much intimidation. In the newsroom, you have people being fired, breaking down in tears, hitting the bottle.... I was paid to go out and take drugs with rock stars – get drunk with them, take pills with them, take cocaine with them. It was so competitive. You are going to go beyond the call of duty. You are going to do things that no sane man would do. You're in a machine.'

In January 2006, not long after the falling out with Max Clifford, Coulson was doubling his exhortations to greater productivity at the *News of the World*. In another memo to senior staff he wrote: 'This is going to be an incredibly tough year.... I'm going to be more and more reliant on home grown material.... But the agenda is simple: How will the *News of the World* break more bigger, agenda setting exclusives?... I'm not looking for decent spread ideas – I want splashes, two-/three parters, long term investigations etc.' Many of these types of features had previously come from PRs like Clifford.

In May 2006, at long last, the Information Commissioner's report, 'What Price Privacy' was published. Quite why data that had been in existence for many months surfaced only then is unclear. It was suggested by the ICO's former investigator Alec Owens that the Commission had been afraid to upset the press, and only published in 2006 when it got wind of the coming storm over Mulcaire's work. In any event the report's impact (if that is the word) was slight. Certainly it did little to impair celebrations on the *News of the World* table at the 2006 press awards (by then in the hands of the London Press Club) when – yet again – it won the Paper of the Year award. Jokes on the table about the paper's debt of thanks to Vodafone and other mobile phone companies were by this time old hat.

The fact that that summer a sport reporter, Matt Driscoll, was cutting up and making allegations of bullying, or that Tommy Sheridan, a Scottish politician, had won a libel case against the paper, were probably of little concern in that context. The man they had been unsure would ever make an editor was riding high.

7

What £330,000 Will Buy You

The paper was winning awards, but the climate had changed from the paper Mulcaire had joined. The interest in celebrity-driven stories was greater than ever, and some of the older guard were feeling less and less welcome. Clive Goodman, a long-time servant, was demoted from the post of assistant editor on the news desk – effectively the control room – reporting directly to the editor Andy Coulson, to a post as a mere news-getter, reporting to the news editor. The pressure to bring in stories or be replaced was insistent, and not what a senior reporter approaching his sixth decade might reasonably have expected.

The pressure was mounting on Mulcaire, too. If another paper broke a big story, there was always – as on any successful paper – an inquest into 'why we didn't have the story'. The fact that, in April 2006, the *Mirror* broke the story of cabinet minister John Prescott's affair with Tracey Temple had a huge effect. It was absolutely a *News of the World* story, but had appeared elsewhere. It was an outrage!

The news desk was coming under pressure for other reasons – to cut budgets. The casual resort to intercepting voicemails was widespread, as *News of the World* reporter Dan Evans testified in court, and if money was to be saved, some thought Mulcaire was expendable. After all, it was argued, there was no mystique to hacking a phone, and some reporters spent much of their time doing precisely that, unassisted by Mulcaire. Of course Mulcaire actually offered a great deal more than that, and those who couldn't get access to voicemails would report back to the desk, which would then have to fall back on Mulcaire's talent for blagging or otherwise identifying PIN numbers.

Mulcaire became concerned that having helped the paper in its mastery of the dark arts, he had become the author of his own obsolescence. Having shown many the way, he might then not be needed, or so he feared. So on occasions, having cracked a particularly difficult number that he knew would be of value to the news desk, he would make a note of the information and change the PIN number again to a number that only he knew, to secure his own role as gatekeeper to that celebrity.

That said, there were other blaggers in the field, and some of the bosses thought they could find another one, and probably cheaper than Mulcaire. Besides, there was no harm done by reminding Mulcaire that nobody was indispensable. The paper's ethos required that everyone be kept on their toes, after all.

So in February 2005,the news desk told the accounts department to stop Mulcaire's weekly payment of £2019. This was the most explicit sign that even Mulcaire, access to whom was one of the paper's Holy of Holies, was not beyond threat. As we have seen, chief reporter Neville Thurlbeck was deputed to speak to the investigator about whether there might be scope for some sort of revised deal, or whether this might be the end of the road.

As we have seen, Max Clifford had just fallen out with Andy Coulson. So, if Clifford was no longer to come to the paper with his stories, the paper would go to him, although without feeling the need to tell him. Clifford's client list would be invaluable, no doubt, so he came under the full scrutiny of Glenn Mulcaire, who confirms that both Clifford and his PA Nicola Phillips had all their calls monitored by him. Mulcaire set about itemising all the calls, doing pattern analysis (evaluating the time of call, the frequency and so on), identifying those who called, listening in to voicemails and so on. 'They wanted a full comm[unication]s profile,' he remembers.

At around the same time, royalty reporter Clive Goodman was deputed to see if he couldn't come to some arrangement with Mulcaire. The pair had something in common – both were at odds with the *News of the World* incumbent hierarchy, but, when working at their best, were considered too valuable to lose. Goodman asked Mulcaire how he was getting on with the news desk. He complained that he was being overloaded, being made to work Saturdays and they were trying to get him to do Mondays too. 'I'm out of the loop,' Clive saidm mentioning one executive in particular who he regarded as 'a nob.'

At around this time, as a sort of insurance policy for himself, Mulcaire asked Goodman to arrange for him to become a member of the National Union of Journalists. Although he had had no desire to become a journalist, and continues to hold most of them in contempt, he felt his chances of continued employment would be improved by having a press card. He also sought to offer 'oven-ready' stories to the newsdesk, and pushed a story about Professional Footballers' Association boss Gordon Taylor, which a freelance friend from Wimbledon was to write up on his behalf. Mulcaire had been increasingly unhappy at how he was being treated by the news desk and by the sort of stories he was being asked to pursue. He also felt out on a limb, his most trusted contact in the office, Greg Miskiw, having left the paper. He began to look around for other outlets. But when Goodman, who he knew of old, got in touch, he was happy to listen.

Goodman suggested a scheme whereby he and Mulcaire would work in tandem on specifically royal stories. Goodman was well-liked and respected by his fellow reporters, and held the record for the number of front-page stories in succession (three), but the demand for royal stories had declined, and they needed to be stronger than ever to get in the paper. More generally, among the upper echelons there was a demand for constant improvement. Goodman had joined the paper in 1995 and risen to become royal editor in 2000, but his stock had fallen. One senior executive in particular did not rate his work and, Goodman later told the Old Bailey, a 'massive chunk of [his] work was taken away'. Having initially got on Ok with Andy Coulson – the pair had gone to one another's weddings – Goodman found he changed after becoming editor. 'He became more aggressive and bullying, I was forever being berated for the lack of quality of my stories; he meant to degrade you'. Goodman found he was attending conference but not even being asked to say what stories he had to offer. 'It was humiliating, and intended to be humiliating,' he said.

In Mulcaire he saw an entrée to all sorts of royal

goodies. 'He floated a trial balloon,' remembers Mulcaire, although Goodman's memory was that it was Mulcaire who proposed the idea. 'I would collaborate with him, maybe with payments being made in cash. I wasn't certain at that stage if they were going to renew my contract, or if I wanted them to, so I thought "hang on, this might work",' says Mulcaire. 'I could see what Clive's personal agenda was, and actually I felt a bit sorry for the way he had been edged out, but I could see how it might work for me as well.' Most importantly for Mulcaire, he hoped Goodman would be his 'ears' in the office, someone to tell him the gossip and who was up, who was down. The 'need to know' rule was all very well, but Mulcaire wanted more reassurance from head office than he had been getting. As Mulcaire was to learn, Goodman was not that well placed to oblige.

A plan was drawn up to ring-fence royal stories, on which Mulcaire and Goodman would collaborate, separate from news desk. Goodman sent Coulson an email that said the following: 'A few weeks ago you asked me to find new ways of getting into the [royal] family, especially William and Harry and I came up with this. "It's safe, productive and cost effective and I'm confident it will become a big story goldmine for us."' For this Mulcaire, known in the office as 'Matey', would receive a fixed rate of £500 a week (a fourth of his previous weekly fee), an arrangement agreed with Andy Coulson, says Goodman. The deal began on a trial basis. Goodman would supply Mulcaire with phone numbers, Mulcaire would acquire the PIN numbers and the reporter would do the rest. 'He didn't come back to me and say I got such and such a story from what you gave me,' says

Mulcaire. 'I just opened the gateways and left him to get on with it.'

Goodman recalled later in court: 'Glenn's skill was to lie and he had access to every type of airtime company you can think of to get information. He would get them to reset the number to default, and anyone who has the default number can access the voice message. Sometimes Mulcaire would do it, sometimes I would do it.... It was a day to day practice and approved by my editor'.

A number of stories with a decent ring of truth began to appear in the paper. They included a tale about Prince William getting lost while out on an exercise, how Prince William had called his brother, pretending to be Chelsy Davy and another about him having had too much to drink the night before. In October, Goodman sent Coulson an email, gleefully reporting 'new project starting to get results, William's office in meltdown'.

In November the story about the Prince having a knee injury, of which only a tiny handful of people knew, appeared in the *News of the World*. The story went down well in the office and, for Goodman, this was a vindication of the arrangement with 'Matey'. 'Our new project is yielding results,' Goodman wrote to Coulson in an email. Such was the flow of detailed information about the princes (what pictures they had in their bedrooms, what their essays were about, who they were inviting to their parties and so on) that they reached that happy state for a journalist whereby they have sufficient information that they need to self-censor in order not to reveal their source. It emerged in court that on a transcript, William is reported saying to Kate Middleton: 'I was pissed but I wasn't that bad.' Clive Goodman, ever under pressure for more and better, was asked by a senior journalist if that line could be used in a story, to which Goodman replied: 'Too much information, would be incredibly dangerous to the source.'

That same month, the trial period was extended. The following week, a second article claimed that Tom Bradby, ITV's political editor, had lent the Prince some broadcasting equipment. This was a domestic detail too far. When Bradby and the Prince met a week later, they concluded this was not just somebody being indiscreet. There was something very wrong going on.

Mulcaire remembers Goodman losing sight of the seriousness of what he was doing. 'This wasn't a normal interception story,' he recalls. 'This had immense security issues attached.' The actual accessing of the royal household's voicemail had been comparatively easy, but there were warnings along the way that concerned him. 'There were security flags left on the voicemails. We were talking about a higher level of clearance. I knew a threshold had been crossed.' He sensed the security services would have become alert to what was happening and would be looking out for eavesdroppers.

'I remember saying to Goodman that we need to cool off. There's a security warning flag on the account, and they don't get any higher than that. If you're not going to stop at those warning signs, you're going to be in trouble. Why he kept crashing in like a bull in a china shop, I just don't know, but he just didn't grasp the gravity of the warning. I told him we need to calm down, go off the grid some time, and I wasn't even sure we'd get back on. It was that serious.' He says that in its haste to publish, the *News of the World* was drawing attention to its eavesdropping. Journalists know that often a story must not be printed too quickly, to avoid making the source identifiable. Once a few days have passed, the possibility that it has seeped out through run-of-the-mill gossip gains weight. But by publishing stories 'before they had even left the room', as Mulcaire puts it, huge risks were being taken. This may have been a symptom of Goodman's anxiety to impress.

Mulcaire's feeling was that any further incursions into what he called royal 'airspace' would be closely monitored henceforth. 'They'll be all over this, I thought. With the Lord Stevens investigation into the death of Diana going on, everyone was at a heightened state of alert. And once you're in that airspace it's hard to turn round and say you have legitimate reasons.'

'If I was on the other side – although actually I regard myself and the security people as basically being on the same side – but if I was them, I'd want to know everything about who was getting into royal airspace, even if they went in and out. Who they were, what were they up to? There are definitely national security issues there. On a professional level, I am immensely proud of having got past their protocols. I don't know how many other people could do that then, and I don't want to claim retrospectively that I was doing it to flag up breaches in security, but I realise now that I, or rather the paper, could have done that at the time.'

Asked if he feels guilty about compromising the security of the royals in order not to reveal some great item of public concern but a piece of the flimsiest tittle tattle, Mulcaire's answer is 'if I had come across anything serious, of course I would have done something about it…. But I would rather it was me than anyone else.' And did it do any harm? 'It's not for me to judge,' he says. 'What I do know is that if things had carried on at the crazy rate the *News of the World* was demanding, everyone across the globe would have been on the grid. It would have made the US's echelon system revealed by Edward Snowden look like Lego. They were relentless.'

Looking back, Mulcaire wonders why it took the Anti Terror squad nine months, from November to August, to get together enough information to arrest him. He strongly suspected he was being watched closely, and that the BT engineers who came to visit his house a couple of months after the Prince's knee story to attend to a 'fault' were bogus and were actually putting a listening device in place.

On 7th August 2006, the Mulcaires drove back from a family holiday in Newquay, Cornwall. They were tired from the journey, and the children went to bed early. It was to be an abruptly interrupted sleep. Early the next morning, as Mulcaire was lying in bed, he heard the steady, throaty roar of a helicopter engine. Soon after came a loud banging on the door. It was 6.00am. Mulcaire jumped out of bed and ran downstairs. The police had come not just to arrest him, but to search the family's house and two cars.

When the police arrest someone at their home, they give them a specified amount of time to answer the door before they break it down. Mulcaire, typically, knew how long that period is, and that he needed to move quickly if he was to minimise his wife and family's terror. (In preparing this book, we discussed whether to specify the allowed length of time. Mulcaire said not to, to prevent the wrong people knowing things they shouldn't know.)

Looking back, he cites a near-cliché: 'The greatest feeling I had as I walked down stairs was relief. It was the first time for God knows how long that I'd come down and there was no cloud. My head felt clear. 'This is closure now', I thought. Those months and years of being overworked, overstressed, training too hard to compensate, medication, panic attacks, not enough sleep, even drinking a little too much. I was real heart attack material, but I felt then all that was coming to an end.'

Within moments the house was swarming with police officers, uniformed and plain clothed. The children, having heard the noise and seen the police vehicles outside, rushed to the top of the stairs. Surely their Dad, who had always taught them to stand up for themselves but always to respect authority, could not be in any trouble?

Alison had no idea what was going on, other than that they had 'come for Glenn'. 'Are you aware that your husband has been intercepting voicemail messages?' asked one officer. She – a less likely gangster's moll could hardly be imagined – looked at him in bemusement. She had no idea what the term meant, let alone that her husband might be guilty of it. 'What are you talking about?', she said. Another mentioned that he was being arrested under the Regulation of Investigatory Powers Act of 2000, which he referred to by its colloquial name of 'RIPA'. She imagined some connection with the Yorkshire Ripper.

As the police led Mulcaire out, she came to the bottom of the stair to give him a kiss. There was no 'I can explain everything', which must have been tempting, given that she seems to have been totally bemused by so alarming an experience, or 'Look after the children'. He said, simply, 'Keep cool', echoing the motto on a necklace she wears, given her by him. He seems to have had faith in her faith in him. And for himself, rather more familiar with both dealing with the law and the protocols of the intelligence world, he slipped into 'say nothing' mode. He says the Bono line just about fits the bill: 'Talk without speaking, cry without weeping , scream without raising your voice.'

'Do you know what he does?' Alison was asked, to which she gave her stock answer: 'I know he works for the *News of the World.*' Seemingly the truth is that, pretty much, that is all she did know. 'All that day I just kept thinking "What is all this about? Why are they keeping Glenn?"' 'The whole day I didn't have a clue,' she remembers. 'I took the children round to a friend's house because I didn't want them being upset staying there. Then I got home, and I still didn't have a clue what was going on. I put the TV news on a 7.00 o'clock, and there it was. We just looked at each other… it was all over the news.'

The shock must have been immense, but at no time did she doubt or the children doubt her husband. If he had done something wrong, she remained unshakeable in the belief that it was for the greater good. 'Glenn's always been very private with his work, and my job was to be at home with the children, do the school run and so on. I had noticed that on holidays he had been a bit bogged down, and looking back I can see that they waited till we came back to arrest him. But they said if he hadn't been there they would have broken down the door.

That same day, the police also raided Mulcaire's parents' home in Fulham. His mother, who lives with the memory of when the police arrived to tell her her first son had been killed in a car crash, was terrified by the appearance of police at her door. She asked if Glenn was alive. Initially, no one answered, a brief silence which, even if inadvertent, still upsets the family.

Mulcaire was detained – as if he was a terrorist – at Belgravia police station, not far from where he was brought up. In his own mind he was detached. This was the end of that particular chapter he thought, one which had seen him get into areas of work that weren't him at all. He rested when he could. He asked for a copy of the *Evening Standard*. Initially this was denied him, but then allowed, only with the front page story – the one about him – cut out. The police didn't want him knowing too much, it seems. He was examined by a doctor, who found him in good condition (despite a lack of morning toast, he still grumbles) and a duty sergeant took pity on him and allowed him a chance to stretch his legs. Outside, photographers waited.

Back at home, his fretful children lay down on cushions in front of the television, turned on Sky News and stayed there all night, perhaps subconsciously hoping the news would change. Mulcaire called home during the evening to say goodnight and tell his wife and children: 'Don't worry, we'll be fine.'

That same day, 8th August, 2006, police arrived – together with Clive Goodman – with a search warrant at *News of the World*. The *New York Times* later reported that 'as word of the detectives' arrival ricocheted around the office, two veteran reporters stuffed reams of documents into trash bags', but were relieved when the police went no further than Clive Goodman's desk. 'We only had authority to do that desk,' said the police, who had a concern that police barging into the affairs of a free press would look repressive. Indeed, there was a stand-off, with senior staff claiming the police were there unlawfully, and there was even a fear that violence might ensue. The police wanted to seize more material from Goodman's desk, but were prevented from doing so, and agreed not to force the issue. It is fair to assume, though, their attitude might have been different had the paper belonged to a less powerful proprietor.

Mulcaire was kept in until late the following evening. Knowing that an answer leads to another question, he said nothing for 36 hours. At one point, after countless 'No comments', he said 'well actually... no comment.'

The day after their arrest, Mulcaire and Goodman were charged with various counts of unlawful interception of communications contrary to s.1(1) RIPA 2000 and conspiracy to intercept communications. The day after the arrest of Mulcaire and Goodman, another SO13 Operation 'Overt' had arrested 25 people for a conspiracy to blow up 9 transatlantic airliners which was at the time the largest Counter Terrorism investigation undertaken. As detective chief superintendent Keith Surtees later told the Leveson inquiry, 'it was against this backdrop that I organised for the material seized from Mulcaire's home address to be examined. There were no available officers within the SO13 Counter terrorism command to carry out this exercise. Following briefings with detective chief superintendent Tim White it was established that 8-10 security cleared officers from SO12 were to systematically examine all the documents and create a spreadsheet of the names and numbers of all people mentioned'.

When he eventually got home, Mulcaire and Alison had a big heart-to-heart. He told her what he had been doing and why. What had started as an acceptable compromise while he was working with Greg Miskiw had turned nightmarish.

'I knew at work he was always doing something for the good,' says Alison. 'He did loads of good work... he would sometimes look at the paper and say: 'I caught that person... I helped them catch him'. To be honest I was never that interested. The kids were so young and I was so busy I never really asked.' At the end he was having to do pretty well anything, regardless of its justification, to keep his bosses happy. Although obviously I didn't think it at the time, but in a way at the end it was almost a relief when he was arrested,' says Alison.

It was clear the police were not going to let the matter drop. These raids were too public, and the people involved too high-profile, for that. The royal princes had had personal information compromised in the process. Working under (then) detective chief inspector Surtees, Special branch officers had found 11,000 pages of scrawled notes, many with mobile phone and PIN numbers on them. The officers inputted the names of 418 potential victims, including a large number of high-profile figures.

In July the police had asked for guidance from the Crown Prosecution Service, given how some of what they were discovering was highly personal, and might involve 'extraneous matters' getting dragged into the prosecution area. On 25th July they were advised that the case against Mulcaire should be deliberately limited to 'less sensitive' witnesses.

At a case conference a few days later [21st August], detective sergeant Phil Williams reported there were potentially around 180 victims. The crown prosecution said later that it had asked if there was any reason to think Mulcaire was in touch with other journalists at the *News of the World*, and they were told not.

The view on the arrests from Wapping was not appetising. This was not one of those instances where a discreetly delivered warning from a bewigged courtier to a grateful subject was going to be sufficient. That meant court, and in all likelihood prison for the pair. And, for the bosses at *News of the World*, whose 'news drug habit' had been glimpsed for the first time by the wider public, that meant making sure that that was the worst of it. The police were bound to want to know more. At the very least, Goodman and Mulcaire needed to be squared. In short, there was a cover-up to be arranged. The loyalty, if that is the word, of most of the *News of the World* staff could be relied upon, partly because most knew little of what had gone on, and partly because they wanted to go on working there.

The problem might come with the two people likely to be punished for what they had done in the company's name. Why should they go quietly when they had been doing what was required of them? Certainly Clive Goodman was disinclined to go along with the idea that he should 'take one for the company'. To his mind, it was the company's responsibility for placing him under so much pressure as to make him cut corners. As a respected royal correspondent, at least as far as his counterparts on other papers were concerned, his loyalty to the company had already been waning. He was regarded by rank-and-file reporters as 'one of the good guys', yet he had been demoted the year before his and showed little sign of enjoying the pressure under which he was expected to perform.

If Goodman blew the whistle on just how extensive the lawbreaking at the paper was, he would expose some of his bosses to unimaginable damage. The Murdoch empire was highly professional and ultra-efficient. If it cut corners, it did so with extreme discretion and always in the public interest, or so it claimed. Yet Goodman was in a position to expose extensive quantities of lawlessness. He had to be neutralised.

Goodman had been arrested at his home in a quiet crescent in Putney at 6.00am on the same day as Mulcaire, Tuesday 8th August. The danger the pair posed was obvious. These were two people a long way down the food chain, doing what their bosses wanted, often under pressure. Why should they stay silent? The day after his arrest, Goodman had been advised by Henri Brandman, the solicitor provided by News International, who passed on information to the company (in defiance of Goodman's wishes, the reporter claimed in court), that he should admit guilt. But, said the lawyer, he should say he was a 'lone wolf', a suggestion Brandman was to repeat six days later, and one Goodman said he felt uncomfortable with. The plan was endorsed by Coulson, who followed up the lawyer's call by ringing Goodman. He told him: 'We're mates, but we'll have to suspend you.'

On the afternoon of Andy Coulson's next day off, the following Monday, he made the short journey to South West London to meet Goodman at Café Rouge in Wimbledon Village. The meeting lasted little more than half an hour.

Coulson had a proposal. The police had raided Glenn Mulcaire's premises but the offices of the *News of the World* too. They had secured a mountain of evidence. Coulson knew how reliant the paper had become on the dark arts, and he knew that some parts of the paper were more dependent on them than others. Each would have their own mitigation, no doubt, but they had broken a law which recognised no public interest defence. In short, there was no excuse and Coulson knew resistance was futile. The matter needed not to be challenged but to be buried – as quickly as possible.

Coulson hoped that if Goodman and Mulcaire were to plead guilty and take their punishments on the chin, there would be no need for the details to come out, in court or anywhere else. That way, surely, the paper could just move on. Coulson knew that industrial amounts of phone hacking had been going on, but he knew too that little of it had been established, and that there was nothing to link the strands together. Goodman and Mulcaire could do so, but, with judicious use of sticks and carrots, why would they?

It would require a hefty inducement, though, for Goodman to agree to keep quiet. In a way that few employees ever manage in dealings with their seniors, Goodman had his bosses over a barrel. But, outwardly at least, the streetfighter in Coulson would not acknowledge the hole he was in.

Summoning as much authority as he could from a weak hand, he explained there was no need for Goodman to lose his job. 'He asked me to plead guilty and if I did so I would be one of the people asked back,' Goodman recalled. Coulson explained that 'through his papers' influence' he had learned that there was no wish for Goodman to go to prison. Goodman later told the court: 'Mr Coulson gave the impression that he had been having some kind of discussions with people who were making decisions about the case... the impression was it was the police and the Home Office. The clear inference was that he had arranged for me not to go to prison.'

Coulson offered him an employment deal as a writer or subeditor. The condition was that Goodman should say his actions were entirely of his own volition, and that he had gone 'off the reservation'. Goodman was not happy at being the only staff member to carry the can, but could see no alternative to pleading guilty. As was the custom among many on the *News of the World*, Goodman took the precaution of covertly recording the meeting, giving himself an insurance policy for use should things turn against him.

He had been suspended by the paper. He later revealed that Coulson had told him he had to do so, but that the editor would feel free to use Goodman's services nonetheless. It was simply a PR exercise, he said. So below the radar Goodman continued to be involved, helping with newspaper serialisations and some re-writing and subediting tasks.

News International had sent the necessary signals to Goodman to say he would be looked after, but executives on the paper couldn't be sure that he and Mulcaire were the police's only target. On 7 September the police wrote to News International to ask for its files on the investigator and details of calls made to him. A week later, its lawyers Burton Copeland replied, having found only one such document, and saying that under protection of sources legislation they would not be handing over their phone records.

Among those whose name appeared as one of Mulcaire's victims – fortuitously, it seemed at the time – was the editor of the *Sun* Rebekah Brooks. She was informed of this (as many of Mulcaire's victims weren't) and on 15th September she attended a meeting with detective chief inspector Keith Surtees, receiving from him an extensive breakdown on what the police knew and what they suspected. With hindsight, this was trusting in the extreme, but then the Met's relations with senior News International executives had been such as to assume they were on the same side. Not only did the police assume good faith on her part, as protocol required, but it went far further than necessary in revealing police thinking. She was told the police were confident of nailing Goodman and Mulcaire for intercepting royal voicemails, that there were 100 to 110 other victims, that they wanted to bring charges against Mulcaire that demonstrated the full extent of his activities.

With hindsight – given how big an affair the phone hacking saga later became – the period soon after Mulcaire and Goodman were arrested takes on a particular weight.

Its significance lies in how little salience it was given by the police, notwithstanding the desire to protect the privacy of the Princes. They had other fish to fry. The commissioner of the Met, Sir Paul Stephenson, later told the Leveson inquiry: 'I do not recall having any substantive or detailed discussions about phone hacking with anyone else during this period. Indeed, it is fair to say that set against the other issues facing the MPS (including counterterrorism issues, the investigation into the 'night-stalker', the reinvestigation of the murder of Stephen Lawrence, very real budgetary challenges, the Olympic security preparations, Government proposals for significant changes to the governance arangements for the police and national structures for dealing with serious and organised crime), phone hacking was not a matter which I prioritised. I was satisfied that it was being overseen by a highly experienced and very senior officer. I was reassured by the fact that to my knowledge the case had been reviewed by the CPS and by counsel.'

The court was later told how in eight months, Goodman and Mulcaire made 609 calls to the voicemail boxes of three identified members of the royal household. One of them, Helen Asprey, personal secretary to the princes, became concerned when she found that messages she had yet to hear were identified as old calls (as if they had been listened to). In one 17-month period her phone was rung 102 times. As we shall see, this was not all, but further evidence was not to become publicly apparent until later.

On 29th November 2006, at the Old Bailey, Goodman and Mulcaire pleaded guilty of conspiracy to intercept communications, just as their paymasters had hoped they would. Goodman's barrister John Kelsey-Fry QC announced: 'Mr Goodman wishes through me to take the first opportunity to apologise publicly to those affected by his actions. It was a gross invasion of privacy and Mr Goodman accepts that is accurate. He wishes to apologise to the three members of the royal household staff and, moreover, to their principals – the Royal Highnesses Prince William, Prince Harry and the Prince of Wales.' A lower bow than the royal correspondent's could hardly be imagined.

It was matched by Mulcaire, whose barrister Neil Saunders, told the court that he also apologised to the royal family, and extended his apology to include Max Clifford, Elle Macpherson, Liberal Democrat MP Simon Hughes, Professional Footballers Association boss Gordon Taylor and Sky Andrew, a sports agent'.

Andy Coulson was anxious to show due humility, and added his own apology, taking 'ultimate responsibility' for the conduct of his reporters. 'Clive Goodman's actions were entirely wrong,' he said, 'and I have put in place measures to ensure that they will not be repeated by any member of my staff. I have also written today to Sir Michael Peat, the Prince of Wales's private secretary, to this effect. The *News of the World* will also be making a substantial donation to charities of the Princes' choice.' There was no mention of Goodman's future on the paper, or indeed Coulson's own. If he had his way, neither would be in any danger.   Sir Christopher Meyer, the chairman of the Press Complaints Commission, chipped in, describing 'phone message tapping' as 'a totally unacceptable practice unless there is a compelling public interest reason for carrying it out.' That sweeping remark highlights a remarkable shortcoming. The PCC code said that there was a public interest defence (and was later cited in mitigation in court), yet the law of the land says there is not, a discrepancy nobody, including the PCC's £150,000 a year head, seems to have been aware of. Given the confusion, it is little wonder journalists came to be accused of taking the law into their own hands.

The judge, Mr Justice Gross, was clear, however, and warned: 'I am not ruling out any options. It's a very serious matter', and told the court he would consider their punishments and the court would reconvene in January. But there was still work to be done.

Elsewhere, the lawyers were getting busy. On 30th November 2005, the day after Mulcaire pleaded guilty, his solicitor Moray Laing, recommended by a friend of Mulcaire, contacted Fiona Spink at News International's legal team, mentioning that he understood senior management were 'keen to discuss the matter with a view to coming to an amicable resolution of any claims [Mulcaire] may have'. The tone was more courtly than menacing, which may have been a relief at Wapping. Nothing happened for over three weeks, whereupon Laing sent the email again, this time to News International's legal affairs manager Tom Crone.

On December 12, Goodman, with his solicitor Henri Brandman and John Kelsey Fry, his barrister, met a News International executive. It was spelt out once again, at least according to Goodman's recollection, that if Goodman didn't implicate others, he would retain his job. If he did, he wouldn't. This was the opposite of a cleaning out of the stables. But Goodman was clearly angry, and reiterated several times that he was not happy with the role he had been handed. He spelt out how the editor had complete control of everything that happened, that phone hacking was a day-to-day practice and approved by the editor, how Glenn Mulcaire's work was 'key to the organisation', that he felt he had been lied to, manipulated and felt very aggrieved, having performed with the full knowledge of some senior people. Addressing such matters lay in the future.

At News International, everything was on hold until punishment for the two 'rogues' was decided. Coulson believed the pair would not go to prison, in which case, it was believed, the affair would probably blow over, amid pious expressions about 'lessons having been learned' and so on. But, just in case, the press office was refusing to answer questions as to whether Andy Coulson had known about the hacking.

Goodman, according to his barrister John Kelsey Fry, was in 'utter terror' at the prospect of going to prison, and was having to sell his house.

Mulcaire was pretty sure he would be given a custodial sentence, but he didn't want to alarm his family in case he was wrong. His protectiveness of his family is striking. He was particularly concerned about the possible effect on his wife, whose uncomplicated sweetness of nature makes her a non-starter as the controlling evil genius that some tried to portray her as. 'We'd say "You're going to prison Glenn, aren't you," and he'd say "I don't know, maybe not,"' says Alison. ('But he did know,' says his daughter Georgia confidently). The night before sentencing, Mulcaire packed a small bag with clothes and books – 'just in case', he said – which he handed to his solicitor. It was at that point that Alison's uncertainty dissolved. There was also some wild talk about how long he would get. An apparently well-informed soul, attempting to soften the eventual blow, and overlooking the fact that the maximum allowed for the crime was two years, mentioned between three and five years.

Nonetheless, on January 26th Clive Goodman was given four months in prison. Glenn Mulcaire was sentenced to four months for conspiracy plus two months for the other offences relating to the five celebrities. (In the event, Mulcaire served 13 weeks with three weeks on a tag. Goodman served just four weeks.)

The judge didn't stint in his criticism. Their behaviour, he said, was 'low conduct, reprehensible in the extreme'. 'This case was not about press freedom; it was about a grave, inexcusable and illegal invasion of privacy. 'It was not pushing at the limits, or at the cusp: it was plainly on the wrong side of the line. It is essential for the decency of our public life that conduct of this kind is clearly marked as unacceptable. 'This was serious criminal conduct to which we must not become numbed. It is to my mind [of] the very first importance to the fabric of our public life that such intrusive, sustained criminal conduct should be marked by immediate loss of liberty,' the judge said. Goodman was motivated by 'career advancement and protection', but his thirst for inside information led him to break the law.

There was not necessarily as much contrition in the air as the judge might have hoped. Mulcaire will still tell friends that it was a journalist who got him into this mess. 'Clive was in way above his head, and he made a grave error by not being careful enough,' he says. 'Clive was worried about his job. He wasn't privy to enough of the real stuff in conference, and wasn't being asked to do enough. He was worried he wasn't getting the stories and was pushing the boundaries as a result.' In other words, the feeling was less: we deeply regret what we did because it is wrong, and more a) we were only doing what everyone else was doing and b) it was only because of a mistake that we got caught.

But the stigma of prison wasn't the end of the damage. Andy Coulson, who had promised to bring Goodman back into the fold after a decent interval, resigned. His carefully assembled statement said: 'I have decided that the time has come for me to take ultimate responsibility for the events around the Clive Goodman case. As I've said before, his actions were entirely wrong and I deeply regret that they happened on my watch.' His hope of Goodman being given a no-custodial sentence had vanished. If there was to be damage-limitation, Coulson was to play no further part in it.

Max Clifford wrote at the time that he couldn't understand why Andy Coulson hadn't resigned when Goodman was convicted. 'We are told they decided a fortnight ago,' he wrote, 'but my suspicion is that the decision was dependent on what punishment Goodman received. If he had been ordered to do community service, I believe Andy Coulson would still be the *News of the World*'s editor.'

Versions vary as to why Coulson resigned. It has been said that the decision was his and his alone, and that he had decided to go a fortnight earlier, but others say he didn't want to go and only agreed to do so after a conversation with Rupert Murdoch's most trusted confidant Les Hinton, on the understanding that he would be back in the fold once the fuss had died down.

Certainly one senior colleague who saw him that day said he seemed in surprisingly good spirits, the blow softened by a substantial payoff. A figure of £600,000 was mentioned in court, but a well-placed Wapping insider points out that while the norm for deposed News International editors is to receive two years' money on leaving the company, Coulson got three (which would take the figure beyond £600,000).

Goodman was in limbo, and now had little or no guarantee that he could make the agreement stick. And there was more. Just a couple of weeks into his sentence, Clive Goodman received a call from his wife to say that he was being dismissed, with one year's money. Goodman was astounded. He had been promised that if he pleaded guilty, his job was safe. Now the company had ratted on the deal.

In other circumstances, the sack would have been no surprise, given that Goodman had not merely broken the law, but intruded on the personal privacy of the heirs to the throne. Given that the press had had a major hand in the death of their mother less than a decade earlier, the black mark this cast on the newspaper can hardly be exaggerated.

But Goodman had every right to feel aggrieved. He was carrying the can for something half the office, seemingly, had been up to. Hinton, gamely but lamely, sought to sugar the pill by saying that in the light of his distinguished years of service to the *News of the World* and in recognition of the pressures on his family, he would receive one year's salary. Asked later, Hinton told MPs he had had discussions with others about the decision – he didn't recall who, unsurprisingly – but that the decision was his.

Goodman had had enough. The payment of a year's money didn't begin to satisfy him. On 2nd March he wrote to Daniel Cloke, Human Resources Director of News International, saying that he planned to appeal against the termination of his employment. This was bad news for his former employers, and had to be kept under wraps. Things were to get worse. Goodman, who had previously told Wapping bigwigs about the complicity of senior staff, went to town with the detail. In an angry denunciation of attempts to stifle the issue, he appealed against his sacking following his release from prison. He called the decision to sack him 'perverse' and 'inconsistent' in that the actions leading to this criminal charge were carried out with the full knowledge of senior staff at News International. 'Other members of staff were carrying out the same illegal procedures…. This practice was widely discussed in the daily editorial conference, until explicit reference to it was banned by the Editor. As far as I am aware, no other member of staff has faced disciplinary action, much less dismissal.'

What had escaped the media at the time Goodmand and Mulcaire were sentenced was the judge's telling remark towards Mulcaire. He said: 'As to Counts 16 to 20 [the phone-hacking of Max Clifford, Simon Hughes MP, Sky Andrew, Elle Macpherson and Gordon Taylor], you had not dealt with Goodman but with others at News International.' In other words, the judge supported what Goodman was claiming. This is worth remembering when looking at subsequent claims by News International to have got to the bottom of the matter. The police erroneously took this assertion by the judge to relate only to lawful research work.

Goodman demanded to be shown emails sent to him by six of his colleagues in the 16 months up to his imprisonment. News International refused the request, but asked a firm of lawyers, Harbottle & Lewis, to review the emails. They asserted that the messages did not provide evidence that the six other employees had knowledge of phone hacking. It was a decidedly partial use of their findings, Harbottle & Lewis later complained in court.

And over in Cheam, the Mulcaire family were having to get by without Glenn. Alison admits she didn't cope well. They would visit him in Belmarsh every Sunday, where he was torn between putting on a brave face for his beloved family and despairing in rage at how his employers had so spectacularly abandoned him. In his absence, Greg Miskiw, under whose news editorship Mulcaire's association with the *News of the World* had started, was in regular contact, an expression of support that the family took as genuine and heartfelt. Certainly it was received better than the earlier suggestion from reporter Neville Thurlbeck that Mulcaire and his family should 'move to a small village in Wales'. They felt they had no more reason to feel ashamed than, say, Neville Thurlbeck.

Ostensibly solicitous phone calls came from another executive, but this one still on the paper. One executive called – according to Alison's memory – every day during the first week that Mulcaire was in prison. 'He used to ring up and say "hello, how are you? How's Glenn getting on? How's the family coping", all that,' she recalls. 'I used to just stonewall… I always said yeah, yeah he's fine. And then towards the end of the call, you could tell what he was up to, he'd always say "Do you still have any of Glenn's emails... are there any emails in the house?" You knew he was worrying about anything that would incriminate other people.'

One day, soon after Mulcaire had learned – in a roundabout way, shall we say – of his release date, he was summoned to the prison governor of Belmarsh's office. He was asked if he was planning to write a book. Evidently, Lord Archer having shed a certain amount of light on his time at Her Majesty's Pleasure, the governor was hoping to be spared. 'Ask a journalist, they do the writing,' Mulcaire told him. But that didn't seem to be the governor's chief concern, and indeed, he had a second question. How had Mulcaire known before even the governor when he was going to be released?

The prison listens in to inmates' conversations, and Alison had been heard telling her husband that a well-connected friend had told her when Glenn was to be released. Glenn, knowing the call to Alison was monitored, had tried to laugh off the information as unreliable, but she, understandably anxious to raise his morale with some good news, had doggedly insisted on the reliability of her information. 'I'm hopeless at all that stuff,' she says. It is only and plentifully to her credit that that is easily believed.

The below the radar fretting of the guilty men was in striking contrast to their public lack of concern. It is a mark of how successful News International had been in sailing serenely on and closing down the hacking story that, within weeks of Andy Coulson resigning, George Osborne was meeting the former editor at a London hotel to talk to him about his working alongside David

Cameron. According to George Osborne's biographer, Coulson joked that on the day he had resigned, both Tony Blair and Gordon Brown had been touch to commiserate, and the fact that the Tories had taken much longer was a mark of how much they needed to up their media game. Anyone who knew the truth of how dirty Coulson's hands were would have been astonished at the affirmation of his unsinkability, as they would have been by his appointment. But few outside News International did.

Coulson and Steve Hilton, David Cameron's loyal friend and proprietorial conveyor of the Cameron message as campaign manager, had already been sizing one another up to see if they could work together. Hilton had given his blessing, and Osborne's benediction (though never in doubt as he had been one of the idea's midwives) was the next stage in his recruitment. If the waves were closing over the affair, publicly at least, that surely suited all concerned.

As the Coulson-Cameron courtship was getting under way, Mulcaire's solicitor Moray Laing emailed News International's lawyers again on 23rd February, this time in rather more urgent terms. He told the company that for legal purposes Mulcaire was effectively an employee of the *News of the World*, and was entitled to compensation. This was based on the paper's degree of control over Mulcaire's activities, the exclusivity of his services and the 'mutuality of obligation' that existed in showing he was treated the same as other employees. He also cited discussions with an News International individualwho on at least one occasion told Mulcaire that if he did not do the work he was instructed to do he would not be paid.

As an employee, therefore, he was claiming unfair dismissal, since the usual procedure had not been gone through. Laing said, further, that Mulcaire had been dismissed in part because of the possibility of his whistle blowing a) on the company and b) specifically on executives who had instructed him to access the voicemails of a number of individuals, including former Met boss Lord Stevens. ('He was the next on my list,' remembers Mulcaire now.) Laing said he had emails and audio evidence to support this claim. Mulcaire would be willing to come to a 'constructive conclusion... in a confidential fashion', he said. He favoured meeting in a constructive fashion, and that if that was not possible, proceedings would be issued.

If News International was worried about what tales Mulcaire could tell, it was doing a good job of pretending otherwise. Once again, Laing was made to wait. The email from the south London employment solicitor to the global conglomerate was ignored for some weeks. This may be a measure of the continuing high-handedness of News International management at the time, plus the fact that the relevant legal affairs person was on holiday for ten days after the email was sent. Even after his return, though, the email went unanswered for three weeks. He was prompted for a reply, and on 26th March he asked for the original to be sent again.

Goodman, too, was still seething. He had a meeting on 20th March with News International human resources, which he covertly recorded. Three weeks later, he met Rebekah Brooks, then editing the *Sun*, at the RAC club for lunch. Brooks suggested he work for her. When

Goodman expressed a doubt that she might be in a position to employ a sacked senior reporter such as himself, she said dismissively: 'I can employ who I like.' But the offer was temporary, not well-paid and – he told the Old Bailey – would undermine any thought of blowing the whistle on wrongdoing, so he turned it down. Asked in court about the job offer, Brooks said she 'wanted to stop him making unfounded allegations against the paper', having been assured by Coulson and others that there was no truth to what Goodman was claiming. (To her answer, her questioner replied: 'to shut him up'.)

Goodman wrote to News International on May 5th 2007, alleging that News International notes taken at a meeting he had attended some months earlier were grossly flawed and misrepresented much of his evidence. He identified 47 inaccuracies, which to those of a conspiratorial cast of mind was more than enough to suggest a shepherding of the evidence towards the narrative that subsequently emerged – namely that the blame was confined to as small a number of people as was credible. Equally, the note taker was evidently not well versed in the saga and can be excused some errors. In any event, Goodman listed a number of inaccuracies. While it was becoming evident that Goodman would probably stay silent about what he knew had been going on at the *News of the World*, it was equally clear that one year's salary was not going to be enough, and negotiations continued for some months. Nonetheless, his former bosses were not admitting to any concerns about the strength of his position.

By this time, the Tories had decided they wanted Andy

Coulson on board. He was in many respects just what they needed, but by any standards Coulson's copybook was shop-soiled. Two people had gone to prison on his watch, and another *News of the World* employee, recently sacked while being treated for depression, was bringing a legal case against him for bullying. The Tories needed to give at least a nod to due diligence and, according to a very senior Tory, wanted to reassure themselves that there were no further legal cases that would compromise Coulson's appointment.

By late April, News International were at last addressing Mulcaire's claim seriously. They met Moray Laing on 10th May, and on the following day Jon Chapman, the director of legal affairs at News International, made an offer for a full and final settlement. It was £80,000, which was £52,600 as half a year's salary, plus £10,000 in compensation. There was also, at Mulcaire's suggestion, a clause stipulating that Mulcaire 'assist/co-operate… in any investigation' into the events that led to the conviction' of Goodman and Mulcaire.

With hindsight, £80,000 looks a good deal less than what Mulcaire might have got. Certainly Mulcaire regrets not pushing for more, although Greg Miskiw at the *News of the World* Manchester office, who Mulcaire believed had his interests at heart, warned him 'if you don't take it, you'll get nothing'. 'It is one of the very few things Alison and I have disagreed about,' he says. 'I knew that a whole lot of people knew what I was doing on behalf of the company, and I didn't want to just roll up and concede, but Alison was worried about where our next meal and mortgage payment was coming from. Now of course she wishes we'd turned it down.'

As May came to an end, Mulcaire came to believe that this was as good an offer as they were going to get, and that he should accept. Now both Goodman and Mulcaire, far from exposing the fact that they were not 'rogues', were coming into line. Relief all round.

It may or may not be a coincidence that Andy Coulson was appointed as the Tory party's head of communications on 31st May. Only the Daily Mail expressed any surprise at the timing of the appointment, although even that may have had more to do with professional rivalry and the prospect of the Murdoch papers being closer to the prospective PM than Associated Newspapers.

Elsewhere, the legal skirmishing over the two 'rogues' was petering out. Mulcaire signed his agreement in the first week of June, but Goodman and News International were still being obdurate. On 10th May, at a meeting in Wapping, he had been told the company was 'minded to reject his appeal' over being sacked. A week later Rebekah Brooks emailed him, offering to send him on a sub-editing course, which a reporter of Goodman's experience could reasonably have regarded as a sideways step at best and which he ignored. On 30th May he was told his appeal had been formally rejected, upon which he announced he said he planned to appeal to a tribunal, which effectively meant going public.

Goodman got his reward for holding his nerve. Three days later, he recalls, he was called by the head of corporate and legal at News International Jon Chapman and offered another £50,000 to settle the employment claim. That was more like it. A few weeks later, after further negotiations, the company agreed a payment of a further £153,000, comprising £40,000 in compensation, £13,000 in legal expenses and a further £90,000 in notice. The company later struggled to explain how the supposedly disgraced reporter, to whom the company had threatened to pay nothing, was now receiving a second notice payment, totalling nearly two and a half times what he had been offered.

To most people, Goodman's threat to expose the extent of lawlessness had been seen off with the help of nearly £250,000. If so, he was not the last to apply such pressure. But executives at the company sought to explain everything. 'There was an issue of a long process,' they protested, 'which... was going to hamper the company's, or the newspaper's, opportunity to get back on track, and I decided at the time that the right thing to do was to settle this and get it behind us....' Jon Chapman agreed that this was not hush money, but was to 'allow the *News of the World* under its new editor to move on' and allow the paper 'to recover as a brand'. The company later said the size of the payment was in part down to its failure to follow statutory procedures. In any event, both Goodman and Mulcaire had been silenced.

Andy Coulson started work for the Conservatives on 9th July 2007. The phone hacking saga seemed to have died a very silent death.

8

'We Don't Need F**king Murdoch.'

The aspect of the phone hacking affair that most impinged on Westminster was the appointment of Andy Coulson to be David Cameron's communications chief on 31st May of 2007. Of all the decisions Cameron had to make as leader, it was the one to cause him the most unshakeable embarrassment. Cameron admitted within months of Coulson's resignation from Downing Street (accepted against Cameron's will) in January 2011 that, with hindsight, he would not have appointed him. And 29th June 2014 he apologised to the British people for having employed Coulson. Yet at the time it had barely caused a ripple in the media.

The first 18 months after David Cameron's December 2005 accession to the Tory leadership were characterised by an engaging lack of preparedness and a charming learn-on-the-job feel from the mostly youthful, tieless cohorts around him. Their eccentric and brilliant guiding light was Cameron's professional blue-skies thinker Steve Hilton, his former colleague and friend from Central Office.

The Cameron project owed a great deal to the blueprint of the man Cameron had been seeking to unseat, Tony Blair. The new leader and his prospective chancellor referred to Blair as 'the master', such was their admiration for a man who had helped turn Labour from the loser of four successive elections into a formidable election-winning machine. Having comprehensively lost three elections, the Tories, led by a new breed of careerist politicians, were not above learning some difficult lessons. And if that meant conveying some uncomfortable truths to their party – and possibly advertising their hard-headedness in doing so, as Blair had done – that was fine too.

One of the axioms of Hilton's thinking was that the old print media was continuing to lose its grip on the national conversation, and that voters were making their choices on the basis of what they had seen on television and in the new media.

So on that issue at least, the Tony Blair playbook was to be flung out of the window. The presumed need to secure the support of the Murdoch papers (the endorsement of the *Mail* and *Telegraph* groups was all but taken for granted) was to be defied. For these young men (mostly) on the make, that particular magnate had lost his power of attraction. In 2006 one of Cameron's closest lieutenants exclaimed off the record, to a journalist: 'We don't need fucking Murdoch.'

Such thinking was understandably the source of some frustration at News International, which had marched in step with Tony Blair for most of his time as Labour leader and which enjoyed the fact that for better or worse, politicians were forever on the phone trying to woo them. Murdoch and election-winners tended to go together. Psephologically they were as inseparable as the chicken and the egg.

But in early 2007, the Hilton media strategy thinking

wasn't cutting the mustard. Notting Hill's clever young media types were delighted when Cameron advocated hugging hoodies on housing estates and huskies in the Arctic, and the newness of it all certainly caught the eye, but the polls didn't suggest it was going down well, and the old-fashioned press worried that the whipper-snapper had gone too far. Further, why was someone as self-evidently traditional as Cameron adopting these outlandish positions? Was there nothing he wouldn't say to win office? With Gordon Brown by contrast – seemingly bristling with conviction and serious intent – about to take over as prime minister and with a snap election a clear possibility, Cameron risked looking rootless and lightweight. He told friends it was conceivable he would have to quit the leadership by the end of the year.

At about the same time, an answer to a nagging problem presented itself. Cameron's lead press adviser, the low-key, ultra-loyal George Eustice, was looking for a parliamentary seat. If successful, he would be unavailable to David Cameron after the election, whenever that came. Besides, Cameron had been feeling the need of a 'heavy-hitter', someone with presence and comment-page experience who would command respect among senior journalists. Many people were approached, but those who wanted the job were not quite right. Those best qualified didn't want it.

The solution was Andy Coulson, recently deposed as editor of the *News of the World*. For him and his predecessor, Rebekah Brooks, the dismissing Goodman and Mulcaire's exploits as a rogue operation seemed to have avoided what could have been an almighty scandal.

(To the bemusement of those who knew how the *News of the World* operated, this close call had done nothing to trim/curtail the rise and rise of Rebekah Brooks. She continued as editor of the *Sun* and to enjoy the support and indulgence of her boss Rupert Murdoch.)

Given Murdoch's penchant for backing winners, his endorsement would add enormous credibility to any politician's ambitions. So just as Cameron's jejune experiment in defying the press barons was coming to an end, the availability of Coulson was perfectly timed. Indeed, there may have been a degree of cause and effect.

The problem, though, was that Murdoch needed convincing about Cameron and Rebekah Brooks was to be the architect of winning him over. With James Murdoch in tow, she set about persuading the media baron. David Cameron, of course, lapped this up. He showed a puppyish and uncharacteristically light-headed willingness to please her and her bosses. Although she has denied it, Rebekah Brooks has been mooted as the person who suggested initially to George Osborne that Coulson, with whom she was effectively still in a relationship, albeit a complicated one, was the person for the job.

Though not renowned as a political player, Coulson promised the sort of knowledge of the real world that the Cameron entourage notably lacked. His modest Essex background ticked the social mobility box, and he was known as highly competent and professional. Who better to help change Rupert Murdoch's privately stated view that there would never be another Etonian in No 10? Murdoch, after all, had agreed to give him a substantial payoff, presumably believing – to a degree at least – that he had been hard done by. Other lieutenants of the Tory leader knew and liked Coulson, including Michael Gove and William Hague, whose goodwill towards the Murdoch papers had been cemented four years earlier by being given a £200,000-a-year column for the *News of the World*. (Hague may not have known – may still not – that in 1998 it had been Coulson's idea to portray the Tory party as a dead parrot, with Hague's head superimposed, on the *Sun*'s front page, or that Coulson had voted Labour the year before.)

Coulson had many attributes, and it would be a mistake to say he was chosen solely because of his News International pedigree. One close Cameron associate said: 'We should talk to this guy, and when he came in, I thought this is the guy, and he did a brilliant job for us. We'd been saying "where's our Alastair Campbell?", and this seemed to be it.' But his News International connections cannot have done his prospects any harm. One account says that Rebekah Brooks edged another candidate, Guto Harri, aside because he was not 'acceptable' to News International. According to a story in the *Mail on Sunday*, 'Rebekah indicated the job should go to Andy. Cameron was told it should be someone acceptable to News International. The company was also desperate to find something for Andy after he took the rap when the phone hacking first became an issue. The approach was along the lines of, "If you find something for Andy we will return the favour."' The story has the ring of truth, but the fact that such a possibility could even be entertained says much about Cameron's new-found desperation to win Murdoch's approval.

When the shadow cabinet was told of the decision to hire Coulson, it was presented as a *fait accompli*, with barely the faintest discussion. Cameron and Osborne were delighted. There was no sense that the appointment needed explaining or excusing, an attitude the press coverage seemed to endorse, perhaps revealing a concern about journalists' need to work closely with Coulson. The editor of the right-wing *Spectator*, Matthew d'Ancona, might have been speaking for Downing Street when he wrote: 'That's a real coup for them because Andy's a very good journalist and highly respected.'

It is hard to credit that more hurdles were not put in the way of Coulson's appointment. With hindsight we can see that Coulson, fresh from presiding over illegality and with several hundred thousand pounds in his hip pocket, was being given a top job, presumably to the delight of his then lover Rebekah Brooks. Certainly, considering what is now known about his immediate past, it is extraordinary that anything other than disaster was expected to come from it.

Moderately well-informed journalists at the time could have told the Tories that Coulson had been reluctant to resign, but it was agreed that a senior head had to roll if the impression of a clean-up was to be convincingly conveyed. Coulson would not have been human had he not thought 'Why me?' when so many others who knew about red-top methods were spared. But as captain of the ship, he acknowledged the symbolic importance of a price being paid. The Fleet Street consensus was that Andy would be 'looked after' once the affair had blown over. For sure, financially he was looked after, whether his resignation was voluntary or not. In News

International, it looked as if he was the sacrificial lamb.

How would Cameron explain the hiring of someone with a questionable recent record? The line he decided to take, a colleague recalls, was that he had been reassured that Coulson's past was nothing to worry about, and later on, if that didn't wash, he would say that, Coulson having lost his job, there was no reason why he should be punished twice. In the event, Cameron didn't have to answer questions about Coulson's past for a couple of years, something which seemed to vindicate the decidedly lax appointment process.

So what had Coulson been asked, when he took the job, and what had he said? This remains a thorny issue.

Osborne had a drink with Coulson at a London hotel. He told the Leveson inquiry that he asked Coulson, 'in a general sense, as you might do in a social encounter, whether there was more in the phone-hacking story that was going to come out, that was not already public, that we needed to know about – and he said "no". According to George Osborne's biographer, Janan Ganesh, on the way back from the hotel, Osborne called Cameron to say Coulson was open to an offer of employment.

A number of people asked David Cameron privately if he was sure he was doing the right thing in appointing Coulson, but his mind was made up. One senior former Fleet Street editor told Cameron the very fact of having edited the *News of the World* meant an editor would have done things that would disqualify him from holding such high office. But Cameron's biggest concern was quite different. He was fixated on the idea that there would be a repeat of what had happened to William Hague, whose media adviser Amanda Platell had written a video diary while in the job and which hugely embarrassed Hague subsequently. If that could be resolved (which it was), Cameron was sold on the idea, and as a tidy-minded politician, he hates going back on decisions. Coulson was to be his media magus, the man to help steer him to Downing Street.

As far as Coulson's own pronouncements are concerned, a certain amount of mythology has built up. The phrase Andy Coulson 'has always denied knowing' (about the phone hacking) became something of a mantra in the media. In fact, it is quite inaccurate. The press bought the most spectacular dummy. When he resigned from the *News of the World*, Coulson issued no such denial, nor did he do so for more than two years afterwards. As former prime minister James Callaghan once said, a lie can be half way round the world before the truth has got its boots on. In the digital age, that should read 'several times' round the world.

Coulson, well-rewarded and heading for David Cameron's office had to walk a tightrope. On the one hand Murdoch had to be convinced that Coulson knew nothing in order to secure his payoff. Murdoch would surely not have compensated a guilty man so generously. On the other, Coulson couldn't publicly deny it in case any concrete evidence came out, because in that case he would have been showed to have lied, which would cause him to lose that job and jeopardise the great News International switch from Labour to the Conservatives.

And so, on 26th January 2007, an enduring untruth was born, when journalists, possibly briefed by people who knew no better, were given the impression that Coulson had known nothing of what royal correspondent Clive Goodman and private investigator Glenn Mulcaire had been up to. It became the accepted truth even though, in Coulson's own statement, there was no such denial. He said merely 'I deeply regret that [these actions] happened on my watch'. The closest anyone came to an on the record denial was when Les Hinton, News International executive chairman, told the Commons Committee on Culture Media and Sport in March that the editor 'told me he had no knowledge of this activity but … [felt he had to resign]'. There was to be no explicit denial for more than two years.

Did this glaring omission not raise concerns when the Tories came to do the due diligence on Coulson? Seemingly not. Indeed, there is no sign of anyone having even noticed. 'Our biggest concern was to check whether all the court cases had concluded, whether there were outstanding tribunals,' said one leading Conservative, perhaps aware that Clive Goodman had launched a case against the paper for unfair dismissal (although surely in normal circumstances a cabinet minister would not normally know that). Coulson's appointment was announced on 31st May. The settling of Glenn Mulcaire's case for unfair dismissal was imminent, but the case brought by sacked sports reporter Matt Driscoll, who eventually won a huge payout for bullying against the *News of the World*, had barely got off the ground.

But who had made sure that there was nothing in Coulson's past that might embarrass the Tories? The answers here are inadequate, and there is no sign it even struck anyone as odd that he had issued no public denial.

Early on in the saga, in one of Cameron's few statements on the matter, he was strikingly vague as to who had reassured him Coulson was in the clear: 'I am satisfied that Andy Coulson was not aware that a journalist at the News of the World was engaged in this practice.'

A version of events has been proposed by journalist Matthew d'Ancona, a defender of Coulson. In his book *In It Together*, d'Ancona claims that Cameron's conversation with Coulson was the subject of wilfull blindness. When Cameron had raised the issue, Coulson had chosen a form of words which suggested he knew nothing of the detail of what the pair were doing on that particular occasion, but didn't deny knowing about the widespread practice of phone hacking. Cameron, we are invited to believe, takes Coulson to mean he knew nothing at all. 'Coulson had said one thing and Cameron had heard – or remembered – quite another.'

D'Ancona's offer of a lifeboat wins points for generosity and novelty, but is still damning for Cameron. Coulson's version – that he said something like 'no, I didn't know what Goodman and Mulcaire were up to' and that that was effectively the end of the conversation – leaves the Prime Minister looking either a fool or a knave. If he is a fool, it is for failing not to spot the evasiveness of his reply, which seems unlikely. Or a knave, because Cameron is perfectly aware of the inadequacy of the denial, but cynically turns a blind eye, knowing that one day, in extremis, he'd be able to accuse Coulson of misleading him. The second option suited them both, but if true, suggests Cameron, by nature trusting and generous-spirited, had no interest in knowing the truth about Coulson's past, only in his ability to help get him into Downing Street. What d'Ancona calls Cameron's wilful blindness in his context is not that of an indulgent parent benignly pretending not to see a child taking the last biscuit. It is taking a gamble, knowing a course of action is highly risky and still pursuing it in the hope that no one will notice.

And for a while, no one did, or seemed to. In the absence of further evidence of phone hacking, the issue seemed to have gone for good. The politics of the affair returned below the public's radar. But it was no less vigorous for that.

Rebekah Brooks and David Cameron had decided they had shared interests. Cameron knew he needed her support if he was to persuade the Murdoch papers to endorse the Tories, and she knew that getting on with prime ministers (potential and actual) never did her any harm. Happily at about this time she was beginning a relationship with Charlie Brooks, a school contemporary of Cameron's brother Alex, whose family lived in Sarsden near Cameron's constituency home of Dean, in Oxfordshire. As we have seen, Brooks has few rivals in her capacity to love-bomb people she wants to get on with, and Cameron, not reluctant, came under sustained assault. Rebekah was constantly popping round at the weekend and bumping into Cameron at one or other home of the illustrious Cotswolds circle that became known as the Chipping Norton set. 'They do see an awful lot of Rebekah,' said a surprised friend of Cameron, struggling to see what the pair had in common.

The ingratiation reached a new level when Rebekah, at the early stages of her relationship with Brooks, a raffish horseman of the old school who had given her a pair of Hermès riding boots, decided she would like to acquire a retired police horse. David Cameron had been brought up in the countryside, had tried and enjoyed hunting comparatively recently and had expressed an interest in taking up riding again. It was a further opportunity to ingratiate herself with Cameron, a prospect Cameron showed little inclination to resist.

The horse story, which oddly given his brief, Lord Justice Leveson regarded as a trivial issue, was one of those microcosms that reveals a far bigger truth, both in itself and as a result of its revelation. In late February 2012, Tom Harper reported in the London *Evening Standard* that Rebekah Brooks had been loaned a retired horse by the Metropolitan Police. This gave rise to a good deal of merriment, and a twitter account @Rebekah'sHorse quickly attracted followers.

Christopher Hope, a journalist on the *Telegraph*, asked if David Cameron had ever ridden the horse, named Raisa. Initially Cameron's spokesman sought to portray the inquiry as not even deserving of a response. Two days later, Cameron sought to clear things up with a denial. 'Since becoming PM I may have got on a horse once, but not that one,' he said, ducking the issue of whether he had ridden the horse beforehand. Eventually he came clean, confirming that he had indeed ridden Raisa and had known that she had been loaned her by the Met. The intriguing lack of candour chimed with Downing Street's denial a year earlier of a claim that he and Charlie Brooks had ever been riding together, which they had.

So why so evasive? The reason, it can now be revealed, is that the horse was acquired from the police by Brooks *partly for David Cameron's use*. It is a story which speaks volumes about both her and Cameron.

In the summer of 2007, over lunch with Ian Blair, head of the Metropolitan Police, Rebekah Brooks and the Met's head of media, Dick Fedorcio agreed that a horse should be provided for Brooks. In September 2007, she and Dick Fedorcio went to the Met's horse training centre at Imber Court to find a suitable beast. Alan Hiscox, the Met's longest serving boss at Imber Court, remembers: 'I got a call a day or two after Ian Blair and Rebekah [Brooks] had seen one another. It was from his staff officer, I think. I was asked if I knew who [she] was. I said I did and was told Ian Blair had just had a meal with her and that she would like a retired police horse. I was told that this would, "definitely be a good idea for the Met Police."'

Hiscox remembers that it was clear 'people in authority' were interested in the issue. 'I had calls from both Dick Fedorcio and Rebekah Brooks's PA asking when a horse would be ready.' In about October, Hiscox went to the Cotswolds to meet Rebekah and Charlie Brooks to check on the riding and stabling facilities near their house where a horse would be kept. He declared himself satisfied with the conditions, and impressed by the stable manager – 'clearly knowledgeable about horses' – who would be giving Mrs Brooks lessons.

What happened next took Hiscox by surprise. He remembers: 'As we were being shown round the stables she told me that David Cameron would also be riding the retired police horse. At the time I did not think much of it, other than to wonder why she told me that. She may have been trying to show off, but it was a curious thing to say.'

Hiscox returned to his office and told his boss that the stables were satisfactory and passed on the information that Cameron would be riding the horse. 'This information would have been passed up the chain and I feel sure Dick Fedorcio and Ian Blair would have known', says Hiscox. The horse arrived in July 2008, but when it was clear it was hardly being ridden it was returned to Imber Court. Hiscox defends Charlie Brooks against the charge that he had not cared for the horse. 'When it was returned the horse looked as if it had been put to grass for some time. Clearly it had not been ridden or groomed much, but there was no suggestion by me that it had been mistreated, as was claimed in the press. Quite rightly, Charlie Brooks was cross at this suggestion.'

'It struck me as quite odd that everyone was so evasive about the retired police horse,' said Hiscox. 'Why did David Cameron's office not say he had ridden the horse in the first instance? I have nothing to hide about this episode and it wasn't clear to me why they were so embarrassed about it. It is possible, I suppose, that Rebekah Brooks was trying to ingratiate herself with Mr Cameron and that she had told him she was going to get it for him, but in normal circumstances it should not have been a big deal.'

As the Brooks-Cameron equestrian bonding proceeded, at about the same time, late 2008, Andy Coulson was asked by a journalist, this book's author, to clear up what at the time might have been a misapprehension. Coulson had claimed, in a private conversation, that in his resignation statement he had denied knowledge of phone hacking. He was subsequently asked, on the record, to clarify where this denial was to be found, which of course he was unable to do (having done no such thing). Having not demurred when confronted with his non-denial, he was also asked, simply: did he know about the phone hacking? The answer he gave begged more questions about other versions of events. He asked to go off the record, giving an inconsequential reply. He was then asked: 'Now, on the record, are you saying you knew nothing about the phone hacking at the *News of the World*?' There was a long pause, and he said: 'I really have nothing to add to what I've said before.' He was given another opportunity to answer the question, but he didn't take it. In other words, he was choosing to continue with his non-denial stance.

This was curious. If he didn't know about the phone hacking, why not say so? If he did know, he had either come clean to anyone who asked him about it, which presumably would have made him unfit for the job, or he had lied. If the latter, why did he not repeat the same lie to me? Or, with hindsight (the d'Ancona version had not been published at that point), maybe he had only been willing to deny knowing about the fine detail of what Mulcaire and Goodman were up to? In which case, what an interesting conversation that must have been.

It was not until July 2009, by which time his ducking of the issue could no longer be ignored, that Coulson made his first public denial. The *Guardian* had just revealed that PFA chairman Gordon Taylor had been paid £700,000 by News International to drop his breach of privacy complaint. The obvious question was why was News International so keen to keep him quiet if they had so little to hide? Rebekah, having just married Charlie

Brooks and been made chief executive of News International, should have been asked the question then, but wasn't. And fortunately for Coulson, he was able to say that he had nothing to do with the settlement, having left the paper some time earlier. Privately he was more worried. He spoke to Cameron's private advisor Ed Llewellyn and told him he understood that the time might have come for him to go.

But Coulson told the House of Commons Media Select Committee 'my instructions to the staff were clear – we did not use subterfuge of any kind unless there was a clear public interest in doing so. They were to work within the PCC code at all times'.

Matthew d'Ancona has reported how, in preparation for a trip to Afghanistan, Cameron and Coulson had undergone training together to learn what to do in the event of being kidnapped. One lesson they had learnt was that if one of their group was raped, the others should embrace him, by way of showing solidarity. When Coulson returned from his Select Committee grilling, in a gesture that shows more decency than judgment, Cameron interrupted a meeting to embrace Coulson.

But privately he was advised that no good would come of Coulson's continuing presence by his side, and the drip-drip of news was not encouraging. Nor was Coulson's confessional assertion that 'I wasn't running sweet shop, Dave.' So Cameron invited Guy Black, his predecessor at Conservative Central Office in the late 1980s and much more recently a fulcrum first of the Press Complaints Commission and then of Press Standards Board of Finance, which oversaw and funded the PCC, to a quiet supper at his home in Notting Hill.

Assuming Black would be familiar with the ways of the press, Cameron, understandably concerned by the continuing revelations, asked Black if he thought he should be concerned. Black reassured him, saying no, apparently believing, as many did, that since the police long had the evidence and nothing new and substantial had emerged, that was that. When surprise was expressed that the worldly Black should believe that to be the case, it was pointed out that Rebekah Brooks was one of the witnesses at his civil partnership ceremony. 'He does believe it, but even if he doesn't, he's not likely to dump on his best man, is he?' said a friend of Black's.

Following the 2010 election, when Mr Cameron became prime minister at the head of a coalition government, he insisted on Coulson staying on board. He wanted and needed him, he felt, and took a gamble on the whole thing going away, a hope that infected his whole office.

Coulson had made himself a key member of the team by now. Cameron respected his opinion and knew he stood for a part of the electorate poorly represented among the rest of his circle. And of course he was well known to the press, particularly his former colleagues at News International, where he was not bashful about using his standing as a former editor when suggesting ideas for his former paper, the *Sun*. While it would be an exaggeration to say that News International editors 'took dictation' from No 10, Coulson's word carried a lot of weight. The headline 'Bottler Brown', for example, accompanied by a mocked up picture of a bottle of beer with Gordon Brown's face on it, after he failed to call a snap election in 2007, was widely assumed in

Westminster to have been Coulson's idea, as was the portrayal of Brown as a tenant who wouldn't budge from No 10 two days after the 2010 election. Dominic Mohan, the *Sun*'s editor from 2009 to 2013, who succeeded Rebekah Brooks, was regarded by Coulson as always receptive to good ideas.

The issue of Coulson's security vetting once he reached Downing Street is often raised, and still there are no satisfactory answers. A minimal check had been done on him in 2007, but to work in Downing Street required a higher level of clearance. However, he was not subjected to 'Developed Vetting', as his predecessor Alastair Campbell had been, which has given rise to a good deal of speculation.

Due probably to an oversight, Coulson is believed to have been privy to files that should only have been seen by those who have been 'DV-ed', because colleagues assumed he had been. But the question of why Sir Jeremy Heywood did not insist on Coulson facing such scrutiny remains unanswered. One serving police officer with extensive high-level experience in counter-subversion reports: 'You can imagine what happened. If the boss wants someone, that's that. So if he says: 'Get him in', all the protocols go out of the window. They jump to it.' Cameron, though, says it was entirely a matter for the civil service.

After Cameron became Prime Minister – thanks in part to the endorsement of the *Sun* – an idea that had been mooted by the Murdoch clan became a concrete goal. News Corporation decided to try to acquire the 61% of broadcaster BSkyB that it did not already own. The decision as to whether this should be allowed to go ahead, or whether it was in breach of competition law, was likely to be a political one. On the government side the decision was put into the hands of a Liberal Democrat, Vince Cable, the Business secretary, but the closeness of Cameron to the bigwigs at Wapping gave rise to suspicion that News Corporation was angling for, and possibly getting, preferential treatment. This concern did not abate with the revelation that in the fifteen months after the election, Cameron had 26 meetings with its executives. The Prime Minister's office had been called upon to compile a list of these meetings, but it forgot several of them, including the fact that Rebekah Brooks (to the surprise of his oldest friends) had been invited to Cameron's exclusive 44th birthday party at Chequers. Small wonder that Cameron was so shifty about the extent to which they socialised, or that, for example, at a point-to-point they texted one another to agree to meet in a marquee, to avoid being seen arriving together.

Some months after the 2010 election, Cameron's director of strategy Steve Hilton was given confidential and legally sensitive information about Coulson's acquaintance with certain aspects of the dark arts. Hilton passed it on to Ed Llewellyn, Cameron's chief of staff, but for reasons still unclear, the information was not passed on to the PM. Cameron did not like going back on his decisions. Besides, why should he, he thought. When under pressure to sack Coulson, he told an aide: 'You can't just sack people on hearsay.' Not that he wanted to get rid of Coulson in any case. On the contrary. Coulson had given Cameron's media operation a notably tougher edge, and the pair had become friends. In their three and a half years together, Cameron was warned that, as further investigations continued, Coulson's past would come back to haunt him, but it was news Cameron just did not want to hear.

Only when the mood music from News International changed did Cameron reluctantly accept Coulson's recognition that he had to go. It was not a moment too soon. In July of the same year it was revealed that Milly Dowler, a kidnapped (and murdered, it later emerged) Surrey schoolgirl had had her voicemails listened to. The story became politically unignorable. The *News of the World* was closed down by News International, Andy Coulson was arrested, the News Corporation bid for BskyB was withdrawn and Rebekah Brooks resigned from her position at News International. The deluge of scandal was threatening to engulf the PM himself. Cameron's closeness to Brooks and Coulson was laying him open to charges of impropriety. He set up the far-reaching Leveson inquiry, to look into the practices of the press. Its scope went far further than many in the press felt necessary, but Cameron was in charge when some fairly major law-breaking became evident. If he was to show he was personally beyond reproach, he had little choice, but it was a move that many in the newspaper world resented.

Cameron's performance in front of Leveson was notable for his nervousness. He said he had agreed with his Cabinet Office Minister Francis Maude MP and his chief of staff Ed Llewellyn about the importance of obtaining assurances from Coulson, and Cameron said the pair had asked Coulson, but Coulson himself had no recollection of any such questioning. Cameron told Leveson he had sought assurances himself from Coulson about phone hacking, in a meeting in the Norman Shaw building in Westminster. 'I remember it was very important that I ask him that question,' he added.

Coulson recalled speaking to Cameron in a phone call in which Cameron said security checks had been done on him. That call effectively confirmed he had got the job. Coulson said Mr Cameron had called while on holiday in Cornwall (seemingly it was the same call). 'Mr Cameron sought assurances about his knowledge of the hacking at the *News of the World*. I was able to repeat what I said publicly, that I knew nothing about the Clive Goodman and Glenn Mulcaire case *in terms of what they did*,' he said. Here was the fogginess that formed the basis of the account published by Matthew d'Ancona. 'In terms of what they did' could mean anything. Asked whether any further assurances were sought by Mr Cameron in relation to the matter, Mr Coulson replied: 'Not that I recall.'

Cameron had told the House of Commons he had hired Coulson 'on the basis of assurances he gave me that he did not know about the phone hacking and was not involved in criminality'.

The reality was that Coulson had been hired on the basis of an assurance he would give only in private. Two years later he did finally give a public denial, but still neither man spelt out what he had said when he was hired. As time went on and the issue refused to go away, Cameron's concern grew. He sought to spread the blame when he said: 'I think on all sides of the House there's a bit of a need for a hand on heart. We all did too much cosying up to Rupert Murdoch.' Finally, in June 2014, after Coulson's conviction for phone hacking, he apologised for his decision to hire Coulson, and strongly implied he had been lied to.

During Coulson's time at his side, Cameron had asked many people, including Rupert Murdoch, who said there was nothing new in the story, and that the police had all the evidence. This, of course, was true. Everybody had been too trusting, nobody really knew how redtop newspapers worked, including the press regulatory body, and the police dropped the catch.

So, it was all the Met's fault apparently.

9

Milly Dowler

The story that transformed the allegations of phone hacking from a tale of marginal interest with little traction beyond the media village was that of Milly Dowler. On Thursday 21st March 2002, the 13 year old schoolgirl took a train at the end of the schoolday at Heathside Comprehensive from Weybridge, but she never reached her home in Walton-on-Thames, Surrey. Normally she got off at Hersham, but this day she got off at the first stop, Walton. There she stopped briefly to go to a coffee bar with a friend. At just past 4.00pm, she said goodbye and began on the ten-minute walk home. She was never heard from again.

At 7.12pm, her father, whom she had called shortly before 4.00pm to say she'd be home soon, called the police. It was a call that was to spark searches of more than 350 locations and countless news stories. If ever there was a story made for the *News of the World*, it was this one. The paper had been campaigning for 2 years for greater public scrutiny of sex offenders, and here was a story that seemed to vindicate that demand. A blameless schoolgirl disappears unaccountably within yards of her home. As the media cliché has it, it was every parent's nightmare, an eventuality most parents find too horrifying to contemplate in reasoned terms.

Stories at the time speculated as to who would want to kidnap a lively young teenager. There seemed to be no reason why she might go missing of her own volition, although police did attend a school disco on the Friday night, for which she had bought a ticket, in the hope that she might turn up there. More than 50 extra police officers were brought in to search empty buildings, allotments and wasteland, and a helicopter with a thermal imaging camera deployed. Local people rallied round with help and expressions of support. A thousand posters showing the girl's face were put up around the area. Milly's father Bob said he and his wife Sally had been 'absolutely overwhelmed' by the extent of people's kindness.

In cold-blooded media terms, it was by any standards a big story. Everyone wanted to read about the Dowler family, whose everyday lives, comparable to those millions newspaper readers in the UK, had been so shatteringly disrupted. Papers vied with one another to solve the case. The chase was on, and the sparring of stablemates, under normal circumstances unseen by the public, came out more than ever. The *Sun*, then edited by David Yelland, had reason to claim the story as its own, a feeling amplified by his personal antipathy for Rebekah Brooks then editor of the *News of the World*. The greatest prize for any paper, of course, would be to restore Milly, as the media proprietorially referred to her, alive and well to her parents. Reporters set about their duties with such a 'trophy' in mind.

As far as what was evident to the public at the time was concerned, the nation was united in its desire to find Milly. The problem was, there were precious few leads. It was apparent that police were checking on Milly's close family, but 6 days after her disappearance, they were admitting they were baffled. 'We are obviously looking into abduction but if she had been forced into a vehicle against her will it is astonishing that not a single person on a busy main road on a bright sunny afternoon saw anything at all,' he said. 'I would have expected someone to register something. A 13-year-old is not going to go with someone against her will without a struggle.'

The idea that she might have planned her own disappearance, for reasons unknown, began to be floated. There was vague talk of a possible 'secret boyfriend', but there was not the faintest sign of one, so this was more about official desperation than anything. The area around the Dowlers' house was the focus of the search, with police checking the allotments, gardens and streams between Walton railway station, her home and Hersham station.

Curiously, Sarah Payne had grown up in Hersham, within miles of the Dowlers. Her killer, Roy Whiting, had been jailed for life the previous year. Police officers from that inquiry had been brought in to advise, but were able to shed little light. A police spokesman said the Dowlers' home 'remains the most fertile ground for possible clues as to where Amanda [Milly] may be or why she has disappeared. The search is with the full and free consent of Mr and Mrs Dowler and none of the family are suspects in this investigation.'

There was a flurry of activity when, two weeks later, the *News of the World* claimed she had applied for a job with an employment agency. On 14th April, the first edition of the *News of the World* ran a story headlined

'Milly "hoax' riddle"', which suggested that messages had been left on her phone after she vanished. Specifically, it reported that at 10.13am, on 27th March, just six days after Milly had disappeared, a woman left a voicemail message saying: 'Hello Mandy. We're ringing because we have some interviews starting. Can you call me back? Thank you. Bye bye.' It also mentioned two other calls. The second edition, which went to press at around 9.30, contained a similar story, but talked in more veiled terms about voicemail messages and omitted the verbatim quote from the agency. In the last edition, the story was changed again. It referred to a '"hoax" outrage', and reported that 'a deranged woman has been posing as the missing youngster'.

Similarly, interest peaked when, separately, a body was found nearby, word getting round quickly, but erroneously, that Milly had been found dead.

The police's obvious struggle to make any progress was causing concern. Mark Williams-Thomas, a former a detective constable in Surrey's child-protection squad, acknowledging the difficulties the force faced, expressed a commonly held concern. Two and a half weeks after Milly's disappearance, he was quoted as saying: 'They don't seem to have a clue what has happened to her.' He added, 'I heard recently that they had taken away a computer from her home, but they seem to have done that only recently, while it should have been one of the first things they did.'

Seven weeks after Milly's disappearance, the *News of the World* managed to have a photographer at the scene when her parents conducted a re-enactment, intended to be in secret, of her walk home from the station. It was not until that September that a shocking revelation was made. Police found the decomposing body in woodland in Yateley Heath, Hampshire, on September 18 2002. Levi Bellfield, by then convicted of two other murders, was found guilty of her murder on 23 June 2011.

The story had exercised a lot of journalists and alarmed the reading public. Its monstrous cumulation was extensively covered, but then it faded from the news pages. There was little new to write, and even the papers that had championed her cause could see little to be gained from stories that would merely amplify the silence. The story exploded again late on Monday 4th July 2011 when the *Guardian*'s Nick Davies reported that Milly Dowler's voicemails had been unlawfully intercepted. It was among a large number of cases revealed by the paper, including many victims of crime, and caused such widespread outrage that it catalysed the closing down of the *News of the World* and the resignation of chief executive Rebekah Brooks, News International's Legal manager Tom Crone, Les Hinton of Dow Jones and one of Rupert Murdoch's closest lieutenants.

Included in the story came a comparably calamitous claim, with an even more obvious human angle – that whoever had hacked into her voicemail had deleted messages on her voicemail. Sally Dowler later told the Leveson inquiry how she had rung her daughter's phone many times before the message box filled up. 'It clicked through on her voicemail, so I heard her voice, and it was just like, "She's picked up her voicemail, Bob. She's alive."' This cruel 'false hope' allegation was the most explosive story of all, with its suggestion that there were no lengths to which newspapers would not go to beat their rivals. Mulcaire's name appeared in the article together with that of the *News of the World*, and the inference as to the culprit was an obvious one.

A storm erupted, the story having become unignorable, even for News International's most loyal outlets. The *Sun* carried a prominent story reporting that Rebekah Brooks found the allegations 'almost too horrific to believe'. The Chief Executive wrote: 'I am sickened that these events are alleged to have happened. Not just because I was editor of the *News of the World* at the time, but if the accusations are true, the devastating effect on Milly Dowler's family is unforgivable.'

David Cameron, called upon to respond during a visit to Afghanistan, said the allegation that Milly Dowler's phone messages had been intercepted were 'quite quite shocking... a truly dreadful act'. The Dowlers' lawyer Mark Lewis said: 'It is distress heaped upon tragedy to learn that the *News of the World* had no humanity at such a terrible time.'

In the public airing of the story about Milly Dowler's disappearance, Mulcaire's name had barely been mentioned. Now he was centre stage. The next day, on 5 July, the *Guardian* published a statement by Mulcaire through his lawyer: 'I want to apologise to anybody who was hurt or upset by what I have done. I've been to court. I've pleaded guilty. And I've gone to prison and been punished. I still face the possibility of further criminal prosecution. Working for the *News of the World* was never easy. There was relentless pressure. There was a constant demand for results.'

This was pretty much the first thing Mulcaire had

uttered in public for four years. Dr Evil, as he perceived the public to regard him, had been lured from his lair to answer charges of being even more shameless and uncaring than he had hitherto appeared. But he said no more, and slunk back into the shadows. That was the story as the newspapers reported it, for better or worse. So far, so public.

The story was not as it seemed, however. Mulcaire, it emerged in court in 2014, had indeed hacked into Milly Dowler's voicemails, and for many, there need be no further discussion. But his claim for mitigation is striking and worthy of every bit as much scrutiny as those journalists who claim they were 'just trying to find Milly'.

As for the 'false hope moment', Mulcaire, looking back 9 years, was confused. He had not confirmed he had been responsible for any such thing. The *Guardian* article of 4 July had not directly accused him, but nor had it cleared him. It seemed that he probably was responsible, but he could not understand how. Beyond the human considerations, the suggestion that he might have deleted a voicemail was an affront to his humanity and his professional sense of self. He had built a lucrative career on treading stealthily. The inept deletion of voicemails suggested a crassness, an artlessness, that undermined the professionalism upon which he prided himself. Only someone lacking his knowhow could have done such a thing, he thought, and yet, from his outcast's vantage point in 2011, cut off from most of those in the know, the newspapers were reporting that he had blundered spectacularly. Was it possible they were right? After the *Guardian*'s allegation, he was distraught. It was a dose of his own medicine, some might say, but he was adamant that his motivation and competence had not been at fault.

In fact, the *Guardian*'s story turned out to be wrong in a key respect. Voicemails had indeed been deleted from Milly Dowler's phone, but they were nothing like as easily explained as the paper had claimed (and, it seems, as the police also believed). Indeed, to this day, there is dispute as to how they came to be wiped. And in inviting the inference that Glenn Mulcaire had been culpable, the *Guardian*'s article sent the investigator into an unprecedented emotional turmoil.

Mulcaire, with his 'Special Projects' role and track record in such cases at *News of the World*, had been straining at the leash to look into the case after Dowler disappeared on that Thursday afternoon in March 2002. When he was tasked, finally. he started a file called Project Dowler, as if to emphasise that this wasn't 'any old job'. Yet, contrary to common belief, he wasn't asked until others had failed. The public narrative which suited many of the others involved in the whole saga has placed Mulcaire firmly in the role of baddie, the man in the black hat at whom the audience boos ritually. And as long as the 'rogue' who had 'gone off the reservation' remained silent, gagged by expensive lawyers, he would retain that role, rightly or wrongly.

So a key fact in the story is the following. The police log revealed that in fact the 'false hope' moment happened on Sunday 24th March. Mulcaire was not tasked to look for Milly Dowler until Wednesday 10th April, nearly three weeks after she had disappeared, almost three weeks after the cruellest privacy invasion of all. It was in few people's interest to point this out, but the *Guardian*, the leader in the field of phone-hacking studies, had let itself down, a fact some of its rivals – never keen on the phone hacking story – were not slow to advertise. In her initial recollection of the matter, Sally Dowler said she thought the 'false hope' moment had happened in April or May, which was indeed after Mulcaire had been tasked.

If someone had deleted her messages on or before 24th March (as seems highly likely), it was almost certainly not Mulcaire. A human story as touching and engrossing as this one had a great many journalists seeking answers. Given how widespread phone hacking was in certain sections of the market, it would not be surprising if someone's zeal had not got the better of them.

Mulcaire couldn't understand what had happened, but the fact that so many people believed he was responsible for the false hope moment was mortifying. His family, too, was devastated. Within three days of the allegation being made, 2 of his daughters, distraught at the claim (that neither for a moment believed), had passed out through worry for their father, by then tarred as beyond the pale. He had journalists outside his front door for days, including CNN with a satellite dish, but he wouldn't speak to anyone. His name was as black as anyone's could be. He worried that even his solicitor believed the claim was true.

'Alison was a total rock,' Mulcaire remembers. He was shocked that something so wrong could be laid at his door by a newspaper. 'She kept me going. She never doubted me... even when I had really dark moments and I thought "I must have done something wrong", she was the one who said "no, you never". You remember what happened....'

Mulcaire, in a depressed state after the Dowler story appeared, met Nick Davies the following morning with his solicitor Sarah Webb. At that meeting, Davies put a number of suggestions to Mulcaire, and asked him about who had tasked him in his activities. Davies had had it confirmed that Dowler's phone had been hacked. Mulcaire did not confirm it, but nor did he deny it. At that stage, of course, while he knew he had intercepted her voicemails, he didn't know that the false hope moment had happened before he got involved. So he was tormented by not understanding how he could have deleted them (when in fact he hadn't done so).

With a large number of civil legal claims against him and facing the possibility of further criminal charges, Mulcaire said very little to Davies. He refused to answer questions that might prejudice those cases, and was unable to recall (as he is to this day) many details of the jobs he did. 'He was trying to get an admission and add to the story,' says Mulcaire, 'but I confirmed nothing'. Davies agrees with this, but says the informal nature of a long meeting (which also gave rise to an abortive attempt for Mulcaire to turn Queen's evidence) gave Mulcaire every chance to steer him away from the inference that he had been responsible, but Mulcaire did not take it. Mulcaire had not been explicitly accused in the article, but as the convicted hacker nearest the scene of the crime, as it were, the juxtaposition was clearly suggestive, and at that stage – not knowing about the date in the police log either – he had no choice but to make the same assumption.

Mulcaire's version of events remains considerably at

odds with the one that, by design or by default, has established itself in the public mind. As we have seen, he believed he was on the side if not strictly of the law, then certainly of humanity. The Dowler case shocked the nation, and the *News of the World*, with its special interest in bringing child abductors to justice, was bound to be at the fore in the hunt for her.

So what had happened? After Milly disappeared on that Thursday afternoon, newspapers readied themselves for a big denouement. Possibly she would be triumphantly reunited with her family, or the polar opposite would emerge, or maybe a waiting game would begin. In any event, the public would be interested, and want to read more.

The *News of the World*, never bashful about its authority in this field, was desperate to 'own' the story. When Rebekah Brooks sets her mind to getting something, she tends to get it. Her news executives were left in no doubt what was wanted – the securing of Milly's release. And if she couldn't have that, the paper was to lead the field. The idea of the paper being embarrassed by another having a better tale – least of all the *Sun*, edited by David Yelland, who had pipped her to the editorship – was too humiliating to contemplate.

As news editor, Neville Thurlbeck was central to cracking it. Experience of such cases suggested that the kidnapper might be someone close to home, possibly a family member. Initial suspicions turned towards Bob Dowler, in whose house were found items suggesting an interest in bondage. To heighten suspicion, investigators discovered that his wife Sally had been unaware of his interest in such paraphernalia until Milly herself had recently come across it inadvertently and brought it to her mother's attention. The easiest assumption – 'the father did it' – must have been a tempting one indeed, for both police and press. But where was the evidence?

It was a day short of three weeks after Dowler's disappearance that Mulcaire was put on the case. The call came from Neville Thurlbeck (it was later agreed in court), although knowing the pair's previous work on what Mulcaire calls the 'greater good' projects, it is probably fair to assume that Miskiw, who had been away the week Milly had disappeared, had been wanting to deploy Mulcaire on the case for some time. To this day, Mulcaire is at a loss to explain why his services were not called upon sooner.

He remembers rushing into his house, having got the call, just as his wife was about to serve their evening meal. 'I've got the lead eye,' he told his wife Alison excitedly. 'I can't eat my dinner, I've got to get onto it.' He went straight back out to his office. Alison remembers his enthusiasm at being tasked. 'He just wanted to find that girl, that's all he wanted. That's what he's like,' she recalls.

As part of his tasking, Mulcaire recalls, he was given Milly's phone number by Neville Thurlbeck, which – according to Mulcaire – he said the police had given him (which Thurlbeck disputes). The fact that the number had come from the police – assuming it had – didn't strike him as unusual. Thurlbeck and Miskiw were forever cooking up deals with the police, trading information and swapping tips. It's what they did.

Mulcaire was preparing to put his standard procedures in such cases into operation, but at this stage, three weeks after Dowler's disappearance, he assumed many of them had already been performed. He checked with Miskiw. He was horrified by the response. Precious little.

'When I asked him what had been done, he was just sheepish and embarrassed on the police's behalf. I couldn't believe the stuff they hadn't done. On a case like that, process goes out of the window. You get what you need. A girl's life was in the balance. You get the info in as quick as possible. Greg was a coordinator, rather than the investigator, so he would listen to me on the best techniques to use on a case like this. I would not be dictated to… I would either do it or not. It was a relationship that worked well, and we both respected the other's patch.'

At an early stage, Miskiw asked Mulcaire to do an FP (full profile) on 'X', a known sex offender who had come under suspicion. Again, Mulcaire did as requested, assuming Miskiw had his own reasons for wanting to know about this character, possibly inspired by his chats with the police. 'That didn't go in the paper. There was no story saying "there's a suspect by the name of X being held"… why did Greg ask for it? That time I think I did ask, but they didn't want to discuss that.' Mulcaire is confident that Miskiw was passing information on to the police that Mulcaire could obtain more easily than they could. This a) helped the police and b) helped oil the wheels of Miskiw's relationship with them, with the promise of a quid pro quo implicit. Again, there was no necessary reason to tell Mulcaire why it was wanted.

Years later, at Sutton Police station, Mulcaire was gratified to have his suspicions confirmed when police told him that they had indeed questioned the man that

Miskiw had asked him to profile. Clearly, Mulcaire believes, someone in the police had given Miskiw the name – or at any rate, Miskiw had acquired it – and Miskiw was asking Mulcaire to find out what he could. Mulcaire was duly tasked to do a quick turnaround job. 'I could do the comms stuff the police couldn't do,' says Mulcaire. 'They knew Greg could get that sort of stuff, and it would have taken them ages with court orders and so on to get the same sort of detail. So what I did was helping both Greg and the police. I may have helped them ask the right questions.'

Mulcaire, nothing if not a passionate man, affects reluctance to point fingers over an extremely raw episode, although ultimately he fails to suppress the human impulses of a father of five. Initially he will only talk about what he would have done. 'Certainly I would take all the family's computers away, and their phones, and make sure I was on top of all the communications everyone in the family had had in the previous weeks.' This is not just completeness for the sake of completeness. As Mulcaire says: 'There are always little giveaways – switches in data patterns and so on – that wouldn't occur to most people. These can be much more revealing than you might think, and I would have expected the police to have been on top of this. There is no reason why the family wouldn't have been happy to go along with that.'

He reflects on what he regards as something of a specialist subject, 'In that first golden hour, you do an FP. You're on an egg timer. Every second counts. You've got to save that girl…. There are a lot of rumours, but you should only work on the intelligence you have gleaned, on the hard facts, as far as possible. Leave out the commonly held 'root causes'. You can go back to that later if you need to and haven't made progress otherwise. Unless you've done an FP, you risk making a big leap into other areas, whereas in fact what you're looking for is on your doorstep. The data mining needs to be done in the first hour, not the first 3 weeks,' he laments. 'When you're brought in between stage 2 and 3 you're just picking up the pieces'

'I would have made sure everybody was profiled. You build a grid, and identify who has phoned her, and get everyone's call history in the last six months... even as that's going along, and it's quite time consuming getting that data in, I'd be working on the MICE format [a recognised acronym designed to whittle down possible motives] Money? No. Ideology? No. Compromise? Ego? No. 'It is more clinical, more surgical more decisive... high direction, high support.'

The central part of his technique in an abduction involves locating individuals via their mobile phones. This is done either by working out the distance of each phone from three given phone masts. As any geometry student knows, if you know the distance of an object from three set points, and draw a circle around each point, you can identify a triangle showing where it is. There is another technique called 'pinging', which is used with digital mobile phones, and is an even more accurate way of locating a phone. So if Milly Dowler had been taken by someone who had been in phone contact with her or members of her family (and they had their phone on them when she was taken), that person should be evident on the grid. 'I would put every cell section on the grid,' he says. 'I'd identify them, turn the numbers around… so you identify everyone who was near her… it's geolocating…. We call it the Bermuda triangle, we don't let anyone out of that triangle… we get them flashed up, turn the numbers round and give them a visit…. With a bit of luck, within an hour you have a great position. Maybe you can say 'these are the three people'… knock on that door, that door and that door… these are the people who were within 2, 3, 5, 10, 20 yards… we're not calling them suspects necessarily, they're people of interest, they might have seen something… let's give them a visit… if you know the number is on the phone… if you ask them, "Why have you got that number on your mobile phone?", their reaction tells you a hell of a lot…. These are not mobile phones floating around on their own, they are with human beings who were in the area at the time…. But it's critical to get to them in the first hour.' Mulcaire insists that such technology, though not as effective as it is now, was available (and invaluable) at the time. 'You have to do immediate data mining as forensic analysis. It makes all the difference in the world.'

But on the available evidence it seems none of this had been done, to Mulcaire's horror. He set about doing it, but a good many horses had bolted. 'It was spectacularly unbe-f***ing-lievable, catastrophic and embarrassing. Given what's been missed, I just thought 'in this sort of case, we're heading for a really bad outcome here. There's only a 5 per cent chance we'll be lucky, and when you get a call that late… but so much stuff just hadn't been done.'

And what of the Dowler family being ambushed by a

photographer in their distress as they conducted a secret reconstruction of Milly's last walk? This is news to Mulcaire. 'I knew nothing about that at all,' he says. 'It's not just that I don't remember that. I know I would remember that if I had been involved. I would not have been involved in something on that scale. It looks very much to me as if the paper was getting drip fed intel from the inside.'

Mulcaire is not the sort of person to sit around saying 'isn't it awful, that poor girl, her poor family' and so on, but his human empathy for the victim and her family is implicit – powerful, even – in what he says. Maybe this shouldn't need saying. After all, what sort of person, let alone a parent, would not be moved by an innocent young daughter being abducted? Yet it is an assertion that needs to be made. His family know what the allegations of callousness towards Milly Dowler and her family did to Mulcaire. If he did wrong (and he denies this, believing he was acting effectively with the state's authority in trying to save a girl's life), he knows a great many people who did much worse, he says. 'My conscience is absolutely clear. I do not have a dark heart, and those who know me know that. In the same situation again, with the same facts in my possession, I would do exactly the same thing again. Given the conversations I had had with my superiors, and knowing they had been talking to the police, I don't see what further authorisation I could have had.'

And yet... his account is so eloquent of his keenness to save a young life that issues like whether his methods were legal are in danger of being overlooked. When he talks matter-of-factly about finding out who had phoned

Milly's parents' phone number in the previous few weeks (as he did, according to detective sergeant Greg Smith's evidence in court), that is of course illegal without a court order. When he mentions 'turning numbers round' – the devining of a person's identity and address from their mobile phone number – that, too, is illegal. It generally requires an employee of a phone provider to break the terms of their contract, presumably for money, to hand over the details. It is something the police can do with the help of a production order, but that can be time-consuming, or so the argument goes. In fact, experienced police officers say that if needs be the person providing the authorisation will often be willing to backdate permission if the perceived need at the time is great enough. Yet one imagines that, had one of these unlawful ruses uncovered Milly's assailant, we would be leaping to applaud the person in question, and any suggestion of a prosecution of the offender would be an outrage. There is, surely, some sort of lesson here.

And, as admitted, he did intercept Milly's voicemails. Transcripts shown to the jury revealed anxious friends asking: 'Please come home. I miss you so much… Hey, Milly, if you get this, call me…. Hallo, Milly. It's just that we want you home.'

He also did a voice analysis on the Dowler voicemails. 'I had the whole download on tape. Alison heard it as well. There was a very distinctive American voice on there. I wondered if she had been taken abroad. That would have been good news, I thought… at least she had more chance of being alive.

Recalling that period, he says now he regards that call as being potentially more significant than the one which later attracted the greatest attention, from a recruitment agency in Telford, West Midlands, apparently using Milly's real name, Amanda, left on Wednesday March 27. As mentioned above, the *News of the World* initially published a version of the message and also has an internal record of the message (worded slightly differently from the one that appeared in the paper, presumably to avoid alerting rivals) saying: 'Hallo, Amanda. This is Jo from Mondays Recruitment Agency. We are ringing because we have some interviews starting today at Epson. Please ring.' The message was actually for a woman called Nana who had a similar phone number, although of course nobody had any clue of that at the time. Mulcaire remembers being concerned that the message didn't ring true.

He recalls now dismissing the call as a hoax, and says he wrote as much on his notes. That, as far as he was concerned, was that. He reported his view back to the office (he thinks to Neville Thurlbeck, but is not sure), and continued with his researches. But at the *News of the World*, this was gold dust. Clearly Milly must be alive. She must have had an argument with her family, it was assumed.

Rather than inform the police, the next day, Thursday 11 April, Neville Thurlbeck sent a team of 6 journalists to an Epson factory near Telford. Thurlbeck told the court later that the decision to hold the information back from the police for 24 hours was made by Stuart Kuttner and Andy Coulson, although the judge asserted that Thurlbeck must have also had a hand in it. Mulcaire had passed the information to his taskers as soon as it reached him, and neither he nor the police knew of the sending of the journalists to Telford. Seemingly, though, The *News of the World* was convinced it was on the verge of getting a world-beating story.

Mulcaire's scepticism was shared by Vanessa Altin, who in a statement to the Leveson inquiry said: 'I, and other colleagues, dispatched by Neville thought the idea far fetched in the extreme. Milly had been missing for several weeks and we were certain she would not have been able to slip in unnoticed and hold down a job at Epson when she was just a child.'

News of the World reporters on at least three occasions called the recruitment agency claiming to be Milly Dowler's mother, asking if they had given work to her daughter. The owner, Valerie Hancox, told police that a 'well-mannered' *News of the World* reporter had come to her house and said he was helping police with their inquiries. 'He asked if I wanted to help Milly Dowler,' she said (in a statement). 'He informed me he was working with the police investigation team.'

But the team in the midlands failed to unearth anything. In fact they were on a wild goose chase. So, although reluctant to reveal to the police that they had been listening to Milly Dowler's voicemails, the paper sought to apply pressure with increasingly explicit references to the intercepted message, hoping the police would 'come clean' about something they might have expected the police to have known about already. In fact, the police, having acquired a production order from Guildford Crown Court, had done a download from Milly's voicemail box on 25th March, the day before the message from the agency was left, and were not to repeat the task for several days. (Curiously, and still unexplained, on that day, the PIN number was reset twice by the phone provider.)

This download, one might think, was surely overdue, and tells more of the story of the police being a little behind the curve. In any event, when confronted with the excited scribe from the *News of the World*, the police knew nothing about the message from the agency and, besides, had their own reason not to respond as urgently as the *News of the World* wanted. For one thing, the force heard that day from their colleagues in the West Mercia police about the reporters claiming to be Sally Dowler, Milly's mother. And as we shall see, they had another reason.

In any event, on the afternoon of Friday April 13, growing increasingly conscious of the looming deadline for Sunday, the *News of the World*'s managing editor, Stuart Kuttner, called the police. This was a new front, a more formal one, in Surrey/Wapping relations. He told them: 'The purpose of this call from the *News of the World* is to alert the Surrey Police to what may be, and I can put it no higher than may be, significant information in connection with Milly Dowler.' This was clearly not something to be ignored. Sarah McGregor, the force's head of communications, put Mr Kuttner in touch with a senior officer. Kuttner went for broke. In his note, Det Sgt Kevin McEntee noted Kuttner saying 'The *News of the World* are in possession of a recording of the message.' The same detective then spoke to the news editor, Neville Thurlbeck, noting: 'Thurlbeck told me he had accessed Milly's voicemail with PIN no 1210.' A little later, Thurlbeck told Sarah McGregor the paper had spoken to the recruitment agency, which, he said, had confirmed that Dowler was registered with them. (The police found later that there was no evidence to support this claim: 'the contrary is the case'.) McGregor told the trial that Thurlbeck had said he had obtained Milly's phone number and PIN code 'from schoolchildren'. In a police report prepared by Deputy Chief Constable Jerry Kirkby, it was concluded that the paper 'had *confirmed* with Milly's school friend that this was her mobile number [my italics]', as if the number had been obtained elsewhere beforehand. This may be a crucial difference.

At the end of the trial in 2014, Thurlbeck said, rather curiously, that he had claimed he had acquired the number through schoolchildren to protect Mulcaire's police sources. Mulcaire is at best mystified by this, citing the fact that Thurlbeck, a registered police informant, was the one with the police contacts. "It just makes no sense at all," he says.

Meanwhile, the *News of the World*'s enthusiasm about its supposed scoop was unabated. This was despite the fact that Milly Dowler was not registered with the agency, and, the mysterious voicemail aside, the idea that she might have did not survive the faintest scrutiny. We also know that the police had not known of the message left, supposedly, for Milly, and that when they heard of it, they were disinclined to credit it with much weight, to the *News of the World*'s undisguised disappointment. In fact, as the paper may not have known, a hoaxer was strongly suspected by the police to have been impersonating Milly closer to home. Over time, the evidence mounted and their belief strengthened, and a year later the hoaxer, a man called Paul Hughes, was imprisoned for 5 months.

It remains in some doubt that the paper had obtained Milly's PIN number from schoolchildren. Glenn Mulcaire is certain not only that he was given the PIN number by Thurlbeck, but that he was told the number had come from the police, a notion that raises all sorts of questions. If Mulcaire is correct, one of Thurlbeck's accounts must be wrong.

Those who doubt Mulcaire might say that he must have blagged the number himself. This is almost certainly wrong, even should one be disinclined to believe his assertion that Thurlbeck gave him the number. For one thing, it is known that the *News of the World* had the number before Mulcaire was on the case. But what is equally important is that once someone had that particular number, it would not be difficult to hack her phone. Milly's was the type of phone that used an unregistered SIM card, which means there was no provider in a position to pass on the key details that would have given access. In fact that wouldn't be necessary. It would take no great expert to identify the provider from the phone number (phone companies are given a range of numbers to give out, so the provider could be easily inferred by anyone with a knowledge of the industry). Once the provider is known, the default PIN code would be easily identified, and it is known that Milly had not changed her PIN number.

In other words, in the first five days after Milly's disappearance (before the PIN number was changed), it was comparatively easy to listen to her messages. Perhaps this was why it was felt Mulcaire's services would not be required. In any event, the answer as to who deleted the voicemails has its source, perhaps self-evidently, with who had the number, and how it was acquired.

Here, there are some clues, even if still no settled

answers. We see in the 'blue book', private investigator Steve Whittamore's record of inquiries from News International, the names of Ada, Robert, Sally and Lucy Dowler, and the family's ex-directory telephone landline (but no mobile), requested by the *News of the World*'s crime reporter Sarah Arnold. The number was seemingly not found by Steve Whittamore, but was subcontracted to another private investigator, John Gunning.

The possible significance of this is great, given what is known about the search for Milly Dowler's number. For having the Dowlers' landline number would have more than the obvious use: it would, with enough guile and indifference to the law, enable a blagger to find, say, the names of those who were called most frequently from that number. And that number would, almost certainly, include their daughter's. We are speculating here, and there is no evidence to say that Gunning did blag the Dowlers' phone numbers. Simply that somebody who knew how to do so could well have done so, but Gunning had that knowledge and is named as having provided the Dowler's ex-directory number. 'Once a blagger had the land line, getting the 'Friends and Family' numbers is the easiest thing in the world', says Mulcaire. As we have seen in chapter 2, it was not difficult to acquire, and that is indeed what Mulcaire believes someone on the paper did.

So, late on Friday 13th, the *News of the World* executives were in a quandary. They believed with great conviction that they had some sort of Dowler story for the paper for Sunday – they just weren't sure what. It was clear that somebody had indeed left a message on Milly's voicemail. The question was why. What did they think they were doing? Had she really applied for work? Or had a hoaxer applied, pretending to be her? In which case, how on earth had the hoaxer got her number? Nothing made complete sense.

Rebekah Brooks, who had been the moving spirit behind the Sarah's Law campaign, was desperate to crack the Dowler case. From her holiday in Dubai with her husband Ross Kemp. She and her deputy, lover and eventual successor, Andy Coulson were in frequent contact by text, voicemail and phone. Nonetheless, a jury conceded that Rebekah Brooks knew nothing about the voicemail messages, so we must conclude that the decisions were left to Coulson, and they went down to the wire.

The paper drew up two versions of its story, one saying the call had been a hoax, and the other reporting that the police were taking it seriously and treating it as a new line of inquiry. After much deliberation, The *News of the World* decided its information was too good to go to waste, although it ended up running a story that they didn't believe, or so subsequent conversations suggested. The account, headlined 'Milly hoax riddle', quoted directly from the voicemail from the recruitment agency. The word 'riddle' is a bit of an old newspaper favourite, a savoury enticement to readers which seeks to disguise the fact that the newspaper has failed to crack the big story. It said, 'It is thought the hoaxer even gave the agency Milly's real mobile number... the agency used the number to contact Milly when a job vacancy arose and left a message on her voicemail... it was on March 27, 6 days after Milly went missing, that the employment agency appears to have phoned her mobile.'

As late as 8.10pm, a *News of the World* journalist called

the Surrey force to say the next day's paper would carry a story quoting the police as saying: 'We are intrigued, but believe the message may have been left by a deranged woman hoaxer thought to have hampered other police inquiries.' The journalist was told the quote was too strong, and asked for time to amend it. The journalist said it was too late, that the first edition had already gone and that the quote would be used in all 5 subsequent editions.' In later versions, the verbatim quote from the voicemail message was removed.

The following morning, the police agreed the following line for media inquiries: 'We are evaluating the claim that Amanda may have registered with a recruitment agency. At this stage there is the possibility that a hoaxer may have been involved in generating this story.' And the following off the record guidance was also adopted: 'At this stage we are confident that this woman attending the recruitment agency is a hoaxer and not Milly. The woman is older than Milly and hence would be able to register at a recruitment agency (would question how a 13-year-old would be able to register for a job)'. On the Monday (15th), West Mercia police, which had been asked by the Surrey force to look into the call to the recruitment agency, came back and said that an employee of the agency had said they had no one on their books called Amanda Dowler, nor had they ever interviewed anyone of that name.

Certainly 'Milly hoax riddle' was a story, but it wasn't *the* story, the one that would thrust the *News of the World* unassailably out in front of its competitors. The paper's top brass were getting agitated. During that week, managing editor Stuart Kuttner got in touch again with the police, challenging their assertions about the hoaxer story and reminding the police they had 'passed on information about messages left on Amanda Dowler's phone... We offered a copy of a tape-recording of the messages.' (In the context, for good or ill, this admission to having broken the law was secondary to the search for Milly which may have played a role in the jury's decision to acquit Kuttner in June 2014). But the police stuck to their guns, reasserting their faith in the story. Crime reporter Ricky Sutton replied: 'This is not true. It's inconceivable... Milly has been up there in person. She has registered and applied for a job at the factory. We know this for 100 per cent.' Of course, he knew no such thing.

On Wednesday 17th, police performed a second download of Milly's messages, and this time picked up the call relating to the employment agency. Two days later, a Surrey officer listening closely to the message concluded that the name sounded more like 'Nana' than Mandy. The officer called the agency and was told they had a lot of ladies from Ghana on their books and that this was a popular Ghanaian name. Further, the agency had indeed spoken to a 'Nana' on 26th March, when she called to say she had changed her mobile number. The following day, the agency had called her about job interviews. How the wrong number had come to be written down wasn't clear.

So when on Saturday 20th April, when the paper went into battle again to say the hoaxer line was inaccurate, the police were ready for them. Mrs McGregor confirmed their belief, but relayed what the officer had concluded the previous day – that the name on the message was 'Nana' and not Mandy, and that the number was simply wrong. (The police later told the House of Commons Culture Media and Sports Select Committee that 'contrary to Surrey police's initial suspicions', the message did not come from a hoaxer but was 'a pure coincidence' and 'of no evidential value'.)

But, she was to tell the court in 2013, she said Ricky Sutton, the paper's crime correspondent, still refused to accept the explanation and had told her the paper was '100 per cent absolutely certain' of its source on the information. He also said the paper was switching its investigation to the north of England, where they believed Milly had applied for a job in a factory. The paper's excitement of the previous 10 days had dissipated.

About 2 weeks later, the *News of the World* had to accept a major humiliation, as it will have seen it. Plans for a reward for information leading to the return of Milly Dowler had been in the air for some time. The problem was that the *Sun*, their stablemates, had had the same idea. Stuart Kuttner was deputed to spell out to the police that this was not what was wanted at all. He sent an email on 1 May saying he was unhappy about the *Sun* being involved, pointing out that his paper had 'better circulation and more resources'. 'Rebekah Wade [Brooks]' he explained, 'has stated that she couldn't do this on a joint basis.' That was supposed to be that, evidently.

The police had the temerity to ignore Brooks's edict. It adopted Solomon's judgment, thanked both papers and said they would gratefully accept £50,000 each in reward money. This prompted a furious call from Ricky Sutton, who said 'You have killed us stone dead in the water' before putting the phone down.

The big question that remains unanswered over the Milly Dowler affair is how the cruel 'false hope moment' that led Milly Dowler's parents to think their daughter might have listened to her voicemails came about. The narrative that has a certain currency, is that the voicemails were deleted not by a human being but by technology. This might have been the result of them dropping off the system, as they are programmed to do, 72 hours after they were left. Or some say the introduction of new 'platforms' over that weekend would have done for the messages.

Neither explanation is satisfactory. The 72-hour explanation won't wash, because other message left in the previous day or two were also deleted. And, all being well, the switching of a 'platform' should have no bearing on whether messages are retained or not.

Detective chief inspector John Macdonald of the Metropolitan Police was tasked with getting to the bottom of the matter. He concluded that we may never know how the voicemails came to be deleted, and he may well be right. He also said there was no evidence to suggest Milly's phone had been hacked before 26th March 2002. This is to suggest that at even though the *News of the World* had paid to get Milly Dowler's family's phone numbers, that nobody had tried to intercept her voicemails during that time, this despite hacking now being common practice on more than one of the redtop papers. Certainly it is a suggestion Mulcaire has trouble believing. MacDonald did confirm that there was evidence hacking had taken place after that, and there was evidence that two voicemail messages may have been manually deleted. Equally they may have been automatically deleted.

There was further consternation at the fact that the police, having been alerted to the fact that the *News of the World* had a recording of a phone message, took no steps later to pursue the matter. According to the Independent Police Complaints Commission report on the matter, 'officers and former officers from Surrey Police… expressed surprise and dismay that it wasn't investigated'. It continued: 'We have not been able to uncover any evidence, in documentation or witness statements, of why and by whom that decision was made: former senior officers, in particular, appear to have been afflicted by a form of collective amnesia in relation to the events of 2002'. It concluded that it was 'scarcely credible' that no one connected to the investigation 'recognised the relevance and importance of the information Surrey Police held in 2002 before this was disclosed by Operation Weeting'.

Mulcaire's continuing sense of anger at the assertion that he was responsible for the 'false hope' moment is palpable. For one thing, as is now generally accepted, he almost certainly could not have been. But there is a boiling sense of indignation that stems from his own personality that continues to frustrate him. Mulcaire sees himself as being on the side of the angels in the whole story. He admits he intruded on the Dowler family's privacy, but for noble reasons. At the time he was tasked, there were precious few clues about what had happened to Milly, and there remained suspicions about the role of Bob Dowler. Further, executives on his newspaper were desperate to appease their editor by solving the crime.

For those inclined to dismiss Mulcaire as a low-life hoodlum, the idea that he believed he was acting on the police's behalf may be incredible (though by this stage of the story, I hope marginally less so). His claim should be heard. He was given Milly Dowler's number by Neville Thurlbeck who said it had come from the police.

This, of course, is a key moment. There may appear to be an irony in an information-getter of Glenn Mulcaire's background needing to be given such a number. It is an idea that in this context positively riles Mulcaire. 'At that stage, when a girl had been missing all that time, you would have to have any relevant details there and then. This wasn't some grubby hole-in-the-wall job. It was a serious investigation, and the fact of being given the number was confirmation that this was sanctioned job.'

It seems clear that Mulcaire's modus operandi was more sophisticated than the police's. In his own words, he was 'pinging and triangulating for breakfast', while the police – for reasons either of technological knowhow or legal obligation (or so Mulcaire believed) – were cumbersome and slow on their feet. As we will see, there are many examples of the police/Fleet Street nexus working together and exchanging information, supposedly for the common good. Individual police officers, confronted by headlines demanding progress on the disappearance of a missing child, might fall back on their friends in the press if they think it might produce results. And even if the number reached the *News of the World* from people close to the Dowler family (as Neville Thurlbeck maintains), that too is plausible, even if, in the case of children, strictly speaking a breach of Press

Complaints Commission rules. As one senior figure in the Met puts it: 'Friends and family in that situation will do anything, they will tell anyone anything if they think it will get the child back.' Few journalists would spurn such an offer. It is what they might do with the number that is more questionable.

Could the false-hope moment have been the result of messages automatically 'falling off' Milly's voicemail box? Possibly, although the number of people with an interest in this being so inclines the sceptic against it, as does the fact that other messages, left less than 72 hours before, were also deleted. Was it a bungled attempt to hack into Milly's messages? More sinisterly, could it have been a successful attempt to hack her voicemails (by a journalist from who knows where?), followed by an intentional deletion to prevent rivals getting a message? For what it is worth, a police investigation has said there was no evidence of anyone accessing the voicemails.

The *News of the World*'s deputy features editor Paul McMullan, who has plenty of experience in the ways of redtop papers, says 'a reporter would do all they could to protect their story... you want to protect your story, esp[ecially] on a Sunday paper.... If you get scooped on a Saturday, it's gutting... you do anything; you fly people out of the country, anything, to keep the competition away from the source. In the Dowler case you would almost certainly record it and then delete it.... But everyone was trying to find her... police were shit, absolutely hopeless. They were so shit they let a murderer wander round for seven years hitting people with hammers.... People abroad have said how lucky we are to have vigorous investigative journalists and we're not tied to just using a useless police force. Bunch of incompetents.'

In July 2012, Mulcaire was again charged under RIPA: this time with both the interception of Dowler's voicemail messages and conspiracy to do so. He admitted the first charge, but resisted the conspiracy charge with some vigour. He was interviewed by the police three times in 2011, having not been invited to speak about the Dowler affair when he was charged in 2006. He told them he believed he was acting not only in the public interest, but also with an 'empowering authority', i.e. with the knowledge of the police. The word 'conspire' has connotations of planning premeditatedly and cold-bloodedly with others to perform a crime, whereas his own interpretation of it was that it was the purposeful deployment of a technique in the hope of saving life.

When he turned up at Sutton police station, he was ready for an argument. He wanted his day in court to explain his position.

I told them 'I did not conspire…. I had an empowering belief to hack phones…. I believe I was doing it legitimately…. I was prepared to go all the way down the line and plead not guilty on conspiracy. I would call key witnesses and paperwork to explain why I believed I was doing it on behalf of the law… it was not like the three other charges [of 2006], which were celebrity-based bits of nonsense. But I was not going to plead guilty to conspiracy.' He says he has the impression the police had wised up to who he was and what and why he had done it. Their tone, by the end, showed more respect than would be due a 'rogue'. 'By that time,' he said, 'they'd got the picture as to why I did what I did. Not before time.

In fact, a lawyer would say that Mulcaire's claim to have lawful authority or an empowering belief is not sufficient to get him off the hook. To have lawful authority, it has to be formally bestowed by an arm of the state. A nod from, say, Greg Miskiw is not sufficient, although Mulcaire's vehemence on the matter shows the strength of his belief. His anger over the case is evident. Soon after that, the conspiracy charge against Mulcaire was dropped. Conveniently, he says. 'do they really want me there, in Leveson etc… police had a lot to lose if they left him in conspiracy charge… they knew full well I was determined to stick with this in a court of law. I would have liked Neville to go "not guilty". I would have welcomed the chance to thrash it out in court. Ok, let's talk about all this.'

Mulcaire maintains a faith in the legal system to get to the bottom of an issue, as long as the evidence is presented in court. He insists he has told no lies throughout his legal odyssey, but as a result of pleading guilty on all charges apart from the (dropped) Dowler conspiracy charge, has deprived himself of the opportunity to appear in court to explain himself.

For those unfamiliar with how the paper worked, this idea of his wanting the whole issue exposed to public transparency may seem extraordinary. But Mulcaire was essentially uninterested in most of the stories he worked on. He wanted to find the nugget, to crack the secret. The finding of it was its own reward, while the parading of it was for others. He often didn't even buy the paper in which they appeared, and he prided himself on not being a 'trophy hunter', as he dismissively referred to some of the journalists with whom he worked. And few of those who were in charge of him discouraged him in that attitude. It suited them to keep things on a 'need to know' basis, not least because once he started asking questions he might never stop. We will see that Mulcaire was something of an expert in the twilight world where official public bodies meet the dark arts, and he knew when it was inappropriate to ask too many questions. And with a young girl missing, it would surely be no surprise if the police were throwing every trick in the book into solving the problem. The police team working on the case, too, were under enormous pressure from their bosses to come up with leads.

And the fact that he might be doing work for the police by the back door was neither discreditable nor surprising. In a different context, his wife Alison recalls one holiday in Great Yarmouth in particular, when she was at her busiest with their young children, in a caravan. She was giving Mulcaire a hard time, because he kept going outside to speak to someone on the paper when she needed help. 'I'm sorry, but we've got to do this, we're doing it for the police.' She says that was a fairly frequent occurrence, and in the Milly Dowler case, he was seeking to free a young girl from her kidnapper.

Neville Thurlbeck had had a remarkable past as the breaker of big stories. His exposure of criminals made dealing with the police a pretty much daily experience. In 2000 he had come close to going to prison for bribing police officers. Thurlbeck was registered as a police informer (No. 281), bearing the codename 'George' and gave a 'substantial volume of information that was 'extremely useful' to Scotland Yard and the security services. In return, Thurlbeck received confidential information from the Police National Computer that enabled him to write about a Labour MP with a conviction for committing obscene behaviour and, separately, a supposed 'stalker' threat to the Queen.

It later emerged that Thurlbeck was actually an unpaid employee of the National Criminal Intelligence Service (NCIS), a liaison body between Scotland Yard's Special Branch and MI5. 'Sources close to' Thurlbeck said that 'people right at the top of News International were aware of his role'.

Following his release, Thurlbeck displayed plenty of insouciant candour when he told the *UK Press Gazette*: 'The police were very impressed about the type of intelligence I was coming up with and that was revealed in court. The judge said it was a substantial volume of information that was extremely useful to police.' Mr Justice McKinnon said the relationship between Thurlbeck and his source was a 'symbiotic one – a two-way relationship with information passed both ways'. The case was thrown out, with the judge accepting Thurlbeck's assertion that no money had changed hands, so no law had been broken. Thurlbeck said at the time: 'When you deal with police officers in the year 2000, the currency is information not money.... The *News of the World* crime desk receives a huge amount of information about criminal activity – and the police have always been eager to tap into that resource. In return policemen give information to us. That is our most valuable currency.'

Mulcaire's self-image is as 'one of the good guys', and it's a belief that has bolstered him through several years of vilification. A weaker man would certainly have crumbled, given the reputational and financial strain he has come under. 'Reputation is one thing, character is something quite different,' he is inclined to say, the latter, of course, being the one that matters. But such faith cannot be self-sustaining forever, and he needs his side of the story to be better understood. Hence his cooperation with this book presumably.

For one thing, he remains enraged that, having put up with being dismissed as a 'rogue' when he was first convicted, it later became convenient to saddle him with numerous other heinous offences. A scapegoat was needed, and he, gagged by lawyers, was ready made. Now, though, he wants a full inquiry into the Dowler case. He persists in disbelieving much of the evidence that has been given in court, and wants all his files returned to him.

There have been claims that the police's own voicemails were listened to. He doesn't know if he did so, but says it is possible and, given his low regard for the police's record on child abductions, quite understandable. For one thing this might have helped find the child, and for another, it was known that in one such case, an officer was having an inappropriate relationship. Again, if that was the case, there was no reason it shouldn't be known about. If it was true, he says, his files would reveal the reason. He estimated a great many (possibly as much as 25 per cent, he says) are still missing, despite attempts to get them back. Those, he says, would tell much of the story, but he says they remain unattainable in the police's safe keeping. 'God alone will flush out those people (who listened to her voicemail early on and made such a mess). It may take a long time, but I can't do to them what they have done to me.'

10

Arms of the State

In a book about life on a redtop paper, the author Graham Johnson talks about the closeness of the police to parts of the press, and how lawlessness can thrive as a result. He ends by saying: 'The police looked upon us as the good guys, or so we believed.' This throw-away remark resonates for anyone looking at the police's performance over the phone hacking affair. The police's faith that essentially that their 'friends in the press' had virtually identical interests to the cops was largely responsible for one of the biggest messes in the recent history of the Metropolitan Police. A relationship of co-dependency became one of exploitation. But it took the police a tragically long time to realise it.

Those who recall a supposed golden age of policing were horrified, and with good reason. In the 1950 and 1960s, the cry 'Send for the Yard' meant the calling in of what might now be called a 'celebrity copper' to investigate. This might be '(Robert) Fabian of the Yard', or '(Jack) Slipper of the Yard', whose name would be known across the land and in whose judgment and inde-fatigability an expectant public would place enormous faith. This aura of rectitude was generally reinforced by an obliging pack of crime reporters which would follow them round the country, waiting to be fed snippets over an innocuous whisky in the hotel bar. The relationship was largely controlled by the police, with the press grateful for what it could get.

There was police corruption, of course, and there was some well reported tales of porn barons and gang bosses bribing police. On a smaller scale, one reporter (now deceased) admitted he kept a 10 pound note in the breast pocket of his jacket in case he thought it would loosen the tongue of a police officer, and buff envelopes were not unknown. There might be a habitual Christmas delivery of a crate of brown ale or a bottle of whisky, just to oil the wheels, but the assumption, drummed into the police from early in their training, was to distrust the press.

Stewart Tendler, crime correspondent for the *Times* from 1978 to 2007, recalls: 'They were told that journalists were always after something, and that one could never be sure how and when something you had told them could cause problems for the officer and his force. But in London the proximity of one of the biggest forces in the world and the headquarters of the national media was bound to wear that hostility down, especially as the Yard was involved for decades in the cases that made the biggest headlines.' Some officers simply didn't take the risk, but, says Tendler:

> ... others saw the media as a useful source of intelligence, part of the armoury of detection or a useful tool for their own advancement by attracting publicity for their work. There have also been others operating from venal motives: for many years police pay was poor.

But as newsgathering became more intense and crime fighting part of the political agenda many other officers lost their reticence and were prepared to meet for a drink or lunch. The more cautious ones either paid for themselves or picked up the bill. Others would simply never meet in that sort of social milieu. They were more likely to suggest a coffee in their office. Others might reciprocate at a later stage.

The details of the wining and dining between journalists and police that Lord Leveson found show how things had changed. Was this corruption? It certainly looked dreadful in hindsight. It looked still worse when an HMIC report found there had been 298 cases of 'inappropriate' hospitality, even if it found that most officers had shown common sense in this area.

The fact that that the police swallowed a pack of lies about a 'rogue reporter' at the *News of the World* in 2006, that as a result the Prime Minister hired one of the leading wrongdoers as one of his closest confidants in 2010, that hundreds of victims of crime had to resort to the civil courts, and that it took nearly 7 years to bring the *News of the World*'s main malefactors to justice, and even longer to identify their counterparts on papers other than the *News of the World*, is a pretty open and shut case of a bungled investigation, at best. Coming after the force's failure to identify the killers of Stephen Lawrence, this would have been bad enough. And given that in the course of the investigation into the *News of the World* it emerged that police officers were being paid for stories by the paper, there was plenty for those inclined to find dark forces at work to get their teeth into. After all, they had plenty of ammunition already. There had long been allegations of undue masonic influence inside the Met. On top of this were ever-present allegations of racism, political bias and suspicions of corruption, compounding a more general loss of deference towards authority. Seemingly the police were not earning the public's trust.

And for those who smelt a rat, there was a more specific cause for concern. In 1987, a private investigator, Daniel Morgan, was murdered in a pub cark park in Sydenham, south London. It was believed that Morgan was on the verge of blowing the whistle on widespread police corruption. Morgan had set up Southern Investigations, a private investigations company, and it was after having a drink with his business partner Jonathan Rees that he was found with an axe embedded in his head. The officer charged with interviewing Rees was also moonlighting for him, which undermined the investigation's credibility from the start. Arrests were made, but all those charged were acquitted, leaving the murder unsolved. Given what emerged subsequently about drugs and police corruption, the idea that Morgan knew too much would not go away.

What made it all the more potent, and did all the more to undermine the police's efforts to get to the bottom of *News of the World*'s misbehaviour, centred on Rees. The *News of the World*'s former crime reporter and later news executive Alex Marunchak was an associate of Rees, and Rees used to sell him stories for the *News of the World* (for up to £150,000 a year, it later emerged). It was claimed many of Rees's stories came ultimately from corrupt police officers, so, regardless of who had committed the murder, too deep an examination of *News of the World* news-gathering might expose some uncomfortable truths about the Met at the same time.

Another was that that in December 2000, Rees was jailed for 6 years, extended to 7 years on appeal, for conspiring with a corrupt police officer to plant cocaine in the car of a woman so that she would lose custody of her children. Any association with a man capable of such a thing was going to need some explaining.

The third surrounded detective chief superintendent Dave Cook, a talented and assiduous detective who, in 2002, became the latest officer to investigate the murder of Daniel Morgan. Because of the sensitivities of the case, Cook and fellow officer Jacquie Hames, a presenter of the BBC's Crimewatch programme, were placed under a witness protection scheme. Nonetheless, they suspected they were being put under surveillance by the driver of a white van, who seemed to be waiting for them at the end of their drive. When police stopped the van, they discovered it was leased by News International through its *News of the World* executive Alex Marunchak. It was later claimed by Rebekah Brooks that they were being watched because of a tip that Cook and Hames were having an affair. In fact, this was no secret. They had been living together for 12 years, had 2 children and had married 4 years earlier. Some months later Cook was able to confront Brooks in person at Scotland Yard. Nonetheless, even though there seemed to be evidence of a possible interference with Cook's investigation, it was decided no further action should be taken. The impression created was that of a bad smell, at best.

Alex Marunchak later pointed out to the *Press Gazette*

that at that time he was the editor of the Irish edition of the *News of the World*, and was based in Dublin, professionally at least. He confirmed that he had been given a tip, that Hames and Cook were having an affair, and merely passed it on, unchecked, to the desk in London. Apart from a 30-second conversation with the newsdesk, he said, he had no involvement in the story. Marunchak also said that he had never even heard of Daniel Morgan, or of his PI company Southern Investigations, at the time of Morgan's death.

While most of the dark allegations were yet to register on the broader public's radar (let alone their denials), those who had looked into it were unimpressed. It is fair to infer that the feelings ventilated in a newspaper article by former assistant commissioner at the Met John Yates in 2013 reflected the feelings of campaigners 10 or so years earlier: 'For many years, [the Morgan family] were lied to, fobbed off, patronised and dismissed as crackpots by the very people who should have been helping them – the police.... It is one of the most, if not the most, shameful episodes in Scotland Yard's history.'

As the phone hacking story developed, further grounds for suspicion about the police's role emerged. The head of the counter-terrorist unit, the body running the phone hacking investigation, was Andy Hayman. He had been brought in as assistant commissioner for specialist operations (ACSO) by the new commissioner of the Met Ian Blair, in February 2005, and just months later, in July 2005, he was in charge of the biggest criminal investigation Britain had ever seen, the search for the 7/7 bombers. He was also in the thick of the action when Jean Charles de Menezes, a Brazilian electrician, was shot at Stockwell underground station in the mistaken belief that he was a terrorist. In 2006, he was appointed Commander of the Order of the British Empire.

Andy Hayman was gregarious by nature, and positively encouraged the mixing of business with pleasure in the company of journalists, frequently holding meetings with journalists and press officers at The Sanctuary hotel or some similarly convivial location round the corner from Scotland Yard. He was as aware as anyone of the influence of the Murdoch papers, and made sure as far as possible that they were kept abreast of developments in the fight against terrorism. The *News of the World* was often a beneficiary of this, its reach to a wide public being used, for example, to publicise an FBI film showing how much damage the so-called 'shoe bomber' Richard Reid might have caused had he not been stopped in time.

But there were questions about Hayman's use of his expense account, of his mobile phone and the extent of his fraternising with colleagues. The fact that 2 months after he decided to resign, in December 2007, he took up the offer to write a column for the *Times*, another Murdoch-owned newspaper, did not look good, as he admitted later. In the 10 months before he stood down, he had met representatives of the Murdoch media 5 times for meals, which also did not help make him look like an ideal Caesar's wife either.

Assuming good faith on the part of senior Met officers, though, the investigation in to the *News of the World* was a humiliation. To understand why, it is necessary to go back to the year 2000. 'Over the years, the

Met had become more and more secretive and cautious: officers had not been allowed to talk to the press without the authority of an inspector or someone of more senior rank, and this attitude had tended to attract suspicion and contempt. The Stephen Lawrence case had put our reputation on the floor, and it seemed to me that we needed to make strenuous efforts to rehabilitate ourselves and restore our own confidence. Perhaps because we ourselves had gone into our shell, the press, for their part, had withdrawn and distanced themselves.' Those words were written in 2005, so still the balmy days of Police/press cross-fertilisation, come from Sir John Stevens, reflecting on his arrival in the Met commissioner's chair 5 years earlier.

Hindsight is unkinder still. 'I myself worked hard to foster good relations with national newspapers,' continued Stevens, 'mainly by being open and making myself available to the editor… Piers Morgan at the *Daily Mirror*, Rebekah Brooks at the *Sun*, Andy Coulson on the *News of the World*, Dominic Lawson on the *Sunday Telegraph*, Alan Rusbridger of the *Guardian* and Paul Dacre at the *Daily Mail*.… Sometimes this policy alarmed my own public relations staff… but on the whole it paid off handsomely.' Stephens was also notably friendly with Paul Dacre, Max Hastings at the Standard and the Barclay brothers, owners of the *Telegraph*.

One journalist Stevens didn't mention in that context was Neil Wallis, then deputy editor of the *News of the World* and an assiduous cultivator of senior police officers. In 1995 Wallis had set up the *Sun*'s Police Bravery Awards, which have been attended by every Prime Minister since. Wallis has said in an interview, 'I was used to dining with senior police officers. There was an understanding we could work together. Paul Condon [Now Lord Condon, Met commissioner 1993-9], [Now Lord] John Stevens, [Now Sir] Paul Stephenson (Stevens's successor). All became Metropolitan Police Commissioners. I was able to talk to them all. Journalists, particularly in the tabloid press, discover things the police can't. Co-operation with the Met can help catch criminals.' The police looked on us as the good guys.

The relationships that Wallis had built up would have been the envy of any senior journalist, and as long as due proprieties are observed, there is nothing wrong – on either side – with journalists and police officers having mutually beneficial relations. So it will have been a shock when Neil Wallis was questioned by police at Hammersmith Police station about his knowledge of phone hacking. In the event, the matter was dropped, but at a time when the police's relationship with News International was undergoing exceptional scrutiny, it gave rise to a great deal of innuendo.

Wallis is by all accounts good company, with those who are his equals and above at least. He was well placed to help John Stevens improve the Met's relations with the press, having written the then deputy commissioner's strategy plan when he applied to be given the top job. Lord Condon, Stevens's predecessor as boss of the Met, had been a reserved presence, not someone naturally comfortable in the company of prying journalists. Stevens's natural gregariousness by contrast must have played well by comparison.

In the new collaborative climate, Wallis's friendliness with Stevens would have been seen as a plus by both his newspaper colleagues and senior people in the Met. The pair would meet over dinner, sometimes in the company of deputy commissioner John Yates, Stevens's right hand man, who was seemingly also destined for the top, and Dick Fedorcio, Scotland Yard's head of press. All being on the same side had convivial advantages, with the assumption that they were all seeking to put bad people behind bars a given. As one senior former colleague puts it, 'John Stevens wrote the book on how to schmooze the press.'

Wallis's friendship with Stevens spawned a friendship between Wallis and Yates, and it was this that was to cause the end of Yates's 30-year career in the Met. Rightly or wrongly, their association was held up as the benchmark of an unhealthily close relationship between press and police. During the Leveson inquiry, the name of Wallis acquired a toxicity it had never previously had, yet all other things being equal, both legitimately claim to have been doing their job – having constructive relationships with people who knew useful things.

Wallis, a keen Man United fan, arranged to watch football with the sociable, upstanding Yates, who supports Liverpool. The pair used to exchange larky emails, texts and blokey jokes, perhaps going beyond what their opponents would have thought appropriate. But there is no evidence of the sort of impropriety that would have attracted attention in other circumstances. . Yates told the Home Affairs Committee when he resigned in 2012 that his integrity was intact and his conscience clear. He had gone to some lengths to ensure that was the case, informing his boss about the end of his marriage, for example, lest, say, anunscrupulous journalist seek to take advantage of the fact.

The Yates-Wallis friendship was well known at the Met. And higher up it was felt important to maintain the best of relationships with Metropolitan Police Commissioners. 'The strategy was, get them on side and everything else will fall into place,' according to one News International insider. 'They'll keep you well stocked with stories. The one who didn't conform in that respect was [commissioner] Ian Blair.'

They did indeed keep them well stocked. One of the *News of the World*'s better known reporters was Mazher Mahmood, famous for being faceless. Mahmood's picture has never appeared in the paper because his stories often involve impersonating someone rich, foreign and mysterious, persuading his victims to team up with him in unsuitable schemes. As a 'Fake Sheikh', he has gulled former England football manager Sven-Goran Eriksson into suggesting that together they buy a football club, and as a bogus Indian businessman he exposed a spot-fixing scam among Pakistani cricketers.

Mahmood is something of a redtop legend, though a highly controversial one, and claims to have helped put 94 people behind bars. (Previous claims to a figure nearly 3 times that size have been scaled down.) His stories involve a high degree of subterfuge and the sort of contact with his victims that in some countries might be regarded as entrapment, so of necessity they sail close to the wind legally. Nonetheless he is an outstanding example of how an ingenious journalist can entertainingly expose the greed and delusions of the rich and powerful.

One senior police officer recalls the sort of collaboration that went on with News International in the early 2000s. 'There was a time when they were all over us, he says. 'Mazher Mahmood was for ever giving us jobs, and us coming in on the back of it. It was always a *fait accompli*, there was no question of us saying: "Hang on, is this one a sensible use of our time and resources?" We just had to get on with it. The commander at the time was quite aware of it. It was generally their management talking to our management, but it always came through a chain of command down to us on the shop floor.' Another senior Met figure echoes this, suggesting that the Met did not appreciate every aspect of the arrangement: 'The deal was always that the paper had to be able to print the story first, then they'd hand the stuff over to us. The stories always used to come in on a Thursday or Friday, just when we were starting to think about packing up, so it generally meant a ruined weekend.'

In a more general sense, the *News of the World* identified itself as being on the side of law and order. Deputy features editor Paul McMullan remembers that subeditors used to write at the bottom of his stories the words 'our dossier is available to the authorities', almost as if that bestowed respectability. He says they also used to encourage him to pass on information to the police, whereas for many journalists there is a squeamishnesss about getting in to bed with an arm of the state. 'I did a story about some swingers up to no good which they wanted to know all about, and [managing editor] Kuttner wanted the paper's reputation defended by helping the police', but McMullan was reluctant and felt this was more about a desire for respectability (undeserved, he felt, given the type of advertisements the paper was carrying and the sort of work he was doing) than anything else.

The mood of friendliness was well established at the top of News International and the Met, and was cemented when Sir John Stevens, as he had become, agreed to write a column for the *Sun*. Handily enough, this was ghost-written by... Neil Wallis. According to Hacked Off, which lobbies against press intrusion, Stevens was paid £5,000 for seven articles in the first year, and £7,000 each for the second. Lower down the chain, staff on both organisations knew the power of the other. Making waves was not encouraged.

So the arrest in 2006 of two people working for the *News of the World* was a shock. Clive Goodman and Glenn Mulcaire had been the subject of complaints from the royal family, no less, so the matter could not be managed away with assurances of lessons learned and so on. It was not to be ignored, although those involved remember a higher degree of discretion than usual was deemed appropriate.

Yet it wasn't a big story, surely. The case – having been treated initially as a serious security issue – was being handled by the anti-terrorist branch, which had responsibility for the royal family's safety. Detective chief inspector Keith Surtees, senior investigating officer on the case, said later that he 'fully understood the rationale as to why SO13 had been tasked to deal with this given the national security implications and the potential consequences of a person having access to such sensitive information'. Surtees was also flying to and from Iraq, attempting to secure the release of a British hostage, and had several other cases on the go. The anti-terrorist branch, too, had other fish to fry. A year earlier, Islamist terrorism had come to mainland Britain when 52 innocent people were killed on the streets of London in the 7/7 attacks. And, as if the emphasise the point, the very day after Goodman and Mulcaire were arrested, police seized terrorists plotting to blow up at least 10 planes travelling crossing the Atlantic from the United Kingdom. It is as a result of that vast plot that the restrictions on carrying liquid on flights remains so stringent.

Nevertheless, the case had to be examined, and in some secrecy. When they started, the police had no idea what had been going on, simply that the royal princes suspected they were being subjected to even closer scrutiny than usual. The police soon found that the voicemails were the issue, but not much more than that. Clearly they were going to have to rely on the phone companies for the relevant data, but, senior investigating officer on the case Surtees reported later, they were not well placed to do so. 'From the outset, the phone companies had not appreciated that this illegal access was possible, nor had they a means by which they could assist us to ascertain how often and how widespread this was.'

Given that several bags full of evidence from Mulcaire's notebooks had been seized, the police had plenty of evidence that if the phones of the royals and their staff had been hacked, so had hundreds, maybe thousands of others. Mark Lewis later claimed he'd been told there were 6,000 victims, a figure that became the subject of some vigorous legal exchanges later on. In any event, other journalists also seemed to be involved. Surtees later testified that in meetings, in discussing widening the investigation to other journalists' hacking, it was 'highly unlikely in our view to be restricted only to Goodman and was probably quite widespread'.

Detective inspector Mark Maberly endorsed this, telling Lord Justice Leveson: 'There were still lines of enquiry that I would have been keen to follow. In particular, I'd identified three names who, if I had sufficient evidence, I would have liked to have spoken to. I accepted the decision that, you know, the resources were not there to widen the enquiry, and I myself was deployed on other anti-terrorist branch enquiries at the time.'

Yet there were further difficulties, aside from the phone companies' professed ignorance. Legally, the crown prosecution was in uncharted waters, for RIPA, the new law on phone hacking, had not been tested in court. The legal advice they had received was that interception of phone messages was only a criminal offence if it could be proven that the message was listened to before its intended recipient did so, rather than after. This narrow interpretation of an untested law became the widely accepted doctrine of the 'unopened letter'. To add to the police's problems, they had learned enough from the aborted trial of butler Paul Burrell in 2002 to know that the princes would almost certainly refuse to appear in court, and would want to prevent further exposure of the contents of their calls.

In early May of 2006, the police embarked on a test period, during which members of the royal household would only check their voicemails at agreed times. This would help the police monitor who else was picking up messages. As before, Clive Goodman was a regular, but also a 'Paul Williams' was doing so, Williams being one of

Mulcaire's pseudonyms. The two candidates for prosecution had thereby unwittingly presented themselves.

Another Williams, detective chief superintendent Philip Williams, and his colleague Keith Surtees, were getting somewhere, while being very conscious of other, real terrorist demands on their time. The plod-like recitation of Surtees's duties is typical, yet revealing.

> Given the sheer volume of operations within SO13 that we were dealing with at the time, it was not always possible to maintain the operational structure. It was often a case of reacting and dealing with matters as and when I could. There were a number of operations I was working on as were all the other members of SO13. There were not infinite resources available and in order to fulfil our primary objective of ensuring public security was not compromised, we had to prioritise each operation according to the risk. An operation where there was the real possibility of a threat to life on a mass scale would always take priority. The advantage of focussing the investigation on the current two suspects was that it would mean the investigation would quickly get to the point where a prosecution could be brought against them and thereby provide protection to the individuals who had been targeted and swiftly prosecute the appropriate offenders.

When people ask why only Mulcaire and Goodman were prosecuted in 2006, one contributing answer lies here, for better or worse.

The decision to narrow the scope of the prosecution meant omitting potentially promising evidence such as the now famous 'For Neville' email. This was a message in which a junior *News of the World* reporter copied a transcript of more than 30 messages hacked from the phones of the Professional Footballers' Association chief executive, Gordon Taylor, and his legal adviser Jo Armstrong. 'Neville', now known to be news editor Neville Thurlbeck, was never interviewed by the police, nor was the message in question included in the police's submission to the Crown Prosecution Service, the source of some complaint and point-scoring later. The police's failure to use that email added to a sense among some journalists that police were involved in covering up the extent of the illegality. Met deputy commissioner John Yates later told the House of Commons Media Select Committee, 'I would say it is 99.9 per cent certain that, if we were to question Neville Thurlbeck on this matter, he would make no comment.' He said that had been the case with Goodman and Mulcaire. 'I have no evidence to put before him other than the fact that this is a Neville, that he has not read it and we know he has not read it because it has not been transmitted by Mulcaire to Neville Thurlbeck.' In other words, expending time on this would be unlikely to take the case any closer to court.

If the police kept the focus narrow for defensible reasons, how is one to explain the fact that David Perry, the crown prosecution lawyer who provided the advice, specifically asked the police if other journalists were involved, at a case conference on 21st August 2006. No, he was told, there was no such evidence, but he couldn't remember which officer told him that. That case conference, held less than a fortnight after the raid on Mulcaire's premises, was not made aware of the 'for Neville' email, possibly because, as Perry acknowledged, it may not have been found at that point.

It was later pointed out that the crown prosecution had had access to the famous bin bags holding what had been found during the Mulcaire raid, so the evidence had been there for them to inspect. They were not alone in failing to appreciate the significance of the bin bags' contents. Head of the Met counter terrorism command Peter Clarke told the Home Affairs select committee in 2011 that even the Met had decided against doing an 'exhaustive analysis' of their content. 'I could not justify the huge expenditure of resources this would entail over an inevitably protracted period', he said.

Many were inclined to believe, whatever the police doing the investigation may have said, that the mood was set higher up. As we have seen, making waves was discouraged, in the interests of the News International-Met relationship. To the sceptics, the investigation looked half-hearted, an obligation imposed less by a desire to expose unscrupulous journalists and more by a deference to royal sensibilities.

Perhaps surprisingly, John Whittingdale MP, the chairman of the House of Commons Culture, Media and Sport select Committee, found himself in this camp. Not a notable hothead as a critic of News International and occasional dining partner of Les Hinton, he said later: 'There was simply no enthusiasm among Scotland Yard to go beyond the cases involving Mulcaire and Goodman. To start exposing widespread tawdry practices in that newsroom was a heavy stone that they didn't want to try to lift.' It was claimed later by the *New York Times* that police had failed to show the crown prosecution much of the evidence against other victims of hacking, and that press officers at Scotland Yard were urging their own investigators not to upset vested interests. The first, it seems, was explicable, given the police's focussed strategy, and the second, if true, appears to have been robustly ignored by the newspaper's source.

Certainly there were hundreds of names of hacking targets on Mulcaire's files in the bin bags, but many fewer that proved criminality, as opposed to general 'research'. Executives whose names appeared as 'top lefts' on Mulcaire's research sheets also escaped on the same grounds: who was to say, let alone prove to a jury's satisfaction, that they had asked for anything unlawful to be done? The police may have thought intercepting voicemails was just a handy trick. They showed no signs of realising it was an industry. As one very senior officer admitted simply in Freudian terms: 'We just didn't think it was a story.' And in one sense, nor did a great many redtop reporters.

What would have been a story, surely, and arguably endorsed the call for stiffer charges against Mulcaire, was the evidence that he had breached the witness protection programme by looking into child killers Robert Thompson and Mary Bell. The police had evidence that, 8 years later, was sufficiently serious to be raised with the Attorney General, that there had been an apparent breach of High Court injunctions that protected their new identities (and that of two others). Yet no action was taken, and it seems 2 senior officers, in 2006 the then

Commissioner Ian Blair, and John Yates in 2009, were not made aware of the evidence, even though, with hindsight at least, some felt the apparent offences were sufficient to warrant alerting the top brass.

Here is further food for conspiracy theorists. Yet even those not well disposed to the police admit that had they taken action, it might well have been necessary to re-settle them yet again, which would have incurred further enormous expense, and there was no certainty of securing a conviction. In other word, the wider public interest was not best served by pursuing the matter. And Mulcaire, after all, insists he did nothing to make them any easier to trace by possible vigilantes, and that any encounter between either of them and a third party was conducted away from their new homes. He says he never let a journalist have their home addresses.

Confidence within the Met that the correct decision had been taken was stiffened by the fact that ultimately the call had been made by deputy assistant commission-er and the head of counter terrorism command Peter Clarke, a highly respected figure among his peers, and a man to whom the cliché 'unimpeachable integrity' is frequently attached. Whereas his boss assistant commis-sioner Andy Hayman was, as we have seen, a colourful character (and as such has attracted a lot of fire), Clarke was more low-key. Hayman was happy to leave the inves-tigation to Clarke, and had fewer than 5 substantive con-versations with him over the minutiae of the case. He said later that he was shown a list of possible victims of phone hacking. 'As I recall, the list... ran to several hundred names. Of these, there were a small number – perhaps a handful – where there was evidence that the phones had actually been tampered with.'

While Hayman's view of the ongoing case was almost certainly of interest to the *News of the World*, there is no reason to think that he behaved other than correctly. Indeed, he was seemingly in no position to mark their card in any event. He told Lord Leveson that he didn't even know when the search warrants were to be made or the search warrants issued. And the suggestion of unhealthy Met complicity with the paper – whatever else it might be – is not sustained by evidence from the day police arrived at Wapping. One officer recalled in a newspaper interview later: 'There was a Mexican stand-off, a lock down, and they wouldn't let us in. Most newspaper desks would do the same if a cop turned up with a dodgy looking warrant.'

It is a mark of the Met's faith in the senior people at News International that when Rebekah Brooks was called in by the Met to be told that, seemingly, she had been a victim of phone hacking, she was given a thorough briefing as to the state of the investigation. Had she been treated with the suspicion that she warranted (given that she was later put on trial, though acquitted), the police would have played their cards close to their chest. Instead, when she returned to her office she was able to give News International legal affairs manager Tom Crone a full briefing on the state of play. She reported that police had a list of 100-110 victims, that they were visiting those who had been targeted most, that the police wanted to show that Mulcaire's crimes were not restricted to Palace people and that at that stage they had no evidence of other *News of the World* staff hacking phones. Tom Crone passed the news on to Andy

Coulson at the *News of the World*. Four days later, Coulson had dinner with Met commissioner Paul Stephenson. Did they discuss phone hacking? Who knows, but Coulson barely needed to. The police looked on us as the good guys.

Deputy assistant commissioner Clarke later described breaches of privacy as 'odious' and 'distressing', but 'to put it bluntly, they don't kill you', a fact of life doubtless amplified by his colleagues in the anti-terrorism force. By including five non-royal household victims of phone hacking in the charges, the crown prosecution felt a shot had been fired and a message sent.

The decision to confine the charges was a get-out-of-jail-free card for News International executives. Although, as we have seen, the heads of its employees Coulson, Goodman and Mulcaire, had to roll, the edifice of lawless phone interception had survived. Through its lawyers Burton Copeland, the paper had given the impression of being helpful to the enquiry but, as one officer involved said later, they 'employed every legal means possible to avoid allowing the police to delve further than Goodman'.

In fact, contrary to what one might imagine, at News International there was a degree of resentment at the police investigation. Ian Blair had followed John Stevens in the top job at the Met, and he was a different proposition. Blair and Stevens did not get on at all, 'and that is an understatement', says a former colleague of both, although both are insistent in denying any ill feeling. Emotionally, politically (one imagines) and intellectually, they were chalk and cheese. Blair was less inclined to accede to the News International way of doing things, and some in Wapping detected his hand in what they saw as the police's unnecessary diligence in prosecuting Goodman and Mulcaire. As Andy Coulson put it in court in 2014, when it was suggested that he had tried to use his influence to ensure the pair were not sent to prison, the paper 'had a difficult relationship with Ian Blair and I did not feel very influential at that time,' adding 'no other newspaper was investigated in the way we were.'

Whatever the niggles about not being above the law, there had to be some ostentatious mutterings about the learning of lessons and the rigorous upholding of high standards. Those who worked at the *News of the World* – though surprised at a prosecution having been brought – knew the paper had had the narrowest of escapes. The police, too, were anxious to move on. They had secured 2 convictions through guilty pleas, 'sent a message' to other journalists tempted to stray and were now able to get back to catching 'proper' criminals.

For some, the decision to charge just Goodman and Mulcaire was a little too convenient. Was there a deal between the police and the *News of the World*? Much later, in 2013-14, it became publicly apparent that not only had the voicemails of members of the royal household staff been intercepted, but those of the royal princes and Kate Middleton too – although this was not something it was felt needed to be made public. One senior figure denies there was any such explicit deal, but the fact that Goodman and Mulcaire were going to plead guilty must have been a mighty relief all round. He says 'There was no agreement, it just became a self-fulfilling prophecy which suited all sides at the time – a sort of passive gentleman's agreement. The police were rushed off their feet with the airlines plot and not wanting to upset the royals, and the *News of the World* more than happy to air only a fraction of their dirty linen.' Mulcaire's view, as someone directly concerned but outside the process, is as follows: 'If I we hadn't pleaded guilty, the princes would have had to go into the box. Minimising royal embarrassment was part of the deal. Everyone apart from me was a winner, although they could have done us on national security grounds, which would have meant a much longer stretch.' So, remarkably, the royal princes and the bosses at the *News of the World* had identical interests, and the police, with much else on their plate, did not rock the boat.

The matter did live on, but beneath the public's radar. The police agreed after the convictions they needed a strategy for telling those who appeared to have been hacked. Should they tell all of them? Anyone whose name appeared in Mulcaire's notebooks? Just those about whom stories had been written? It was agreed that just a handful of people in sensitive positions should be told. Those who complained later about the cost of Operation Weeting can surely not criticise this earlier, presumably cost-based decision.

But News International had some 'afters' to address. Mark Lewis, a Manchester-based solicitor with an interest in privacy, had represented the Professional Footballers' Association and its chairman Gordon Taylor. Previously he had had dealings with legal affairs manager Tom Crone at the *News of the World* over pictures taken of Taylor with Joanne Armstrong, the PFA's in-house solicitor. The paper believed the pair were having an affair. Lewis applied for an injunction on the grounds of both privacy and the story being untrue. Crone refused, saying the story had been obtained by 'proper journalistic enquiries'.

Lewis remembers it as a curiously defensive response to a run-of-the-mill legal inquiry. His sense of being onto something was hardened both by Tom Crone's willingness, unprecedented in Lewis's cases against News International, to meet Lewis at his Manchester office, and by his opening remark 'we thought this had all gone away.' After that meeting, on 3rd May 2007, Lewis set the legal wheels in motion, launching a case against the paper and against Glenn Mulcaire, and demanding to see relevant documents from Mulcaire's files.

This was getting dangerous for News International. But on the surface, all was calm. After the flurry of activity that followed the jailing of Mulcaire and Goodman, and the departure of Andy Coulson, Colin Myler had become the paper's new editor. He was considered a safe pair of hands, one well versed in the ways of the redtops. In February 2007 Myler asked the Press Complaints Commission to give a seminar on privacy issues and undercover journalism and emailed every member of staff individually, and written to them at home, with the PCC code of practice. *News of the World* staff were told of a new clause in their contracts that meant a failure to comply could result in summary dismissal. In March Les Hinton reassured the House of Commons's Culture Media and Sport Select Committee that the stables did not need further cleaning out. He said 'I believe absolutely that Andy did not have knowledge of what was going on'. He was asked if a rigorous internal inquiry had been conducted. He replied: 'We went, I promise you, to extraordinary lengths within the *News of the World*' to find further evidence, and was 'absolutely convinced that Clive Goodman was the only person who knew what was going on'.

Hinton was not alone in asserting that the paper's methods were spotless. Managing editor Stuart Kuttner was similarly confident. He told the Today programme that February that only one *News of the World* journalist had been involved in illegal phone hacking: 'It happened once at the *News of the World*. The reporter was fired; he went to prison. The editor resigned.'

In late May, the Press Complaints Commission obligingly published an exculpatory report, declaring it had no reason to doubt the claim that Goodman's hacking was 'aberrational' and that there was no evidence of systematic phone hacking at the paper. Two days later, just to put the most public of seals on things, Andy Coulson was confirmed as David Cameron's head of communications.

At around this time, Clive Goodman was making a number of extremely serious allegations about widespread unlawful behaviour authorised by senior executives, but only those senior executives were privy to his claims. As we have seen, he settled his case that summer for around £250,000. By November of that year (2007), though, the *News of the World*'s last editor Colin Myler felt free to tell his colleagues at the Society of Editors: 'In the Goodman case, his activities were indefensible, but were isolated to a single journalist…. The editor resigned. He wasn't personally culpable for what

Goodman did but he did the honourable thing and took responsibility – a principle we rarely see in public life these days.... There are lots of bad and uncaring people out there. We are on the side of good not evil. Right not wrong. Justice not injustice.'

The world knows now that Goodman did not act alone. So what had happened to the 'rigorous' internal investigation that had been supposed to root out the wrongdoers? Whatever they discovered produced no radical action, at least as far as exposing what had happened in the past was concerned, even if safeguards were amended for the future. So how had they failed to find the source of the stench? Someone close to those looking into it said: 'They have always told friends they knew nothing about what went on – that everyone had read the code, been told to obey the rules.' Yet the investigation was laughably incomplete. Why wasn't there a proper inquiry? 'Don't ask me,' says a friend. 'But the fact that they didn't shows you the level of confidence that it didn't need to be shut off.' In other words, the penny hadn't dropped. The story was not going to go away but – in their attitudes at least – Murdoch's people were behaving with as great a sense of unshakeable entitlement as ever. And why not? Politicians were falling over themselves to be in Rupert Murdoch's good books, and surely *nobody* was interested in phone hacking?

That summer, the game was to change again. In August, Rupert Murdoch won control of Dow Jones, giving him one of the prizes he had long sought, the *Wall Street Journal*. He insisted that he bring his great confidant Les Hinton over to New York to help him oversee it, and so at the end of that year, Hinton crossed the Atlantic.

According to journalist Michael Wolff, Rebekah Brooks hoped she might move up to fill Hinton's shoes. Murdoch, though, wanted to promote his son James, but was unsure how far he should do so. Previously he had promoted his son Lachlan to be News Corporation's deputy operations chief, but it had not worked well. Knowing he was the boss's son, as opposed to someone who had unambiguously earned the title, many members of staff had all but ignored him. Roger Ailes, boss of Fox News, called Lachlan 'callow' and 'unsubstantial'.

'Rupert didn't want that happening to James,' recalls one close associate, 'so he made sure he was quite the biggest fish in the pond.' Rupert made James chief executive of News Corporation Europe and Asia, which meant he was in charge of News International in the UK, as well as many other things. 'Running News International was the rounding off of his education,' says the source. 'Rupert backed off for two years in order to let James run things. Rebekah was the go-between between James and Rupert. She was the one who told Rupert what was going on. James hated it at News International, being a guy with a background in TV. It wasn't his thing at all. He didn't want control of News International, whereas Rebekah was desperate to have it.'

The evidence James Murdoch was to give to the Commons media select committee endorses that impression. He had arrived at a smoothly running ship (with the obvious exception of the ongoing legal concerns), and to a degree had to go with flow. He also knew that his father had enormous faith in the ability of Rebekah Brooks, so it would be understandable for him to be guided by her. James Murdoch inherited the phone hacking mess, but his attempts to clean it up or even were undistinguished, at best. There was an opportunity for the company to start afresh, but it was shunned, presumably because somebody concluded that opening the Pandora's box of Mulcaire's files would be a disaster. It was decided, probably by default, to fight fires as they flared up.

One such was the continuing Gordon Taylor case. On May 24 2008 Tom Crone told Colin Myler that PFA chief executive Gordon Taylor's legal team have 'fatal' evidence and pointed to the so-called 'for Neville' email proving 'we actively made use of a large number of extremely private voicemails'. They sought outside counsel's advice, calling in Michael Silverleaf QC. His verdict was predictably bad. On June 3, 2008 Silverleaf told Crone that News International had a 'culture of illegal information access.' He also warned it would be extremely damaging to the publisher's reputation if that info became public' as a result of the Gordon Taylor case. There was, he declared, 'overwhelming evidence of the involvement of a number of senior journalists' in relation to accessing information about Gordon Taylor.

A week latera meeting was held at which, allegedly, it was made clear to James Murdoch that hacking was not restricted to a single journalist. It later emerged that Murdoch had been sent an email mentioning the 'nightmare scenario' of Taylor having discovered the involvement of another journalist in phone hacking. Murdoch said he failed to read the email properly.

Things went from bad to worse at the end of June (on June 27, 2008), when a judge in the case ordered Mulcaire to identify the journalist in question. This had to be prevented at almost any cost. Gordon Taylor was promptly offered a £425,000 settlement, to include his legal costs, which brought the figure to around £700,000. Two associates of Taylor also received awards, raising the total for what would otherwise have been a run-of-the-mill privacy issue to around £1 million.

The Taylor settlement was astonishing. It was a vast sum, and spoke volumes for News International's nervousness. Executives later claimed unconvincingly that the alternative, to fight the case, would have ended up costing a comparable amount. The problem for those who were confident of there being many similar victims was that the settlement was a secret. Until, that was, on 8th July 2009, Nick Davies revealed the details in the *Guardian*. The paper reported that journalists for whom the Prime Minister's communications spokesman was responsible 'were engaged in hundreds of apparently illegal acts', that police knew 'two or three thousand' mobile phones had been targeted, that executives 'albeit in good faith', misled a parliamentary select committee and that police had failed to inform many of the victims. To those who had been following the case, it seemed like a great leap forward.

To the police, though, it was underwhelming. The Met's new commissioner Paul Stephenson asked John Yates for his view. Should the police re-open the investigation? After just eight hours he decided no, it shouldn't. This surely, was a major stitch-up, or so it seemed to many. The *Guardian* had not only revealed the extent of the wrongdoing, but also police knowledge of it. Why was no further action to be taken?

But for Scotland Yard, there was nothing new. Met

deputy commissioner Yates said later: 'The *Guardian* had raised a lot of issues. It was a bloody great story but the question was: was there anything new in it for us? The answer was no there wasn't.' Yates was concerned that the claims in the *Guardian* had come from unnamed sources, and that the payment to Taylor, while strikingly large, was in itself proof of nothing. 'I held a series of meetings with the senior investigating officer. We looked at what the CPS had said. It was a landmark case and we still don't have case law on it. To have given the go-ahead for a full review of a case of that nature would have involved 4 or 5 people and 5 or 6 months work and a lot of resources and in July 2009 why would I do that?' At the same time, the director of public prosecutions Keir Starmer, who had 'ordered an urgent examination of the material supplied to the CPS', also concluded on the basis of his department's researches that there was no new material that could be fruitfully examined. The fact that Starmer had lunch with Rebekah Brooks the following month aroused a degree of interest. It took place in the company of his then director of comunications and the *Sun*'s political greybeard Trevor Kavanagh at their offices, and covered the role of the Director of Public Prosecutions, the Crown Prosecution Service and the Human Rights Act. Strikingly, for reasons unknown, one issue was not on the agenda. 'Phone hacking was never discussed,' says Starmer. This non-discussion was perhaps down to it remaining an issue for a few obsessives and still didn't loom large on the national radar.

The Met also knew that Murdoch's power was undiminished, and reopening the case would cause a lot of trouble. One officer well acquainted with the Met's thought processes recalls: 'It was certainly part of our thinking – perhaps the single most important part in deciding whether to investigate further – knowing that the *News of the World* would stonewall and claim they had cooperated fully, which would mean that it was most, most unlikely that any requests for additional (and incriminating) information would have been met.'

In hindsight, it was a calamitously bad decision. Yates admitted later to a journalist it was it was 'pretty crap'. He was to tell the Home Affairs Select Committee that at that time the *News of the World* 'appears to have failed to co-operate in the way that we know they should have... we didn't have the information we should have done'.

There is no reason to doubt the reasons he gave for it, but other considerations should be added. One is the feeling that if so saintly a figure as deputy assistant commissioner Peter Clarke had concluded three years earlier that further resources expended on phone hacking rather than counter-terrorism were likely to be wasted, why would anyone argue? 'We did tend to say: "Why doubt Peter Clarke's view?"' said another very senior Met figure. 'It wasn't a concern about corruption or cover-ups or anything, it was the opposite. We had so much faith in Peter Clarke's judgment that we didn't review things afresh as we should have done. That was definitely part of the problem.'

Another is that pressure to have the case re-opened had been led by the left-of-centre *Guardian*. Executives at News International attributed its keenness on the story to the paper's generally anti-Murdoch stance. In short, it was all 'political', they said. The fact that the likely next Prime

Minister had a former *News of the World* editor at his side added to journalists' appetite for the story. One very senior officer involved in the case said he thought the perception of the story being a groundless anti-Tory smear did infect the police. 'I just thought…. "What is this? What *is* the *Guardian* on about?" It was a minor issue… were we naïve? Yes, in hindsight we certainly were.' Another officer involved in the case said: 'We thought it was political, but should have known journalists don't go on like that unless they have good reason.'

The decision could not have done more to feed the conspiracy theorists. In a PR sense, it was certainly the wrong decision, as it stoked a belief that the police were complicit in a cover-up. Yet, remarkably, there are still those attached to the Met who believe that even if the case had been reopened in 2009, it is doubtful how much would have been uncovered. They would certainly have had to go through the bin liners rather more assiduously than they had. But who would have talked to them? News International had shown no inclination to come clean, and its journalists were all back in harness and unlikely to make trouble.

To compound the police's evident lack of enthusiasm for the case, a mounting number of instances were identified where victims of Mulcaire's hacking were not informed of the fact, despite police promises. This was partly because it was unclear whether they had actually had their voicemails intercepted, partly because some were simply unidentifiable, and partly for reasons unaccountable. It is fair to assume that the police simply decided in 2006 that it was too much of a distraction and too expensive to catalogue all the victims and inform them. Various criteria were adopted at various times, but these were not rigidly adhered to, with the result that some illustrious targets were left in the dark. Among these was former deputy prime minister John Prescott, whose name was found in Mulcaire's files but whose phone may not have been hacked. Prescott was furious that he was not informed until years later. It has been claimed by Peter Clarke that John Reid, as Home Secretary, was given a briefing about the phone hacking affair. Reid denied this, saying: 'I can categorically say that I did not receive any briefing from the Met suggesting that there was widespread hacking including MPs and the deputy PM.'

Campaigners and the growing number of lawyers pursuing civil cases against News International were stupefied by the decision not to re-open the case. In November of that year, as if to add to the mounting incredulity and with timing worthy of Gilbert and Sullivan, the Press Complaints Commission published a second report, once again failing to find evidence of further wrongdoing. Three months later, as the general election loomed, the House of Commons Media Select Committee, after a marathon tussle over the correct wording, concluded that it was 'inconceivable' that Clive Goodman had acted alone, and soon after, another victim, Max Clifford, announced he had been paid £1million to drop a legal action that would have named the others involved.

The police did sit up and take notice when in September 2010, the *New York Times* published a 6,000-word inquiry of its own. It quoted former *News of the*

World reporter Sean Hoare, saying that Andy Coulson had actively encouraged the hacking of phones, and contained a number of witnesses, by now willing to speak on the record. John Prescott announced he was seeking judicial review over the police's handling of the case, having learned that his name was in Mulcaire's files but nobody had informed him, allegedly because it was feared he would leak it to the press. And, wonder of wonders, the police announced they were to re-open the enquiry, though looking only at new evidence. The director of public prosecutions Keir Starmer announced (though few noticed) that the interpretation of the law on phone hacking was to be widened, to include messages already listened to by the intended recipient. With the ending of the doctrine of the 'unopened letter', surely now the police's job would be easier? In early November, at last, the police interviewed Andy Coulson, by this time working in Downing Street, but afforded him the courtesy of being a witnesss, rather than interviewing him under caution. Was the New York *Times* article, at last, to be the turning point? No. In December, police said they had found no new evidence.

Given how much the black bin bags could have revealed about Mulcaire's taskers, this was getting silly.

The straw that broke the camel's back came from one of the lawyers representing the celebrity victims. Solicitor Mark Thomson had been beavering away in his small office in the Strand, bringing his legal expertise to bear to make the police let Mulcaire's victims see the files relevant to them. Fourteen months earlier it had been confirmed that his client Sienna Miller's name was in Mulcaire's files, and 5 months earlier he had asked for an order to make the police hand over Mulcaire's notes that related to her. Eventually, on 15th December, the 'top left' name of the person who tasked Mulcaire was revealed as being that of someone until then claimed to be blameless.

Who knows if the development was even mentioned when David Cameron and James Murdoch sat down to a cheery Christmas dinner at Rebekah Brooks's Cotswolds farmhouse a week later, but it cannot have been a very happy festive period for News International's lawyers. If ever the 'rogue reporter' defence took a body blow, this was it. The news meant the police had to change its position – this was unignorable, a point not missed by Keir Starmer, who could not allow the Met to ignore the mounting accusations. And News International now needed a new version of events. The previous one, involving a rogue reporter, had become laughable.

January 2011 brought another torrent of developments. The crown prosecution announced a comprehensive review of all the phone hacking material, following the Sienna Miller development. Andy Coulson resigned as David Cameron's director of communications, saying it was difficult to give his job its full attention. Operation Weeting was set up by the Met, under deputy assistant commissioner Sue Akers. It emerged that Gordon Brown and Tony Blair and their families were concerned that they had been victims of phone hacking and had asked police to investigate.

And News International came up with what the police had been waiting 4 years for. 'Significant new evidence', in the form of emails about Tessa Jowell and David Mills, Lord Frederick Windsor and an adviser to John Prescott, was handed over. This was a game-changer. Where previously the police had believed News International bosses, and later had had mounting scepticism, here at last was concrete proof that all the talk of rigorous investigations had been nonsense. News editor Ian Edmondson, suspended before Christmas, was sacked.

The steam train was now rolling, the police were desperate to make amends, and the handing over of the emails marked the unavoidable change in News International's position. The company had appointed new executives to handle the case, and a great many civil cases were settled in recognition of past wrongs. Quite where the blame lay remained a moot point, one the police were going to look into. In April, three executives were arrested under suspicion of unlawfully accessing voicemail messages, but that was just the start of the carnage.

For the police, though, there was a problem. News International had an automatic archiving system for email installed in 2005, but some executives had opted out of using it. So as it happened, very few of, for example, Rebekah Brooks's emails survived her time in some of the company's most senior chairs. Hardly any emails remained from the years 1999 to 2005. Nearly 4.5m emails from 2005 to 2010 were purged by News International as part of a routine clean-out in September 2010, but 1.49m had subsequently been recovered from other sources. Jurors also heard that Brooks' old hard drive from her office in Wapping had been removed before the computer was thrown away after an office move.

Further evidence had been emerging casting doubt on

the police's impartiality. John Yates, as we have seen, was a known friend of Neil Wallis. The *News of the World*'s former executive editor's name had not been mentioned in the context of the phone hacking scandal, and Yates saw little problem in their association. In early 2009 Wallis's daughter Amy had applied for a job working with the Met, and Yates forwarded her email of application to the head of the Met's human resources, saying Wallis had been a 'great friend' to the force. The boss of HR reportedly said she was keen to accommodate Ms Wallis 'particularly in the light of her father's position/relationship', although she later said she had no memory of having said that. Amy Wallis was given a 6 month contract and a more secure position subsequently. Though she was clearly talented, the proper procedures had not been followed. Again, this didn't look good. (Wallis was later to point out in mitigation that deputy commissioner Tim Godwin and Catherine Crawford chief executive of the Metropolitan Police Authority had requested work experience at News International for their children, which just compounded the sense of cosiness. He forgot to mention head of communications Dick Fedorcio's son doing work experience on the *Sun* in 2003 and 2004, and former Met commissioner Ian Blair's son doing the same in 2007).

Further inappropriateness came to light when it was revealed that Met commissioner Paul Stephenson, head of the Met, had an operation on a growth on his femur, and accepted an offer from a friend, Stephen Purdew, to stay at Champneys, a health farm in Hertfordshire, of which he was the managing director. The stay, which included considerable amounts of physiotherapy, was worth around £12,000. Stephenson reported that he had accepted it because he felt guilty at the amount of time he had taken off work, and wanted to speed up his recovery. The problem for Stephenson was that Neil Wallis was responsible for the spa's PR. By this time, Wallis had come to great prominence for his work at the *News of the World* and the police investigation was continuing. There was a clear conflict of interest.

The press made merry with the story, which was moving into the realms of hysteria. If as blameless and decent a figure as Paul Stephenson was seemingly 'on the take', was there no senior police officer who was not compromised in some way? Inside the Met, there was sympathy for Stephenson. A close family member had suffered a major bereavement, a former colleague points out, and there had never previously been any suspicion of impropriety against him. Indeed, he may be open to the charge of excessive honesty and even naivety. Courtesy of the *News of the World*, his Met colleague John Yates had enjoyed expensive meals at Scalini, Scotts and the Mandarin Oriental Hotel in London, which had helped enhance a developing caricature of high living at the Met. Other officers had also laid their work habits open to misinterpretation, so, knowing that there was increasing suspicion of the motives of some on his staff, Stephenson had brought in measures requiring them to declare anything that could look as if it created a conflict of interest. Thus by declaring his own recuperation at Champneys to the Metropolitan Police Authority, he sealed his own fate. Had he not declared it, he might still be in the job today. The fact that his declaration was publicly available, and that it took a while for the press to notice it, suggests somebody may have tipped a journalist off that it was there, but there is no evidence as to who, if anyone, that was.

On July 4th, The *Guardian* reported that Milly Dowler's voicemail had been hacked. This caused, as we have seen, the stratospheric development of the story. Previously the issue could be dismissed as being only of concern to whingeing celebrities and navel-gazing media types. Now it was about gross intrusion into a ghastly human tragedy. In the following fortnight David Cameron launched what became the Leveson enquiry, the *News of the World* closed down, Andy Coulson and Neil Wallis were arrested, the Murdochs dropped their bid to buy BSkyB, and Rebekah Brooks, Les Hinton, Met chief Paul Stephenson and Assistant Commissioner John Yates resigned.

Yet more mud was thrown at the Met when it was revealed after he left the *News of the World* in 2009, Neil Wallis was asked to submit a tender to Scotland Yard to offer PR advice for two days a week. One of the reasons the Met chose Wallis was that he would offer the Met access to Andy Coulson, and thus to his boss David Cameron, then regarded as likely to be in Downing Street after the election. At that point, as everyone was very quick to point out, Wallis appeared to be a spotless figure. Such doubts as there were were linked only to the fact of his being questioned by police, and those faded again once the matter was dropped.

When Paul Stephenson resigned, he spoke, seemingly, for many in the police, when he pointed out the curiosity of Cameron having appointed Andy Coulson to be his communications chief. The message was, if the PM, with all the back-up of the state at his disposal, had Ok'd Coulson, it was no surprise if others did so too.

Though Stephenson later denied having had a swipe at the Prime Minister, it was not an attack Cameron appreciated, later raising it with Stephenson in person, according to police sources. Cameron's remarks to the Leveson inquiry in 2012 were a reflection of a continuing frustration, one senses: 'Yes, I accepted [Coulson's] undertakings but so did a number of other organisations,' he said, citing the Culture Media Sports Select Committee, the police, the Press Complaints Commission and the jury in a perjury trial.' Even the Prime Minister was playing the blame game.

While some of the cases of unhealthily close links between police and press could be explained as arising from forgetfulness as to how it would look from outside, much less ambiguous instances were coming to light. As part of the supposed clean-up, cases of police officers (and other public servants) being paid for stories were emerging. A large network of 'coppers-on-the-take' had been built up, and News International, now desperate to be seen to be cleaning up its act, was throwing its sources, and some of its journalists, to the wolves. It was as different from the situation in 2008-9 as could be imagined. One Met officer, April Casburn, was sent to prison for offering information to a journalist on how the phone hacking investigation was proceeding. It could not have done more to blacken the police's name. The sense of an inept, complicit force was irresistible to many. Many careers have been ended by this story, some through the bad faith of certain individuals, some through incompetence, some through sheer naivety.

Among those accused of turning a blind eye was Craig Denholm. He was a detective chief superintendent in 2002 and was in charge of the search for missing schoolgirl Milly Dowler. As we have seen, Stewart Kuttner contacted the Surrey force and played them he had a recording of the message from the employment agency. The Independent Police Complaints Commission later said the Surrey force had been afflicted by 'collective amnesia' over the case. The search for Dowler had been led by Denholm, and the IPCC concluded that the *News of the World*'s accessing of the voicemails had been known about 'at all levels' and that it was 'hard to understand' how Denholm could have been unaware of it. While the search for Dowler would have been his main preoccupation at the time, Denholm did nothing subsequently to draw attention to the paper's interception of voicemails, let alone blow the whistle on it. 'Denholm had a chance to lift the lid on the whole thing, but didn't', says one former colleague of the Surrey man. If his silence in 2002 was understandable, his continued holding of his tongue as the investigations continued and while the police were known to be looking for evidence was remarkable for an upholder of the law. 'Denholm could and should have acted in 2002, 2006 and 2009. Heaven knows why he didn't', said a former colleague.

There is the key issue. It's fair to assume that most police were unaware about the possibility of listening in to voicemails. Those who did know probably concluded it wasn't a hanging offence, that they had a great many more important things to attend to and would never have imagined how widespread it was. So when they were reassured by News International people that nothing was amiss, they were relieved. People on whose side they thought they were said there was nothing in the story, and they were trusting enough to believe them. If, as Labour former minister Alan Johnson asserted, they were either 'evasive, dishonest or lethargic', the last of these seems most appropriate. There was dishonesty, in that clearly there were individual officers who were on the take from reporters, but the police is no monolith. That does not mean there was an institutional cover-up across the board by senior officers. In their case, the crime was being too busy and too trusting, a naivety that complemented the belief that 'it wasn't a story'. The case of Daniel Morgan's murder is appalling, but this case teaches us that before looking for a conspiracy, eliminate the cock-ups first, and there are plenty to choose from.

If there was a conspiracy, it was of a curiously British type, and a most almighty cock-up resulted. Having been alerted by the Palace to a possible national security issue, the police satisfied themselves that it was no such thing, more like an issue they regarded as being the responsibility of the press's regulatory authority ('we are not a trade regulator,' said a senior officer very early in the process.) As such, it was a serious one, but not sufficiently grave to require anything as alarmingly democratic as the Royal princes going into the witness box. In a spirit of deference, the issue needed to be both addressed and put to bed, and with minimal royal embarrassment, so when it became clear that Goodman and Mulcaire were willing to plead guilty, pretty well everyone was happy. Had more searching questions been asked, the taxpayer would have been spared having to fork out millions on Operations Weeting, Elvedon and Tuleta years later, and the Met would have been spared quite reasonable complaints, from within its own ranks and beyond, about the diversion of nearly 200 officers from the job of fighting 'real' crime.

11

Spooks

If the news gods wanted to ruin Glenn Mulcaire's children's school summer holidays, they could scarcely have planned anything more devastating than what happened on 4th July 2011. More than four years after he had been released from prison, and just as he felt he was re-emerging in the world of work, things had started to go wrong again, and often in inexplicable ways. A few days earlier, as the legal wheels continued to turn and more and more victims, often at the urging of a burgeoning group of lawyers, came forward to claim compensation, his former *News of the World* boss Greg Miskiw telephoned Mulcaire out of the blue. The pair had not been in touch for a year or so.

The *News of the World* was by now fighting an increasingly desperate battle to prevent the truth about the extent of the paper's lawlessness coming out. There was a huge amount at stake, so lawyers were being followed, witnesses watched, threats issued. Three executives had been arrested in recent weeks, and the picture looked bleak. Rebekah Brooks had been confronted with something pretty serious, too. On 23rd June 2011, she contacted her ex-husband Ross Kemp to say she needed to talk to him about phone hacking. She also asked her PA Cheryl Carter to find her notebooks from 2002 and 2003.

A few days after the 23rd came the call from Miskiw to Mulcaire. He was saying goodbye. He told Mulcaire that he had decided to go abroad, to Florida. Mulcaire didn't really know why he was going, but it was hardly a surprise. Whatever was coming next was not going to be good news. 'We will always be close. You're one of my top 6 best friends,' said Miskiw, who seemed to realise that clouds were gathering, but did not spell out in what form. Mulcaire says: 'It was a very odd phone call. I have replayed it in my mind a hundred times.' It was what Miskiw didn't say that made its mark on Mulcaire.

Within days, the *Guardian* had run the story saying that the *News of the World* had hacked and deleted Milly Dowler's phone messages, thereby encouraging her parents to believe she had picked up the messages and therefore was still alive. As the article effectively invited the reader to infer that Glenn Mulcaire was responsible, thus began the worst period of Mulcaire's adult life. The opprobrium he attracted as a result came in a deluge. He was as disreputable as it is possible to be. For a person whose self-image is of someone who tries to 'do the right thing', it was shattering.

We have seen how the story exploded from there. But looking back, Mulcaire wonders about that phone call from Miskiw. Had Miskiw known what was coming? He may have done, as he was presumably still in touch with people at News International. Mulcaire suspects Miskiw did know. 'If he did, to ring up and say "I'm one of your best friends" and not give me a heads up... I find that extraordinary,' says Mulcaire. 'Maybe he thought it would get out that he had told me, or that the conversation was being listened to, which I assumed. But if he had something to say, but couldn't spell it out, so we had to use some sort of code or subliminal message, he knew me well enough to know that I would be able to draw an inference. But he didn't.' That was the last time the pair spoke until a fruitless approach was made in the preparation of this book.

The Dowler claim, as we have seen, inflated and infected coverage of the phone hacking story for years, but the legal process ground on unrelentingly. More and more legal letters arrived at Mulcaire's house, telling him that another celebrity was demanding that he reveal who had tasked him to intercept their voicemails. Lawyers had long been including him in their claims, in the hope of putting pressure on him to give evidence against his former bosses. Though under enormous pressure of a different sort, he showed no signs of buckling. He had been advised to say nothing by his lawyers and, after a hiccup when Rupert Murdoch publicly expressed surprise that Mulcaire's fees were being paid by his company, his legal costs were covered (although he had to take legal action to ensure that). So indifferent did he become to the writs that he failed even to open most of the letters, throwing them on the floor and allowing them to pile up in the corner of the family's kitchen.

The Weeting Inquiry had been set up in January 2011, and the police – humiliated and uncomfortably conscious of the need to get it right this time – were trying to leave nothing to chance. A total of 185 officers were employed on the 3 operations (into phone hacking, illegal payments to public officials and computer hacking), at an expected cost of £40 million. Whereas previously the process of informing victims of phone hacking had been performed unenthusiastically and incompletely, this time no hostages were to be left. Eighteen months after its inception, deputy assistant commissioner Sue Akers, who ran the three Met investigations, said just over 1,000 likely victims of phone hacking had been identified, from an estimated 4,700 names in Mulcaire's files, rather fewer than initial estimates had suggested.

Many of the files were little more than hand-written scrawls of uncertain intent. The originals of those files were formally confiscated, so Mulcaire had no legal claim to them beyond that of any defendant in a criminal case. The vast majority of the entries contained personal details, the dissemination of which would breach the data protection laws. But lawyers representing victims were allowed access to digital images of the relevant pages, though often in redacted form. The court demanded Mulcaire only see them on a computer in his solicitor's office, but he persisted in calling them 'my files'. This, he insisted, was not out of a particular proprietorial feeling towards them, but because he said they would show his motivation and, in particular, who he was working for. Yet in many cases, he says, the 'top lefts' (the names of his tasker, usually written on the corner of the page) were absent, seemingly torn off, and some pages were missing entirely. He couldn't understand why.

When in December 2011 Mulcaire was arrested for the second time, it followed the awful claim that he had deleted a key voicemail message on Milly Dowler's phone. Having carried the can, with Clive Goodman, for the voicemail interceptions in 2007, he was horrified to have the issue brought up again. Yet since the story had exploded, the police had had an obligation to do the job properly this time, so, though he was annoyed, he was not entirely surprised. Once again, his house was raided. This time the police's arrival was even more invasive. They came back and took away the rest of his files, as if acknowledging that they should have taken them the first time.

Alison Mulcaire remembers the second raid being worse than the first. 'They wrecked Georgia's bedroom, and broke lots of glass. They picked up the bed and bashed it on the ground and were pulling stuff off the radiator. I was terrified, the girls were screaming. I thought it was some kind of a setup. The paperwork they had had a chance to take the first time had never been touched, so they looked at all the same stuff again. They were just nasty.'

A day or two later, she, who even at that late stage knew very little about her husband's work, was asked to come into the local police station on the following Monday. 'I remember crying from Friday till the Monday, worrying about what they are going to ask me. On the Sunday we had Sam's first communion, so it hung over that horribly.' She was asked, she says, 'the most ridiculous questions, like "were you the one in control of the phone hacking?", "Who was working under you?", "When did you first meet Rebekah Brooks?"'

This time, several more people at the *News of the World* had been arrested. The true story was to be given a chance to emerge, Mulcaire trusted. He had always said that he had acted for the greater good, but felt he had had little opportunity to explain himself. In the context of the Dowler claim, this time, at least, he believed he would get a chance to spell out his position.

Conversely, though, a different legal tack was being pursued. Nicola Phillips, former assistant to Max Clifford, was pursuing her case against Mulcaire and News International, and was demanding to know who had commissioned Mulcaire's work. Although he wanted to spell out his position, he was being advised by his lawyers not to do so, on the grounds that he was not obliged to self-incriminate. It was a finely balanced decision, but in the end he followed his lawyers' advice and fought the case as far as the Supreme Court, opting not to reveal the names. He did this partly in the belief that that way, at least, he would avoid being charged a second time.

But in July 2012 the Supreme Court came to its decision, and Mulcaire lost. He was to be forced to reveal who had ordered him to intercept voice messages. This was the decision that Mark Lewis and a string of other lawyers had been hoping for. And only a few days later, on 24th July, the Crown Prosecution Service announced that he would have to return to court, to face charges relating to Charles Clarke, Andy Gilchrist, Delia Smith and, crucially, Milly Dowler.

During his three interviews with the police in May 2013, he had spelt out his 'belief system'. He told them how he believed the *News of the World* was working hand-in-glove with the police. While this does not reach the statute's narrow definition of explicitly stated 'lawful authority' through an 'empowering belief', it illustrates Mulcaire's fierce conviction of his motives that were internationally trashed when the Dowler allegation was first made in 2011. If there was an explicit authorisation on the part of the police, it has still not been uncovered.

His critics might doubt his motives where snooping on celebrities is concerned. But nobody could doubt the force, the self-belief and the humanity with which he speaks of crime against the young and innocent.

In one statement to the police, Mulcaire speaks of having been given information about a possible suspect: 'I was given information, led to believe he was in custody, to find out information about him, between the eyes…. To make sure that he could be clear on certain dates and my information on my notes will confirm that. So that's where we're at regarding lawful authority and it was more than evident in my corner work, it was more than evident on my Project Dowler in the notes saying 'Tell the Police' you know, you can't, there can't be any other key points that I can put on that piece of paper in regards to what I believed at the time. My mission statement at the time was to find that little girl as quickly as possible.'

By the third interview, he felt he was getting somewhere, that the police were coming to understand his point of view. A detective inspector, previously absent, joined the interviewers. One officer, Emma King of the Weeting investigation, in particular, seemed to 'get it', he felt. He was also treated rather more accommodatingly than before, with a 'where would you like to sit, Glenn?'

But for his lawyers, his stated motives were not enough to provide a defence in the eyes of the law. When it came to confronting the legal hazards ahead of him, he was advised to plead guilty on all counts. He admitted he had hacked the celebrities' phones but insisted unshakeably that his work on the Dowler case was done with good intentions. When it came to pleading on this charge, he played his cards close to his chest.

> I wasn't sure who I could trust during that court process and didn't even tell my lawyers how I was going to plead. I wanted to have my say in court, and was prepared to go all the way down the line and plead not guilty on conspiracy. I wanted to call key witnesses and paperwork to explain why I believed I was doing it on behalf of the law. It was not like the three other charges, which were celebrity-based and I felt fell into a different category. I wanted to explain in court why I thought I was acting with police agreement.

He pleaded guilty to the interception of celebrities' phones, and that of Dowler, but he refused to admit guilt to 'conspiracy' on the Dowler charge, as mentioned earlier. In his mind, the connotation of a conspiracy was sinister and based on bad faith. By pleading 'not guilty' he hoped he would have his day in court. That way, he believed, he would be able to explain to the judge why he had done what he did, and how he had always told the truth during legal proceedings.

But he never got his chance to explain himself in court. Others against whom the charge was laid pleaded guilty, but when he refused to do so, the charge against him was dropped. His fox was shot. So instead of throwing himself on the mercy of the court, he is now reliant on his own efforts, supported by the documents taken from his home in the 2 raids.

To someone who is not familiar with Mulcaire's notes, there is no way of knowing what documents are missing.

There is no index, and the sheets of paper were only ever written *ad hoc* and for his own use. There was no filing system that would identify any gaps. But Mulcaire is certain that files are missing and wants to know why. In some cases he thinks he knows, but he does not want to speculate or point fingers without hard evidence. In one case in particular his wife Alison confirms his account, having seen the originals herself.

The police have acknowledged that some individuals' files – around 20 according to one estimate – were held back for 'operational reasons'. This term relates to files on people still of interest to the police, and, to speculate, may include taskings on terrorists or paedophiles, the largest two categories that fell within his early 'Special Investigations' work for *News of the World*.

But among the most startling absences are files relating to the Milly Dowler case. In his remarks at the end of the trial, Mr Justice Saunders rejected the idea that Mulcaire had been working on behalf of the police. He said: "Mulcaire knew perfectly well that he was hacking Milly's phone to assist the News of the World to obtain a story by finding her." He went on to say he did not intend to hear evidence on the issue of whether Mulcaire was assisting the police because he was "quite satisfied that it is incapable of belief". Some on Mulcaire's team took these remarks, made on the day of sentencing, to signal the fact that he was to receive a suspended sentence, as if to offset any criticism that Mulcaire was being let off lightly. In any event, he was indeed given a suspended sentence.

As the judge suggested, he had not seen all the evidence on this, but it seems very few people have. Mulcaire insists, and is supported by his wife Alison, that a handful of sheets, with a 'top left' name on it, are missing, and that one or more of those sheets bear the name of a third tasker, whose role in the affair he believes to be crucial. That person cannot be named for legal reasons, but Mulcaire insists a whole new chapter to the story will emanate from that document, if it is ever made public. He has given that name to the police, and he sees no reason why it should not be made public once any necessary legal processes have been exhausted. The fact that Neville Thurlbeck, through his barrister, called Mulcaire's claim 'intrinsically ridiculous' seemed merely to strengthen Mulcaire's belief. More significant, he says, was the silence of Greg Miskiw on the matter.

There are other files that are equally perplexing. The deployment of Mulcaire to look into the royal princes' relationship with Guy Pelly, a gregarious student at Cirencester agricultural college, is one. The Queen is said to have told former butler Paul Burrell that 'there are forces at work in this country about which we have no knowledge'. For those, like Her Majesty, who detect a sinister hand, and who heard references at the Old Bailey to mysterious representatives of the secret state, Pelly's story has plenty to offer.

It is well known that what started the phone hacking scandal was a complaint by Prince William that he suspected unlawful means were being used to acquire stories about him. A blunder by the *News of the World* made it obvious to the Prince that they had written about an event 'before the story had even left the room'. What is more easily forgotten is how the *News of the World* had been targeting him and his friends for some years. The young princes had every reason to loathe the press after the high-speed chase and death of their mother in Paris in 1997, and in subsequent years they appear to have indulged themselves extensively. In February 2000 the *Sunday Times* reported that royal bodyguards were becoming increasingly concerned about drug use by people who hang around the Prince. Elsewhere there was a story about Tom Parker Bowles, son of Camilla, having been caught taking cocaine. Helpfully 'a family friend' was reported as saying: '[Prince Charles] is happy that his son is wise enough to know how to keep away from such things.' 'Family friends' tend to pop up when potentially damaging stories are being sanitised with the help of expert press handling.

But the extensive bacchanalia at the Rattlebone pub in Sherston, Gloucestershire, just 5 miles from Highgrove, was enough to set tongues wagging, whatever else may have been going on in Wapping. The story wouldn't go away, and kept getting that bit closer to the throne itself. A story by Mazher Mahmood and Clive Goodman said that Prince Harry was using cannabis, and that his father was shocked at how often he did so. Guy Pelly, a friend of Prince Harry since prep school, was singled out as being a bad influence, and was named as being the person 'who introduced Harry to cannabis in June [2001]', reported a well-placed source. The same family friend explained how seriously Prince Charles took the matter, and how his sons were 'on their guard against such a thing ever being allowed to happen again.'

Further drugs exposés were run in January and February 2002. Attempts were made in senior circles to isolate Pelly. Mark Bolland, Prince Charles's deputy private secretary, managed to defuse the worst aspects of the story while painting the Prince in a benign and sagacious light. The Press Complaints Commission obligingly agreed that the matter was 'an exceptional matter of public interest', so there was no unpleasant talk about anybody's privacy being invaded.

Just the engineering of the story and its impact said plenty about powerful forces. Mark Bolland was the partner of Guy Black, head of the Press Complaints Commission. The pair took occasional holidays with Rebekah Brooks, then at the helm of the *News of the World*, and in 2006 she was to be a witness at the couple's civil partnership ceremony.

The fly in this agreeable ointment was that the Princes were quite happy jogging along as before. Indeed, Pelly was lodged at Highgrove the weekend the *News of the World*'s story appeared, and the princes were photographed 'shoulder to shoulder with shamed pal Pelly in a brave show of support at Twickenham'. The pictures enabled the princes to talk of the importance of loyalty to friends, and once again for Prince Charles to emerge as a beacon of regal magnanimity. It also became apparent that Pelly had in fact been in Australia when much of the naughtiness took place, and his supporters are proud to point out that his lawyers had all the allegations against him withdrawn.

The sense remained – and remains – that somebody had been trying to put some distance between the princes and Pelly. Pelly was regarded as bad news, rightly or wrongly, and Palace insiders, far from being scandalised by the intrusiveness of the press (on this occasion at least), show few signs of regretting the matter having been brought to a head. If he was targeted, was it by somebody at the Palace (or thereabouts, though not Bolland, it should be emphasised) feeding dirt to the press for them to 'stumble on'? There is some evidence, as we shall see below, to encourage that view. Or, less sinisterly, was it simply a matter of the Princes' media handlers making the best of a difficult news story that had emerged after a great many local rumours and some assiduous sleuthing (which included voicemail interceptions)?

Mulcaire worked extensively on the story of the princes' supposedly wild friend, and when Pelly took legal action against the *News of the World* some years later, Mulcaire's records had to be handed over. On the files it became apparent that Mulcaire had targeted Pelly and many of those close to him. The legal papers on Pelly's behalf claimed Mulcaire 'recorded in his notes that [Pelly] had an MI5 profile', concluding that 'this information was obtained unlawfully by the Defendants'. Those familiar with royal protocol express surprise at this: if there was a concern about those in the princes' circle, surely it would appear on a police (royal protection) file, rather than an MI5 file? But someone familiar with the episode (neither Mulcaire nor anyone in Pelly's camp) insists that it was indeed an MI5 file.

News International's response to this is revealing. Its press officer said there was no reason to think that 'Mulcaire or *News of the World* had access to MI5 files'. She also said the company's interpretation of the evidence was that Mr Mulcaire found out about the MI5 profile from a hacked phone message, a version of events consistent with the prevailing narrative.

Though News International's response seems to

encourage this view, it would surely be highly surprising, bizarre, even, for MI5 to be so casual as to leave a mention of Pelly's file on a voicemail message, ripe for any techno-savvy snooper to pick up.

This leaves a third option, that there was someone supplying information, presumably either for money or because they believed the public ought to be told.

Mulcaire says that the top page of the relevant Pelly file is missing from those he has seen, but he is pretty sure he was tasked on that project by one of his regular taskers. His memory of the case is not good, but he says it doesn't surprise him that there was a reference to such a file in the *New York Times*'s story that revealed it in October 2011. It was not his job to filter out which jobs he was to do, and which not. He was under contract and trusted his employers to act responsibly. If information had come in from the security services or the police for him to work on, that was a matter for them.

Does he agree that his work might, wittingly or unwittingly, have been prompted by MI5? Given what he calls his 'belief structure' as to what he was doing, he remains confident of his ground, without feeling able to go into details. If the security services had some involvement, was it official or unofficial? In other words, was it the work of a 'rogue', to coin an unfortunate phrase in the context, or did the revelations about Pelly have some sanction from above? Mulcaire, whose own attitudes have little truck with drug-taking, will not be drawn. Speaking more generally, he says simply: 'It wasn't unusual for MI5 to initiate an exercise on people... there were times when a bad press was needed to move things on. It was known as a black project.' So did he know, or have suspicions, at the time that he might have been helping blacken someone's name in the interests of the royal family? He would not comment.

Some believed that the story which exposed Max Mosley's sado-masochistic tastes was delivered with an MI5 postcode, as it were. Mosley, when President of the body that runs Formula 1, used to pay for sex parties, and the husband of one of the participants alerted Neville Thurlbeck to the story possibilities. It was arranged that she would film their next encounter, complete with German overtones, and on 30th March 2008 a story headlined 'F1 Boss has Sick Nazi Orgy with Five Hookers – Son of Hitler-loving fascist in sex shame'. What followed has been well documented, and Mosley said the orgies lacked the Nazi theme that the *News of the World* had claimed. He was expected to slink off, humiliated and embarrassed at the intimate details that were revealed of his preferences. But he took his breach of privacy claim way beyond what had been expected by lawyers, who had hoped a sense of dignity would get the better of his indignation.

Was this brought about by MI5? Probably not, although there are many in motor racing circles who believe Mosley was targeted. Mosley is thought to believe that the motive was money, having identified the individual concerned, although he does not rule out one of Thurlbeck's MI5 contacts having told him of Mosley's tastes. Mulcaire later did some work for Mosley under the umbrella of Quest, a large security company for whom Lord Stevens now works, too.

For a journalist, the world of the private investigator is a nightmare to get involved in. Mulcaire counters that the world of journalism is a snake pit and that nobody can be trusted. Mulcaire's world is one of tradecraft, suspicion and constant security checks. He's inclined to launch into a lighthearted riff on what deviousness those he is in conversation with might be up to. Unprompted, he will make jocular accusations about secret cameras and listening devices. The tone is always jokey, but it suggests a man who finds relaxing difficult outside the company of family and close friends.

Having been blocked in his attempt to make it into 14th Inc Duke of York, as related earlier, he immersed himself in a number of courses, while getting a toehold in the world of tracing and surveillance. There is no corroboration for the following story, but it is very much part of the Mulcaire narrative. Nonetheless, it is very much part of the Mulcaire narrative. When he went for an interview at Worldwide Investigations in the early 1990s, he was told it was due was to start imminently, requiring him to take a cab to get there on time. The cab driver struck up a probing conversation, which Mulcaire believes was a test of his discretion. Having reached the chambers, he realised there had been no tearing rush after all, but felt he was being closely observed. He met a series of people, before meeting the boss, a distinguished-looking and evidently well-travelled former police and military figure called Steve Rowlands, who asked him to start the following Monday.

Is this the delusion of a hyper-wary wannabe James Bond, or was this the first time he came on the eager and public-spirited young security services' radar? If so, did it lead to anything?

Mulcaire's reluctance to be drawn invites speculation, but he will not provide answers. By the 1990s, as we have seen, he had done a good deal of work for Argen and Worldwide Investigations. These companies were useful to the security services, being quick, discreet and cheaper than maintaining investigators on staff when there was insufficient work to justify their salaries. So occasional checks, tracing and background profile work would be parcelled out.

Once Mulcaire joined the *News of the World*, he expected to be helping fill its pages with the paper's traditional fare. He did that, but frequently, while doing work for the investigations unit, he was also asked to provide 'profiling' information on a number of people under suspicion of having terrorist sympathies, seemingly which the police needed doing. Very often, no story would appear in the paper, but Mulcaire would be confident that his handler, usually Greg Miskiw, would have found a mutually beneficial home for whatever nuggets he had been able to find. Mulcaire did not see it as his place to ask what the information was wanted for.

There appear to be just under a hundred names of people on whom he was asked to perform some sort of search and about whom no story appeared in the *News of the World*. Many of the names in the files are Arab-sounding, and include men who have since gone to prison for terrorist offences. Some, it is clear to those who see the entries, were tasked by his customary handlers at the *News of the World*, or the tasking corner is missing. There are other files, says Mulcaire, that have been retained by the police and which, Mulcaire says, also relate to serious crime. When asked about the tasking on those files, he is not forthcoming but says simply that he wants to see the originals.

Mulcaire's belief is that his bosses on the paper were often using the information he provided to 'grease the wheels', to help provide the police with information they could not easily acquire otherwise, which could be swapped or bartered for information about stories for the paper. It is not hard to imagine how such a relationship might build up. If an investigator can tell the police that Suspect A, previously on their radar but now missing, was now living at such and such an address, that information is invaluable. If the police believe the source is credible, he or she is unlikely to doubt its reliability, nor be needlessly officious about how the information was acquired. If noble ends ever call for questionable or unorthodox means, surely this was a harmless enough. And, best of all, it was free from the scrutiny of pesky journalists. In any case, rightly or wrongly, it could probably be denied without any comeback. If a terrorist was thus more likely to be put behind bars, so be it. All parties could happily consign themselves to the side of the angels.

Thus was Mulcaire happy to feel he was doing his bit to help confront antisocial elements. He didn't ask where his information was going, but the known links between the police and News International suggested they were on the same side. On that score, if he felt he was working for the security services, albeit at one remove and deniably, that may be correct.

One case possibly in this category is what he calls the Etch-a-Sketch story. He was in the car, near their home in Cheam, with his wife, and received a call from Greg

Miskiw. He wanted him to drop everything as he had an urgent job. Mulcaire explained that he was driving and couldn't stop, but he asked Alison to write down the details of what needed doing on the nearest thing to hand, an Etch-a-Sketch board. The details, Alison remembers, were of someone with an Arab-sounding name, which she dutifully wrote down. The pair returned home and Mulcaire got down to work, transferring onto note pads and logging the details, later calling Miskiw with the details of the man's whereabouts. The man's arrest was on the television news that evening.

It was suggested during the 2014 trial that there might be some significance to the fact that Andy Coulson had been reassured that Goodman and Mulcaire would not be sent to prison. According to Goodman, Coulson had understood from 'the police or the Home Office' less than a week after the arrests that there was no desire to press for a prison sentence as long as Goodman pleaded guilty'.

Coulson wanted Goodman to plead guilty, so this may have coloured his reporting of what he had been told, but those of a conspiratorial cast of mind may be delighted by the thought of Mulcaire and Goodman being given preferential treatment. Rather more disappointing to them will be the fact that they didn't get it, and went to prison.

Mulcaire's claim to exceptional levels of access to people's phones is the subject of much fascination among those in the investigators' profession. One former *News of the World* employee said that when he was said to be able to divine someone's PIN number, in fact he couldn't. (And of the few people would could, they did not generally include those who answer calls for phone providers.) They claimed that, some years ago, what he did was call the phone provider (posing as an employee of the company) and get them to reset the PIN number to the factory setting. This would then allow him to get into the phone and reset the PIN number to a setting of his own choice, which he would then pass off as the one the target had been using all along. It requires a degree of skill and deviousness, but is not the awe-inspiring trick of great repute in some circles.

However, more recently it has been said that Mulcaire did acquire the ability to obtain PIN numbers. These numbers are 'double encrypted', and, by repute at least, the only people who have that capability are the security services. Again, this is an aspect of tradecraft he prefers not to discuss.

Mulcaire's ability to obtain what was previously thought unobtainable made him ripe for exploitation in a cash-rich environment like the *News of the World*. The need to both pay and protect sources offered cover for all sorts of abuse (and a great deal of conspiratorial nose-tapping), much of which may never be accounted for. It was precisely the sort of thing that the management had been trying to clamp down on, though of course not at the cost of alienating a genuine source. One such case, possibly, was the occasion referred to in court during the evidence of Stuart Kuttner, the *News of the World*'s managing editor, when he wrote a memo to himself about a meeting he had at the home of Clive Goodman, the royal reporter, two days after Goodman's 2006 arrest. The note says 'Glen [*sic*] approached CG & intro CG to senior "spook"…. sd [?] leftovers from SIS bugging.'

The note continues: 'Told Andy this from the start.' Kuttner was questioned about this, and asked: 'Obviously this "spook" would be committing crime by handing over intercepts?' Kuttner agreed, 'assuming there is some validity to this'. He went to on to say that in his experience Goodman, with whom he was said not to have good relations for some years, was inclined to embellish, a line used on several occasions by some of those on trial. Andy Coulson was asked in court about the matter. On a day when his memory was evidently below par, he said he was sure he would have remembered such a development, and that he would have told Goodman 'that is the best story you have ever had'.

Goodman told the court that Mulcaire had said some of the royal phone information he had acquired 'was a by-product of information gained by the security services but I have no way of knowing if this was true.' Goodman said Mulcaire had introduced him to someone he said was a 'serving spook' but as far as he knew 'it could have been his next door neighbour'.

Mulcaire refuses to give the name of this mystery person, but a smile comes to his face at the mention of it. When challenged about his identity, and told that it was fundamental to the relationship on which the book is written, Mulcaire agreed to talk about that person's identity on condition that he was not named here. There is a need for natural discretion here, but this journalist can confirm he has little reason to believe there has been a breach of the Official Secrets Act.

So what was the point of the meeting? Was it to convince Goodman of the brilliant quality of Mulcaire's contacts, in order to get yet more cash out of the office?No, says Mulcaire, who repeats that he signed for all his cash payments. On the 'senior spook', he says, as he has said many times, that he was worried Clive Goodman did not appreciate the seriousness of listening in on royal household voicemails, and that the meeting was intended to remind Goodman that he should be aware of the risks they were taking. He hoped it would also help Goodman 'regain his place at the top table', which would enable both of them – fearful for their jobs – to know better what the bosses were thinking.

Another such example came from Sean Hoare, who spoke to the indefatigable Jo Becker of the *New York Times*, who wrote many stories about the affair. In one, when he was trying to locate someone for a story, he told of how he came across 'pinging'. He approached Greg Miskiw, gave him the cellphone number of the person in question and was amazed when Miskiw returned later with the person's precise location, in Scotland. The cost of this service was about £500 a time. Hoare asked how he got the answer, to which Miskiw replied 'It's the old bill, isn't it?' 'At that point you don't asked questions,' said Hoare.

Mulcaire laughs at the idea that it was the police. 'I'm not saying who it was, but I can tell you it wasn't the police!' Somewhere along the line, somebody was doing well financially out of pinging. Mulcaire insists he was not a beneficiary, because he always signed a chit for every payment he received. So, if there were ghosts in the machine, at least some of them must have had bulging wallets.

12

Postcript

As was mentioned at the beginning, this book has sought to shed a little light on 'how we got here'. There remain a great many unanswered questions, to do with Milly Dowler and the 'false hope' moment, the extent of the missing Mulcaire files, the precise chain of command at the *News of the World*, the degree of official complicity with the paper's unlawful means, and doubtless more will emerge that relates to other forms of information-gathering (computer hacking, bank fraud, payment to public officials and so on) that this book has not been able to examine.

To be continued....

Author's Note

Writing about phone hacking and press regulation has become absurdly polarised, and given the customary pieties about the importance of a vigorous, rumbustious free press, it is surprising how little interest there seems to be in finding common ground in the middle. This book was not meant to throw stones at anyone, but it is clear something went badly wrong, and I write as someone who can't imagine not being a journalist. Justice John Saunders put the legal side in the Coulson sentencing on 4 July 2014: 'There is a certain irony in seeing journalists, who have shed light in dark corners and forced others to reveal the truth, being unprepared to do the same for their own profession.'

From the time when I was first scandalised and fascinated by some news methods, many have patiently indulged me on the subject and I owe them a great deal. There are countless people involved in the story who (if not named may recognise themselves in the text) are owed huge thanks. Lack of space, a vague stab at discretion and a fear of forgetting someone gives me a lame excuse for not naming them here, but Francis Elliott, John Mullin, Lisa Markwell, Heather Holden-Brown, Matthew Norman and Mary-Ellen Field have all given generously and paid heavily. The degree to which they inwardly rolled their eyes at my latest rant varied, but all were unfailingly polite and constructive. Thanks are also due to Martin Rynja of Gibson Square for believing in what this project was trying to do. Most thanks of all are due to my family, who have suffered considerably during the writing of this book and whose generous and entertaining support I do not begin to deserve.

I have always been keen to write a book on phone hacking, even if only for cathartic reasons. But, where were the publishers, hammering on Glenn Mulcaire's door? There were precious few. There are limits to how much a passing public interest can be exploited in a book, and in the eyes of most in the book trade, Mulcaire was beyond it. 'Good subject,' one eminent publisher told me, 'not sure there's a book in it.' And when told such a book would contain the testimony of the man at the centre of the storm, the disdain grew greater still. Mulcaire, after all, was the person accused of deleting the voicemails of a kidnapped schoolgirl, giving her unimaginably distressed parents a cruel moment of false hope. He had not just done it once or twice. His job had been invading the privacy of thousands of people, all for private gain. This was inexcusable. He may be telling the truth, but who says he deserves to be listened to?

I have had plenty of moments of thinking the same thing myself. How could I team up with someone so monstrous, someone for whom law-breaking was casual?

Graham Johnson, a former *News of the World* reporter, wrote about his relationship with the law in his book *Hack*: 'I never stopped to think if any of this was illegal. To tell you the truth, I didn't care. There was a definite feeling that we, the *News of the World*, were above the law, and that we could do anything we wanted. Who was going to turn us over? No one. Why? Because that was our job. We turned people over, not the other way round.' What is to be gained by allowing a criminal to recount the whys and wherefores of his inexcusable behaviour?

Quite a lot, I concluded. To seek to explain is not to justify. He was the man charged with these tasks. Having served his time, he is in a better position than most to understand the motivation of many of those involved. How could so many experienced journalists lose all sense of judgment and publish stories that with hindsight seem bound to have brought them discredit. Johnson also wrote that 'reporters and editors began to build personal fiefdoms based on their access to inquiry agents. The types of personality that the *News of the World* attracted were greedy for power and status; once they realised PIs were an instant fix the phenomenon created a kind of arms race to see who could get the ones that would break the law further and faster.' If one such person was prepared to talk to me, great.

And there were so many other questions. How (or perhaps why) did the police come to ignore so many clues? Who knew what was going on? Mulcaire was also in a position to offer a corrective to a version of events that, still, after eight years, offers little that is definitive. His version would be partial, of course, but of all the participants bar Clive Goodman, it was less likely than anyone's to be coloured by the threat of a spell at Her Majesty's Pleasure.

And besides, Mulcaire is an interesting personality. My profession is surely about more than writing people off as cardboard low-lifers, toffs, fat cats, six-times-a-night lotharios, killer bimbos and love rats. There might just be some light and shade. In a story as big as this, shouldn't that be brought out? He is a private investigator, not a journalist. While part of him is the dutiful professional who does what his patron pays for ('at heart, I'm a loyal dog', he has said), another part of him sees his exceptional sharp-wittedness being used for the public good. He is not short of self-belief and can be impetuous. His early years are characterised by schoolboy mischief, but also consistent acts of humanity and public-spiritedness. His mother's greatest upset was on hearing the judge denounce him in 2007 for telling lies. Even aiming off for a mother's blind loyalty, surely there was at very least an interesting human study here and more than likely a great deal more. As someone famously said in a very different context, where did it all go wrong?

But most importantly, I believed in his anger. If this was a con, the grandest blag of all, it was an astonishing performance. It did not look bogus to me, and although he had clearly done a great many things he shouldn't have done, his sense of justice had been affronted. Even if he was a cold-blooded, dark-hearted crook (which didn't seem to me the case), he had been dumped upon mightily by his bosses. He and Goodman had carried the can, and nobody believed they were solely responsible.

On one occasion, in front of his wife Alison, I put to him a suggestion that I had heard, that he had been offered an enormous bonus for finding an abducted child. He exploded. He turned to his wife and said 'Have I ever mentioned that? Has it ever occurred to you that might be true? I can't believe that... I can't believe it. How low will they go? I want to know who put that about! I want to know! That is disgusting.' It all but ruined the evening. He was visibly upset for about half an hour, constantly returning to the claim. I could not tell him who had passed this on, but when I went back to my source I had no sense there was any substance to it. Libelling Glenn Mulcaire was a free-for-all. I quite fancied kicking the tyres on some of those tales about him.

This was complicated. Two wrongs do not make a right and criminals are forever falling out, arguing and getting into an escalating whirl of complaint and counter-complaint. But this wasn't like that. Glenn held certain individuals responsible for what had happened, but even though he has been on the financial breadline for years, he didn't seem to have it in for them personally. There was no talk of retribution in dark car parks, settling scores and so on. Of course he was furious about what had been done to him and, strikingly, to his family, his anger was more with the corruption of abstract ideas, like loyalty, the truth, the greater good, a notion he constantly returned to. The morally irretrievable criminal mastermind that News International had wanted us to believe him to be had a confoundingly well-developed sense of right and wrong. This was no Ronnie Biggs indifferently flicking v-signs to the world. A crook, a cynic, simply wouldn't bother with being angry. He would have moved on to become a burglar, a computer fraudster or an identity thief, and Mulcaire, with his capacity for dissimulation, would be in a position to do that with some success. But he insisted he wanted his own position explained and the world put to rights.

There were plenty of people who wanted to write him

off as a fantasist, a wannabe Johnny English and an out of control hoodlum. But few fantasists (etc) are paid over £100,000 a year. So who is he?

This not a book for the insider particularly, or for techies wanting to understand the finer points of how cellular phone masts work. Because there are so many sensitivities at stake, there are more unattributed quotes than I would like, and many participants in the story were unavailable to corroborate parts of it, having failed to answer calls, letters or emails. Nothing should be inferred from the non-naming of some of those who worked with Mulcaire, even if they have already been convicted. This is done to avoid creating legal problems of identification in case others are charged in the future.

The last resort of the scoundrel is to say 'trust me', but I will just have to ask the reader to trust me that the quotes are used honestly and because, I hope, they represent a view of the truth. The mistakes, of course are mine, and if I have been unfair or credulous towards anyone, that too is my fault. But this book is an attempt, aimed at anyone who might be interested, to explain how we got here. There will be plenty of unanswered questions, and those without a degree in psychology may be left as baffled as I am by the performance of some of the participants. It is in part a study in deniability, a look at how one person's work, the consequence of which was read by millions, was supposedly not known about by anyone. When Mulcaire was caught an entire corporation just shrugged and said 'Not me, guv'. It was a ludicrous denying of responsibility.

The writing of this book has been an education. I have learned things about my trade that I didn't know, and which its regulators certainly didn't know. I have also learned that Glenn Mulcaire is a proud man. Once or twice I tried to remember what he had said about something, and checked with him the next day to be sure I hadn't mis-remembered. On one occasion I put the words 'I wince at some of the things I did' into his mouth. He did not 'wince' at all, he told me. No, no, no. He did what he did, and most of the things he did were a source of great pride. If a journalist misused information that he had provided, that was a matter for the journalist's conscience. I suggested that he needed to earn the right to be listened to, such were the crimes of which he was accused, and that surely his only defensible position would be to express contrition. As this book seeks to show, sometimes he did, sometimes he didn't. But most evident of all, to my disap-pointment, is his mistrust of many journalists. How can they live with themselves, he would ask? How could they endanger a child's life for the sake of getting the story before a competitor? And how could a journalist be so driven as to be the cause of him going to prison?

'If journalists got me into this mess, maybe it needs a journalist to get me out,' he has said more than once. This book does not seek to get anyone out of any mess, nor does it seek to excuse. All it can do is offer the man a fair hearing. This is his platform.

Neither Glenn Mulcaire nor his family has received any financial benefit for their cooperation with this book.
Where surnames changed over time, the current name is used throughout: Rebekah Brooks (rather than Wade) Kimberly Fortier (rather than Quinn).

Appendix

'In a way I don't care what is in this book,' Mulcaire has said several times. 'What I want most of all is that people know I do not have a dark heart, that people know why I did what I did over Milly Dowler. What I was accused of would have finished off many people. I can't stand the idea that people think I could have done what I was accused of.'

So long has Mulcaire remained silent that it is tempting to expect that when he does express himself, it will be about how he had to carry the can while others got off scot-free. That situation has now changed, of course, because others have been called to account. But while frustration remains at previous claims that no one knew what he was up to, the wound he feels over the Dowler accusation, that he caused the notorious 'false hope' moment, is deep. He returns to it constantly. It caused illness in his family, endless heartache at home and resulted in his name, hardly spotless, being blackened yet further.

His lawyer Sarah Webb drafted a statement on his behalf, which he authorised, apologising to the Dowler parents, but he wishes he had used different words. He would have liked to have explained what he believed at the time, and above all wants to do so now. His words are those of a proud man injured.

'It is the elephant in the room,' he says. 'I know a lot of people have moved on and want to talk about other things, but I want people to know what was really going on there. When the Dowler thing happened, people who hardly knew me but knew about me and what sort of family I have came up to me and asked if I was ok... some people said "this isn't right, doesn't sound right". I went and played football alone with my son when I was being called every name under the sun... it's very hard to forgive that and what was done to me.'

The truth is that Mulcaire *did* intercept Milly Dowler's voicemails. He pleaded guilty to doing so, but his plea was that, to use the legal term, he had an 'empowering belief' that, having been given the number, he was doing so on behalf of the police. And by general agreement, confirmed by the judge in the 2013/14 trial, he first listened to the voicemails over a fortnight after the false hope moment, having not been tasked till then. His frustration lies in the idea that he could have been so inept as to delete a message and thus cause such distress, and that his motives in intercepting the voicemail was motivated by the kind of 'trophy hunting' that can afflict journalists.

His fondness for journalism as a profession is minimal. Those who come fresh to journalism are often shocked by the strength of the rivalry between newspapers. Some stories are of interest to the public because of their human component, like, for example, the abduction of a child. For newspapers, that fact is a given. Their job is to provide added value, to cover the story better than their competitors, every day to outdo the other side. Usually this is for the benefit some common purpose, like the finding of a missing child, in good health, akin to members of the public combing a field in parallel, united by a common goal. Such rivalry between media outlets tends to be harmless (or peevish as when the *Sun* and *News of the World* refused to offer a reward together), but not always. In the case of Milly Dowler, in 2014 the judge said this 'unforgivable' decision to withhold that information could have placed Dowler in 'avoidable danger'. 'We are human beings first' is a line journalists could do with bearing in mind.

Mulcaire is scandalised when that line is crossed. 'I don't know how some journalists can live with themselves,' he says. 'What about ringing up an agency pretending to be Bob Dowler, or Sally Dowler? It's outrageous. Impersonating, in hindsight, a dead girl's mother? I hacked Jade Goody's phone in 2001/2, but way before she contracted cancer. They put me and her together, and said I'd done it when she had cancer. Anyone who knows me knows I would never do a thing like that.' He also expresses frustration at the conflating intrusion into the health of Gordon Brown's family – by others – with his own work. 'The only thing I did in the case of Gordon Brown was to get addresses and do background checks. The story about his son and cystic fibrosis appeared in the *Sun* in late 2006 and was nothing to do with me. In any case, I had been arrested by then and wasn't working. In fact, I wasn't in any communication with anyone, apart from the odd one from Greg, with suggestions about legal matters, and from Neville with his "helpful" advice to get out of town. Cheeky bastard.'

Doesn't blagging require a degree of dishonesty, so that in effect you were, to put it crudely, a professional liar? How do you feel about that?

'That's just bread and butter, doing my job. There is a difference between merely telling the truth and actively seeking it out. And there are occasions when lying is the only way to find out the truth. I am not ashamed to say that, and it seems to me a defensible code. But I wouldn't impersonate one of the Dowler family. I'd find a million other ways of doing it rather than that. People have pretended that's all right. When a child goes missing you just drop everything. The law doesn't really come into your thinking, or I'm not sure it should. I assumed the police had done all sorts of checks when I was asked to look into it, but I was told they had not done the most basic checks and searches. I was astonished.'

After the police reopened the phone hacking investigation, Mulcaire was charged with intercepting Milly Dowler's voicemail and conspiring to do so. He strongly resisted the second charge, believing it had connotations of a dark plot, rather than something with nobler aims: 'I did not conspire… I believe I had an empowering belief to intercept phones… I believed I was doing it legitimately…. I was advised I would have my day in court if I did that, but they dropped the conspiracy charge against me. In one way of course I was pleased, but it meant I didn't get the chance to make my case in court. Had I done so, I would have been able to shed a lot of light on the whole affair. My question to them was: "have you got the guts to go 'not guilty' on the Milly Dowler conspiracy charge if your intentions are good?" I would have liked more than one of them to go not guilty. That way we could have had the whole thing out in court, which I would have welcomed. But then they pleaded guilty after years of denying anything to do with this stuff. I just hope they can live with themselves.'

There is still a sense of grievance, a feeling that it suited no one for him to get up in the box and say his piece. 'My hands have been tied. They took me out of conspiracy straightaway. Did they really want me there in court, at Leveson and the IPCC, the select committees and so on? The police had a lot to lose if they'd left me in the conspiracy charge... they knew full well I was determined to stick with this in a court of law. I got a good mark from the judge. He understood what was going on. I remember the judge remarking that it was a brave decision. "We don't need Mr Mulcaire here, let him go." I made the distinction between special projects and other stuff. At the end, at last, they seemed to get the point about the distinction between the lawful authority stuff and the rest.'

The days after Dowler 'false hope' moment allegation have clearly had a huge impact on Mulcaire. His children were intensely concerned about their father. 'We know what Dad's like, we just know he wouldn't be either incompetent like that or so callous,' says Georgia, his 20 year old. I was really touched to receive a very supportive letter from Father Bernard, my local priest at St Christopher's Church. If it had been a News International story, it would never have run. Three million fans of the paper believed in our ability to get the details right. I must have been doing something right.'

In the whole story there is a danger that the Dowler episode, ghastly as it is, crowds out all the other cases. What about Soham, where two girls, Holly Wells and Jessica Chapman, were abducted and killed. Mulcaire was active there too. Some suspects had their phones hacked and, he believes, the police knew about it (or certainly do now). Why is that file also not available, he asks.

'Again, on Soham... I cannot find the file. I would like

to know who the taskers were. I would not have done that without lawful authority. I found a lot of information on various people there. It was probably Greg. He would have given me *carte blanche*. I did a lot of work involving people who went off the grid, but I'm not allowed to see that material. It's a protected file. I want to show what my belief structure was. I wasn't doing it for a story. I wanted to get those children back. I can accumulate information, or give it back…. I would produce the currency which bosses could barter. If I could get any clinical detail on a child abduction, I would. How that was used by the tasker, you know, the journo, is up to him. They were the broker. He would give stuff to the police that the police couldn't get in their timelines. I was that much quicker than them, so of course what I was able to provide was useful to them.'

This is a slightly different argument, surely. Either you say you were doing it with the police's knowledge and authorisation, or, simply, that it was being done (in a way the police may or may not have guessed at) and much of the information was then fed to the police in exchange for other information about the inquiry?

'You give the police bits and pieces… whether you give it all to them is up to the journalist, that wasn't my call. To my mind, there are three sorts of power in this game knowledge power, positioning power and tasking power. As soon as I give you that knowledge power, you've got all three… it's the intelligence triangle. When you're in that position, you're in a better position than the police. You have autonomy, all the cards, which the police don't have, because they have to get production orders and so on.'

The issue of Mulcaire's motivation, both past and present, has returned constantly in the writing of this book. His insistence on having acted for the greater good should be clear by now, but his current spur is harder to PIN down. Is he motivated by anger? The question has become contentious. He says anger is a negative emotion, that he should not be angry and will happily recite that it poisons the soul. But for someone who carried the can for the practice that kept the news machine fed and was scapegoated while the similarly guilty looked on disapprovingly, takes some stomaching. He does not want it thought he is angry, but no other word does the trick. He is more than peeved, but not particularly vengeful towards those who sat on their hands when he went to prison. He just wants his motivation understood. 'I have always believed that you should retain your emotional control, that you should be better, not bitter.' He may not want to be angry, but it strikes me he is.

It is easy to dismiss Mulcaire with a black and white reference to the law. If he broke the law, does that mean he is beyond rescue? To those whose privacy he plundered (or enabled to be plundered by others), maybe he is. But he has some conditions which he says were ingrained from his early professional life, which mitigate law-breaking. These are that better outcomes must be the result, a person's actions mustn't undermine rule-following in general, rule breaking must be the only means to a better outcome, and that the collective obligation is to uphold the rule of law but individual duty is to do what's best, inside or outside the law.

Since the phone hacking scandal exploded, precious few people have defended the run of the mill redtop journalism from which it grew. Politicians and newspaper editors have argued about how the post-Leveson rules are to be enforced while barely mentioning what those rules should be.

In short, is it a legitimate story if, say, a married professional footballer is cheating on his wife? What if he is receiving millions in sponsorship deals from companies which believe him to be a pillar of probity? They greyness of the borders left them virtually imperceptible in the most competitive part of the market. Only Paul McMullan (former deputy features editor at the *News of the World*) has been brave enough to defend the 'anything goes' principle, while many have hidden behind claims of ignorance or spurious claims of defending the public interest. McMullan, with more honesty than many of his fellow practitioners could summon, told the Leveson inquiry: 'I see [journalism] as a noble profession which sometimes requires ignoble acts and believe passionately in freedom of speech which is indeed occasionally safeguarded by those acts.... Just because exposing devious self-interest, ineptitude and corruption which taints many in the public eye requires a devious and illegal route itself does not make it wrong.... The job of the whistle blower and the brave journalist who condones and uses illegal means to bring this corruption, false representation which debases our democracy to the public attention is one to be cherished and protected, long may it continue.' In short, the law ought to allow a public interest defence for law-breaking.

Where is Mulcaire on all this? How does he feel about the case of someone like Sienna Miller, who was tormented by 360-degree intrusions into her private life? In hindsight he says he agrees that such trawling in the hope of picking up a titbit, cannot be excused. But what about her entire existence – her friends and family – coming under extreme scrutiny to prove something of little ultimate importance? And what about intruding into people's bank accounts and so on? How can that ever be defensible, whoever they are?

'I agree that fishing exhibitions are indefensible. If there's a greater good, fine, but otherwise not. The fact that I did it, for a bit of tittle tattle, I agree, is wrong, but I don't feel I'm particularly qualified to make that judgment. I do know that I would not be happy if my own daughter was behaving like that, but maybe that is not the point.'

Those expecting heartfelt outpourings of remorse on this issue from Mulcaire are likely to be disappointed. The cost-free, easy apology is not his style. He does not want to say sorry insincerely, seeming to regard it as dishonourable.

'I don't know how I feel about this. I feel things have moved on for me. If I had been asked about this in 2006, maybe I would feel worse about this. But now, with the Dowler case and others, and being charged a second time, I feel I'm back on the trauma mill and it's hard for me to stop adopting a siege mentality. I was punished the first time round, when others weren't, when I was acting under their instruction, so now my defences have come up again. It's hard for me to feel fully unqualified remorse on some of those privacy issues. They ask me to apologise for a second time, although actually it was the *News of the World* that apologised to her. I know it's not Sienna Miller's fault how badly this has been handled, but how many times can you apologise for something?'

By way of his own mitigation, he says an action can be

wrong but a person can still be blameless. 'People around me made the choices... they were journalists, lawyers and others who were very successful and I trusted them. But after the Dowler allegation there was a club mentality against me, and the whole game changed then. All bets were off.' And he returns to his insistence that his notes show how he was tasked, and that when he was asked to look at a victim of crime, for example, it was not presented as such, but was merely slipped into a batch of jobs to work through.

After the case was reopened, Mulcaire had to decide how the renewed criminal issue related to the continuing civil cases. He had a brief opportunity to turn Queen's evidence and tell all to the police, which would involve a major process of 'cleansing himself' to ensure no skeletons came out of the closet at a later stage to undermine his credibility. Would that jeopardise his position in the civil cases?

'Once you've gone through that trauma once, been arrested at gunpoint, had your house raided, with your kids watching. I didn't feel I owed the police anything. My elderly parents got raided, with my mum housebound and ill and my dad's moveability is pretty much zero...You pay the price, you go through that trauma mill, you spend longer than the average time in prison... then to rehabilitate yourself, get back to doing some investigation work for Lord Stevens's unit in London, get back on your feet a bit, and then the game-changing moment comes with Milly Dowler. To be Public Enemy No 1 is beyond belief. It is gut-wrenching to see the effect it has had on my family. To go through that phase again, two kids collapsing, your wife in a dreadful state. The media goes after you... and then as you are trying to keep your family's morale up… on top of all that, my wife gets arrested… for money laundering! It was the first time she has ever been in a police station, or had had anything like that happen. Imagine the kids seeing that, people at school seeing that, in the community locally. If you had seen all that immense emotional baggage my wife had to carry around. I couldn't face all that again. I was also arrested for perverting the course of justice and money laundering, because they thought all that cash that had gone from the News of the World had gone to me. They just ran the same uniform mentality gunboat diplomacy, raising the anxiety of co-dependents. They should have been a lot more grownup about that. They should have had a serious conversation about what I was doing and why, but they didn't want to do that. So after all that, being arrested for a second time, with my mum (a signatory on one of his company documents) being interviewed by the police for a second time, seven years on – after which I was released without any charge – can you wonder why anyone would want to give Queen's evidence?'

If there is more than a degree of animus there, he also has a more cerebral explanation.

'Certain people have been in this story for five minutes, and for them self preservation is paramount, so they have chosen a cut-throat mitigation. I have held my position for seven years. That degree of self preservation leads to self deception, because it will make you do anything to save yourself and you persuade yourself to believe things that are wrong. And that will lead to self betrayal. Once you are there, you are led into a situation of either trying to correct it, which is a flushout, a cleansing system, or you are wise to it and you try and learn from it and you gain experience from it… I chose the latter, otherwise I would have given Queen's evidence.'

In short, as he told a friend, he's not a grass. Or is it that he did not want to 'cleanse himself'. Surely all those company documents invite suspicion that that might be the case? Why were there so many different names of companies, and why did he keep using different names, as emerged in court? In 2007 you had to pay back £12,500, which was the maximum the judge decided you could have had in cash from the company. And the police initially accused you of money-laundering, and wondered where all the money had gone. Do you have anything to say to that?

'The company name thing all started with John Boyall, when people set up limited companies, and people would just put down relations' names and so on as company directors, and you'd just change the name slightly every year, just to minimise tax, which to my understanding lots of small companies do. I didn't have an accountant, and my mother kept my payment documents, which doesn't seem to me such an extraordinary thing. But I am unhappy with what was said about me and money in court. It was said that I had used lots of different names to try and bamboozle people, which all fitted the Walter Mitty thing they have tried to pin on me, but it's just not true. What is true that I used two names for undercover work, which were Paul Williams and Dr John Jenkins, but on my children's life, the other ones they used for me… I had never heard of them, and I certainly didn't ask to use them. Matey, Mr Lemon, Mr Strawberry, Alexander, all those. Greg used to occasionally call me Alexander, if he wanted to flatter me, as in Alexander the Great, and in the office I heard they talked about an Alexander project or something, but that wasn't my idea. And the other ones – I never even heard of them until they came up in court. They must have been names they used in the office. The police went through all my bank accounts and found nothing wrong. There was nothing to find.'

'I said to them, I signed for every single payment I had from that company. If you can find the Lamborghini and the house in the Bahamas, please show me. You can have them. I thought of doing what Fletcher did in Porridge, when he was accused of money laundering. He needed a new patio, so he told them he'd buried it under his crumbling patio. The police dug it up and found nothing, because there never was anything, but they had to put things back to normal, so the police had to redo it all and he got a new patio out of it. Alison was accused of money laundering. Can you imagine that? She was never actually shown the documents on which they arrested her. We all wanted to see the documents but never did, but it did sound as if someone had cooked them up. It was absolutely ridiculous, outrageous. Someone must have made a decision somewhere down the line to let that information come out in the interview process. I actually wanted Alison to be charged and to get my hands on that, the legal team weren't allowed to get their hands on that. That's not right. That is abuse of process.'

On the subject of abuse of process, two other questions suggest themselves. Why did he go as far as the Supreme Court in order to prevent having to name his taskers, as requested by Nicola Phillips, PA to Max Clifford, who wanted to know who had hacked her phone and why. And why did he not pursue an 'abuse of process' argument? Some lawyers felt that because the police had had his files for several years and then had to return to the fray, he could claim he had been treated unfairly.

On the supreme court argument, he says: 'I was advised by my legal team to take that all the way. We had a very long and heavy session in chambers, and there were a lot of civil claims coming through. At the end of the meeting the chambers made a massive, very powerful case against me incriminating myself, so for me to go against that would have been pretty unusual, and they thought it unlikely that, as I had been charged and sent to prison before, that I would be charged again for some other thing they thought I might have done, so I shouldn't take the risk by incriminating myself. The irony is at the end I still got charged on 4 counts, so following their advice didn't help me… and on the second one, on abuse of process, that is partly why I decided not to take their advice, even though logically maybe I could have brought a stronger case. I chose not to, because if I had come out of that case having won, people would still have gone into a court of law and blamed me, and I wanted to try and clear my name as far as possible.'

Do you wish now you had gone for an abuse of process case? 'I don't like to look back with regrets, all I can do is listen to the advice I was given at the time and the powerful argument they made at the time and take a decision based on it.'

You have made reference to 'the man upstairs'. How important is religion to you?

'I am very wary about talking about that. I don't want people thinking I am some kind of David Icke figure who was driven by religion to do this or that. At the same time I am not going to deny my faith. I was brought up with it, I believe in it, I enjoy it and I think it gives my children a very solid and admirable framework for life. I know I have to live with the consequences of my actions, and I know I can answer for them. I also ask myself how some journalists can live with themselves after what they have done. I don't wish bad on anyone but I do look at some of the things that have happened, at some of the victims of crime, for example, that the paper went after, and, yes, I enabled the paper to get into contact with, and I wonder how they can look themselves in the mirror. I feel bad that work I did made it possible for those things to have happened, of course, but I do not feel they were my responsibility, something I have to answer for. In many, possibly most, of the cases I did not know what use the PIN numbers I was providing were being put to. Had I known, of course I would have done different things.'

The shock of hearing about those innocent, often grieving people he targeted, or enabled to be targeted, will probably never fade. In some cases, though, he would point out that at the time they were put under scrutiny, some may have been under suspicion themselves. The quantities involved will keep others sceptical, but Mulcaire says he would welcome a chance to discuss in public any piece of work with those who tasked him.

How do you feel when the court hears you say 'Go on, say I love you and it's 25 grand'. You may say you were exposing a cabinet minister's affair with a married woman, and that that is something the public has a right to know about, but surely it's not very classy, is it? In fact doesn't it suggest a rapacious indifference to his feelings? Or the jury also heard you saying 'fuck' when you accidentally deleted a message. The bit about the tape proves you are mortal and can make mistakes, but more generally I mention that because in many conversations with you and in the way you bring up your children, it is clear that dignity and good grace are important to you.

'If I said that, that was because that was what they offered. Don't ask me if it ever materialised, because it didn't. They led me on that. As for the idea of being given an incentive…. It's a bonus, just like bankers get bonuses. Don't tell me everyone else works for free? I've never met a poor doctor. If they weren't motivated by money they'd work for free. I don't have to justify an incentive of £25,000. I was just working for need, to feed my family, not greed'

Because a certain amount of NoW cash remains unaccounted for, some continue to speculate as to where it might have gone. There has been a suggestion of one or two executives having an expensive drug habit. Was Mulcaire aware of any such suggestion? He seems shocked when I put it to him.

'Well, if that was the case, I never saw any evidence of it. I would be really surprised. Anyone I dealt with knows how strongly I feel about that sort of thing. I don't even like even being with puffheads, so anyone who wanted to do that knows I wouldn't approve. I like a drink, and my children are old enough to like the odd glass of wine, but anything beyond that just isn't us at all.'

A friend of Mulcaire who is very familiar with police work says of Mulcaire's belief that he did much of his work on the police's behalf: 'There is no way the cops would have asked Glenn themselves. Someone may have told him "the cops need your help." It looks to me as if Miskiw was so out of control he had his own private police force in Glenn and led Glenn to believe that his work was being sanctioned by the police.' Given all that, do you feel you were too trusting? It's not a great mark of friendship that when Mulcaire left a message to ask for Miskiw's help, Miskiw told Alison: "I hope it's not financial."'

'He came to stay at my house when he was in London, he and I did some great work together, he called and visited my wife a lot when I was in prison. I felt we had a good relationship. But in hindsight the people he was working for needed him to be doing that, to keep an eye on me and make sure I wasn't going to rock the boat. He was useful to them and they needed him, so once again someone, in this case Greg, was deriving a use from me. In the later stages, he was upping his own value inside the company because he was the only one I was talking to. And when he called me to tell me he was going to the US but didn't tell me about the huge storm that was coming over Milly Dowler, that really changed my view of him, although I can't be 100 per cent certain that he knew about it. Alison and I always liked him, but he was always distant. Maybe we were just being used all along. Obviously I would find that very disappointing. And I am disappointed that he didn't feel able to help with this book. He knows the truth about me, and about what I have gone through. I could have done with a hand from him.'

Do you think he exploited your desire to do greater good work by telling you the work was for the police when actually it wasn't, and that in that respect, you were a victim? Somebody who has known you a long time said about you: 'Victim is strong word, but he was naïve. He made that decision to get into that position where he could be exploited, and I don't know how much he expected to be doing all that celebrity stuff.' Someone else, who knows Mulcaire and Miskiw well, when asked if Miskiw was a friend to Mulcaire, said: 'No, Glenn was a contact to Greg. They were not close. Greg's quite a detached person emotionally. He's not that kind of person. Glenn came across as quite friendly and warm. Was Greg cold-blooded? He took his job very seriously.' So how does Mulcaire feel about that now?

'Naivety is a strong word. The word Greg used to use a lot is "schmoozing". He would be very keen on schmoozing people. That means, offer incentives to people. It's a ladder game and they help you up the ladder, but then they keep control of the ladder, so you have no control. I've seen that done plenty of times with other people, and I suppose that is what happened with me.'

You have lived with this, and with yourself and with your conscience all this time, and there is plenty of conviction behind what you say. A friend of yours, a former senior figure in the police, has said: 'To his credit, Glenn has always been completely consistent in saying that he believed he was doing it for the greater good. Now whether he was told that or not, I don't know. He likes to think if the cops can't work it out, they would send for Glenn. I am not sure about that and can't be certain that is true, but he may well have been told that. Certainly he has always been very very discreet, to my knowledge.'

Your father-in-law has talked to me about his anger. 'What about all the good work Glenn did, for the good?' And his wife has talked to me about Glenn having to work round the clock and you telling her 'I have to do this for the police'.

But to someone who doesn't know you, who looks at the thousands of files and what they have read about you, is there anything you can say that you aren't retro-fitting your past, you know, re-writing history, to get yourself off the hook? Because a great many people will want to write you off as someone who believed he had superhuman powers, in short, as a fantasist.

'I know I am not a fantasist, or a Walter Mitty or an obsessive or any of those things. I have faith in my ability, and I know what my motives are. It doesn't matter what people think of you, it's what God thinks of you. Let me see all my files , and all the people who tasked me, and find out why so much stuff has been held back, and then we'll see who the fantasist is. Somebody, at some level, has held things back. Conspiring to commit an unlawful act is a bad thing to do, and I know I didn't do that on Milly Dowler. I am the only one who has consistently told the court the truth on that story. I think there should be a proper public inquiry on the Dowler case. Just let me have all my files and leave me there to defend myself. That will make clear who is telling the truth. I challenge all those people involved to see me in a court of law, with all my documents, and then we'll see who is telling the truth. The files on my work with Quest have also been put into quarantine with the police. Again, if people knew about the sort of work I did for them, they wouldn't use names like that.'

It should be said, for legal reasons, that the police themselves insist that only a few files have been held back, and those are for 'operational' reasons. One senior figure close to the Weeting investigation said: 'After what has gone before, we'd be mad to hold back any files. I just can't imagine why people would lay themselves open to that charge. That is the sort of malpractice that could bring a trial to an end.'

The aftermath of the 2006 trial requires you to look back on a version of yourself that is, frankly, unflattering, some would say greedy, even. You have said your head was turned by the money you were earning, but through blagging, you persuaded a lot of innocent people to do things they would not normally have done, yet you say you have no regrets about that?

'My big regret is that I didn't recognise the spike, as I call it, the massive build-up of phone interceptions in 2004-6, due to the huge amounts of pressure in the office and coming from the office. I feel I was still doing good work then, but often it was not the sort of work I wanted to be doing. I had too much faith in what I was being asked to do and the people who were tasking me. Many of the jobs were slipped in front of me in a bundle using quite a different pretext.'

'But on the serious investigations side, on many of those jobs, as far as I was aware, I was working on behalf of the police. I've got nothing to apologise for, and I never will…On many jobs, I was much quicker than the police, and I make no apology for that. Don't tell me about production orders next week or the week after. If it was your daughter, would you stop and say 'hang on, we've got to do this by the book'? You've got to do anything you can to save that girl's life. You don't get given jobs like that, with people who have done great work, immense work, you don't get contracted with someone like that unless you've got outside form, and I was very proud of where I worked, of working for Rupert Murdoch, who, incidentally, I don't believe knew anything about what I was doing. But I wasn't always proud of some of the individuals I worked with'

It seems to me you have a very high level of self belief, and you have had to be strong, for yourself and your family, to get through this. You did some work for Lord Stevens at Quest, but since 2007 you have not had a lot of luck. You studied employment law, and toyed with setting up a couple of companies, one to help individuals with counter surveillance and one, Celebrity Makers, to film people holding parties, but with the resurfacing of the story you have had a struggle, not least financially. You have managed to stay in your house, now with an interest-only mortgage and a couple of years ago you were made bankrupt for non-payment of £187,000 in tax. (The non-payment was traceable to documents found at News international, which seems to confirm that his payments were indeed signed for. As with his tasking files, they were to be his undoing. (Mulcaire says an agreement was in place with the revenue to repay tax but after the Dowler allegation was made the deal was taken off the table, a source of further grief: 'an agreement is an agreement', he insists.)

But do you ever worry that a part of you is in denial? That quantity of work, which you say was slipped in under a different pretext, can't just be brushed aside and its consequences blamed on the journalists you were helping, can it? Maybe you have told yourself certain things because you wanted to be sure you hadn't lost your bearings. It seems to me that people with a lot of self-belief are particularly inclined, more than most of us, to re-jigging the past expediently, and in not following much of the coverage of the trial and so on, you have averted your gaze from your past. You have talked extensively about your belief in what you were doing, but I suppose I am asking more about the extent to which you have questioned that certainty in yourself. Is there something in that?

'I made a distinction between tittle tattle and the serious investigations. I know what the difference was, and I did a deal with myself that one was the price to pay for the other. And I still insist a hundred per cent that we did some great work on the paper early on. What happened was that it all became just a process, just job after job. I was being piled up with work and yes, I was being paid well to do it, and in that situation I don't think many people with five young children would just walk away. Plus, I didn't realise that a lot of what I was doing was illegal. If I had, would I have kept all those files? I have told you I regret not recognising the spike for what it was, but then again, it wasn't like I was enjoying it then. My health was in a terrible state, I was working day and night just to try and keep them happy. I do wish I had walked away, but if I had, I would have been unemployable and could have been bad-mouthed as an investigator in that world.'

The world of private investigators seems unlikely to be clasping Glenn Mulcaire to its bosom. The above-board, respectable side of the profession are likely to say that he should have joined one of the trade's associations and, at the very least, stayed within the law. Others, less scrupulous, will say that he has let the side down. You shouldn't keep records, they say, suggesting that there's something almost comical about keeping all those files believing there was nothing wrong with what you were doing. And you kept them twice, of course, so they were there in your house when the police came the second time.

The effect of all this has been to disrupt much of that world, in which some investigators skated pretty close to the law, but were discreet and the information was used judiciously, so nobody was to know if the law got broken. I suppose you might say that was an arm of the privatisation of justice, a racket in which most newspapers colluded to varying degrees. How do you feel about that, not as it relates to you particularly, but as a general view, and do you ever wish you had signed up to one of the investigation profession's trade bodies? Do you think, one way or the other, they might have helped avoid what has happened?

'I didn't want to join a professional body. I didn't want to put myself on the grid. I had done loads of courses of a variety of sorts, which I would rather not go into, and was keener to do more military style stuff. I think it is a legacy of my grandfather, who lived with us when I was very young. He had been in the war, and he was a great hero to me. I would very much like to be able to live up to him. He was in the Irish Guards in the war, and later worked in the War Office. The way he dealt with some really major family situations was just so impressive. Plus, when his own wife died, the way he dealt with that. That's what leaders are made of, I thought.'

'You have suffered a prolonged period of anxiety attacks and depression, and have been on Cipralex, escitalopram, beta blockers and valium. Your financial position has also been very precarious. After 2007, you got a qualification in neurolinguistic programming, you did a course in employment law, were a senior investigator at Quest and did work for another large company. And then the allegations about Milly Dowler came out, which obviously made things difficult for you, but when the dust has settled a bit, you must be wanting to get back to work?'

'I have managed to keep things together, and I must have something to have done that. I have been called all sorts of things, and I expect I'll be called a great many more, but I know what sort of person I am, and I have had a lot of support from really good people with good families – people like Dickie Guy [a Wimbledon goalkeeping hero from the 1980s], a good character and a very nice man, who makes sure things are done right. People like that wouldn't support me if I was what some people have painted me. And I am confident I am a very competent investigator. All I really want is to get back to the starting line.'

Acknowledgements

I cannot express enough thanks to my personal committee for their continued support and encouragement; Dr Ruse, Father Bernard, Martin Smith, Rod Fletcher QC, Gavin Millar QC, Teus Young and my uncle big T. This also applies to my late brother stephen, Grandma, Grandad (war office) whose wisdom was light years ahead of others.

The support from Gibson Square has been invaluable along with my literary agent Heather Holden Brown whose genuine caring nature is refreshing in todays business climate. Any proceeds due to me have been donated to charity.

Finally, to my caring, loving and supportive wife Alison my deepest gratitude. Her encouragement kept me focused so i did not become a prisoner of woe..the ultimate safety valve.

Glenn Mulcaire, 2 July 2014

Publisher's Note

In view of ongoing trials no index has been provided.